Engaging
VIRTUAL MEETINGS

Engaging VIRTUAL MEETINGS

openers, games, *and* activities
for communication, morale, *and* trust

JOHN CHEN

WILEY

Published by John Wiley & Sons, Inc., Hoboken, New Jersey.
Published simultaneously in Canada.

Library of Congress Cataloging-in-Publication Data is Available:

ISBN 9781119750888 (Paperback)
ISBN 9781119751021 (ePDF)
ISBN 9781119751014 (ePub)

COVER DESIGN & ILLUSTRATION: PAUL McCARTHY

Printed in the United States of America

SKY10021378_092320

Contents

Acknowledgments

A book is the distilled knowledge of an author into approximately 300 pages. While a book shows an author's name, it takes a team to do the hard work and energy of distilling. I acknowledge my amazing team.

Pre-2000, I imagined a world where you could do virtual team building. In 2000, we formed VirtualTeamworks.com; despite big interest, nobody bought. In 2011, I became the author of *50 Digital Team-Building Games*. In 2020, the coronavirus impacted the world. Zoom expanded from 10 million users to 300+ million users.[1] Microsoft Teams grew 37% in one week to 44 million users.[2] It is as if more than the entire US population moved online in just two months.[3] It is April 25, 2020, as I write these acknowledgments. Now, suddenly everybody is interested in virtual!

I have been practicing engaging virtual meetings for over 35 years, from playing Atari video games with friends to building the Association for Computing Machinery club online at the University of California at Santa Barbara to forming the "Dudes" (non-gender-specific Dudes) at Microsoft (dudes@microsoft.com) to hooking up the first webcams at the Association for Experience Education (AEE) to presenting at the Association for Talent Development conference to running the first geocaching (geocaching.com)-based team-building program for Adobe in 2001 to using our Geoteaming app to run over 200 programs in a year to running my entire company on Sharepoint, OneDrive, Microsoft Office, and Bookings to running our team meetings and customer meetings on Zoom since 2016.

I live in Seattle, Washington. On March 6, 2020, as reports of the coronavirus started to emerge, I decided to launch a new virtual training program to help people who were working from home. The class was a hit. With help from people like Jennifer Clifton who posted on LibraryJournal. com,[4] I conducted multiple training courses for engaging virtual meetings. I have been practicing 35 years for this moment, so I was able to navigate online swiftly. I was able to create order out of chaos. I was able to get work done. I was able to create emotional safety to handle the stress. I was able to teach others.

Let me say that again: "I was able to teach others." My friends went on to form happy hours to reunite communities and families. My clients were able to teach virtual team building in countries like Slovenia, Taiwan, and Saudi Arabia who were *all* having the same stay-at-home experience. My coach was able to save a dying online meeting that was celebrating an American military family member. My girlfriend was able to get even more work done with a top cancer research company. My client was able to take a 200-person mission-critical four-day face-to-face conference for a Fortune 100 company online successfully.

And I can teach you. I acknowledge you for getting and opening this book. I acknowledge you for having the desire for engaging virtual meetings. I acknowledge you for the time and energy you invest in this book and related material. I acknowledge you for having the courage to be a leader of positive change in your community. I acknowledge that I want you to get at least a 10× return on your investment in this book. I want to know you personally. I want you in my community.[5] I want to hear your story of creating greatness where you are. I want to hear of your amazing team results. I want to write about you in my next book. I want to hug or high-five you when it is possible again. I know the only way we beat this virus is with teamwork. I know the only way we survive as a species is through teamwork. I acknowledge you and your part.

I would like to acknowledge the many people who made this book happen. You will see that I attribute many of the initiatives to people all around the world who helped me. I crowdsourced the title of this book with over 100 people. I have tested and provided video clips of every initiative so you can *see* them in action. I have many readers of the book who are the best spelling and grammar police I have ever met. I acknowledge each of you; this book would not be the distilled knowledge it is without each of you.

Thank you to:

Alicia Ellen, Allison Kundel, Ananda Ybarra, Angel Hanson, Ann Kelley Humes, Anne Chen, Ashley Vandermeyden, Ben Kenyon, Beth Assaf, Beth Hughes, Bethany Freeman, BJ Stewart, Brad Cochrane, Brian Calvert, Bryan Roth, Caitlin Allen, Carissa Zenorini Hobbs, Carole Newton McManus, Carolyn Rettberg Browning, Carrie Zimmerman, Catherine M. White, Cathy Mason, Charva Brown, Chewie Wicket O'Quinn Cummings, Chris Saeger, Christie Crystal, Christine Clacey, Christine Wagg, Connie Baker, Crystal Wang, Cynthia Clay, Daniel Green, David Ford, Debbie Ann Schneider, Deniz Senelt Kalelioglu, Devin Stubblefield, Dina Phinney, Don Jones, Donna Cunningham, Ed Cohen, Fei Chua, Gerie Ventura, Gil Peretz, Godwell Khosa II, Heather Zrubek Forteith, Ian Arvin Ortega, Irma Bacho Suntay, Jack W. Peters, James Bishop, Jan Keck, Jana Victoria White, Janet Roberts, Jegatheeswaran Manoharan, Jen Gonyer-Donohue, Jen Graves, Jen Poyer, Jennifer Nance, Jessica Levin Sullivan, Jim Krotz, Joanna Grillo Darmanin, Jo-Anne Rockwood, Jody Lee, Julie Rocks, Julie Watne Hall, KC Frankenburger, Keristian, Larry G. Jones, Laura Schlegel Kagle, Lien Ngu, Lori Finn, Maggie Barr, Marc Ryser, Marguerite Berry, Mary Ann Wethington Cunningham, Mary de la Fe, Matthew Donegan-Ryan, Michelle Cummings, Michelle Turner, Naomi Tucker, Nicole Donnelly, Nicole Kaup, Paula Johnson and her husband,

Penny Laine, Perry Lam, Ping Liao, Priomz Karlin, Ramona Ridgewell, Sheila Schneider, Shelby Sewell, Stefania Contri-Vecchi, Stephen Koch, Suk Wai Tham, Syed Nurul Afsar, Tanya Phillips, Tawna Renee Pangborn, Terry Onustack, Tracy Stuckrath, Trevor Lui, Tricia Hartley Simmons, Trishann Couvillion, Valary A Oleinik, Vicki Allgood, Wanda Colon, Ziva Grgic, and Zoe Omega.

Special thanks to my oldest sister, Ruth Chen Knipe. She completed the first draft review to help me make my book deadline. Ruth has been helping me ever since I was born. Thank you, Ruth—I love you so much; thank you for helping me learn how to be so engaging in this world.

Final thanks to all of my friends who help create psychological safety for me and others. In a virtual meeting I was invited to, my mentor, Ed Cohen, created a space safe enough for an attendee to write a poem and share it with a large group. This person was clearly uncomfortable but felt safe enough to share. It became the most engaging part of this meeting as we watched this person's bravery. I hope this book helps you create these high-engaging moments.

Introduction: Virtual Meetings Don't Have to Suck

Ed Cohen

Ed Cohen, former chief learning officer at Booz Allen Hamilton, led multiple companies to the number-one spot on both the ATD BEST Awards and *Training* magazine Top 125 annual lists.

Whether you are working from home or an office, virtual meetings can often be a dreadful experience—but they don't have to be.

Do your virtual meetings drain your energy?

Do you multitask and lose focus during virtual meetings?

Is video exhaustion real for you?

Has this happened to you? You have a meeting. You log on. The host puts up a slide deck and talks continuously for 60 minutes. You log on to your next meeting and everyone is talking at the same time so you can't understand anybody. You sign up for a webinar. When you log into the session, the chat feature is disabled. There's no Q&A, just a one-way endless set of slides and lecture, so you open up your email and half listen. You log into your next meeting. The speakers are using cheap microphones, making it difficult to understand them. Another speaker has weak internet, so she keeps freezing. Someone takes a call without muting the microphone. The host doesn't know how to mute, so you're stuck listening to the call. You log into your next meeting and a presenter's child walks in demanding to be fed. You log into your next meeting and the meeting host gets a delivery, setting off their dog to bark protectively. You chat a suggestion to them to mute and he yells at his dog to be quiet. You ask for co-host responsibility and he declines. You log off and fall into bed.

Engaging Virtual Meetings shows you the key secrets to having your attendees say, "I have more energy, not less, after 60 minutes meeting with you!" When you read and apply the techniques found in *Engaging Virtual Meetings*, you will learn how to:

- Create a powerful virtual presence
- Create a smooth flow so attendees don't talk over each other
- Look great and convey professionalism
- Engage everyone even if only one person is talking
- Guarantee that everyone feels engaged and heard
- Powerfully close your meeting and take steps to make your next meeting even more effective

John Chen is the CEO of Geoteaming and the author of *50 Digital Team Building Games*. He has been meeting virtually for over 35 years and he is not only expert in creating engaging virtual meetings, he's my go-to person when I want to be sure that my online meetings, webinars, and conferences are successful. Follow the steps in the ENGAGE method and your team will communicate more effectively, easily complete work, and morale will be raised, especially when you can't be in the same room. Take your meetings to the next level. Everyone will feel engaged and energized. Make better decisions and use more collaborative tools.

John has worked with more than 2,400 companies from Barcelona, Taiwan, Shanghai, Saudi Arabia, and America. From meetings with 2 people to over 2,000, he has helped virtual meetings become incredibly engaging. And, through his extraordinarily unique approach to team building, he has helped teams become the top 1% in the world at what they do.

When you read *Engaging Virtual Meetings*, you will notice that you and your team can meet virtually, comfortably, for hours. More importantly, your team gets things done. Your boss will notice your leadership and you will look forward to your next meeting.

Here's what others say:

I have more energy after virtually meeting you for 60 minutes than any other virtual meeting in my life!

Donna Cunningham, clinical research associate, Seattle Genetics

You got over 200 people around the world in every time zone engaged! That's incredible for our first major conference that moved from face-to-face to virtual. THANK YOU!

Charva Brown, Fortune 100 company

Read *Engaging Virtual Meetings* and get ready to learn openers, games, and activities for communication, morale, and trust . . . *now!*

In author John Chen's words, for 80% of the value of this book, read Chapter 1 ("The ENGAGE Method for Leading Great Meetings") and Chapter 2 ("Preparing for Virtual Meetings").

The technology for virtual meetings is continuously changing and evolving. That's why I highly recommend you consider becoming part of the community of Engaging Virtual Meeting enthusiasts by joining the free Engaging Virtual Meeting Facebook group at fb.com/groups/EngagingVirtualMeetings.

If you have any questions that are not covered in the book or you need a current answer to your virtual meeting challenge, ask it there and you will have access to a community of people who want to help you. I hope to see you there.

Virtual meetings that *actually* don't suck! YES.

PART 1
Principles and Preparation for Engaging Virtual Meetings

1

The ENGAGE Method for Leading Great Meetings

If you want engaging virtual meetings, then learn the ENGAGE method. The method has been refined over the past 35 years and has a remedy for the most common virtual meeting problems. ENGAGE stands for:

Engage and interact with every attendee.
Never lead a meeting alone.
Good looks.
Air traffic control.
Get productive with virtual tools.
End your meeting on a high note.

A Brief Overview of the ENGAGE Method

Engage and interact with every attendee. If you want engagement, engage! If you want your next virtual meeting to be engaging, then try different ways to engage your attendees. Greet all of your attendees as they arrive. Have every attendee check in. Ask your attendees to chat. Keep track and check in with the attendees who haven't said anything and give them the opportunity to pass if they don't want to contribute.

Go to bit.ly/evmengage to see a video of a professional host giving a demonstration of engaging and interacting with every attendee.

Never lead a meeting alone. If you want engagement, assign an attendee or someone you invite to a meeting a role in the meeting (after you have trained them). Roles include chat engagement, muting and unmuting, renaming, and security. Any or all of these roles can be delegated. They must be engaged to do their job and it allows you, the host, to focus on connecting with your attendees.

Go to bit.ly/evmnever to see a video of a professional host working with a producer as an example of never leading a meeting alone.

Good looks. If you want engagement, look good. Take a shower. Dress up. Frame your face. Clean up your background. Turn on your lights. Wear your company gear. Wear bright colors.[1] Like Bruno Mars says, "If you want to show up, then show out."

Go to bit.ly/evmgood to see a video of multiple backgrounds evaluated for good looks.

Air traffic control. If two or more people talk at the same time, no one can hear. An engaging meeting is when you understand what is said. You can help by creating air traffic control. From physical to virtual hand raises or other types of talking sticks, help find a way for attendees to communicate without stepping on each other's auditory toes. Until a videoconferencing platform perfects simultaneous audio, use air traffic control.

Go to bit.ly/evmair to see a video of a professional host demonstrating air traffic control.

Get productive with virtual tools. A virtual meeting is about getting work done. We all have to meet to get our job done. As the host, you need to value the time even more, because as soon as you log in, you start an invisible timer to each attendee's "I'm done" factor, or when they cease to be productive. Virtual meeting fatigue is real and you're doing everyone a favor if you can get your collaborative work done and get back to nonvirtual meeting work. Arrive on time. Plan. Value each other's time. Make decisions everyone buys into. Document your decisions. Get out. Your attendees will feel valued and more engaged if you can host productive virtual meetings.

Go to bit.ly/evmget to see a professional host working with attendees to get productive with virtual tools.

End your meeting on a high note. You want your attendees to have more energy after your meeting. Product teams did research on product demonstration meetings. They discovered that if you end your meeting on a high note, customers are more likely to buy your product.[2] Your meetings are exactly the same. If you can find a way to end positively, your attendees are more likely to come back and they are more likely to be engaged. Ask for feedback. Do a cheer. Play a video. Celebrate success. Say thank you. Then log off.

Go to bit.ly/evmend to see a professional host end their meeting on a high note.

The ENGAGE Method in Depth

Engage and Interact with Every Attendee

As the host of a virtual meeting, one of the ways to create engagement is to engage with every attendee.

Engaging every attendee solves one of the biggest problems with virtual meetings, which is logging in and feeling left out. Every attendee wants to feel valued and know that their work is meaningful. All you have to do is engage them, which you can do by talking to them, by chat or by one of the many virtual tools available to you.

In a one-on-one meeting, you'll find it easier to be engaged in the conversation. As more and more attendees join your meeting, you'll have to think about different ways to engage with every attendee. The following is an easy activity to engage with every attendee.

Check-in

Goals: Show how checking in with every attendee can make your meeting more engaging. Ensure that every attendee's audio and/or video is working.

Time: 5–30 minutes
Participants: 2–25
Technology: Audio, video, chat
Category: Opener

Game Summary: Have every attendee check in by saying their name, location, and where they work.

Rules: Attendees must raise their hand to speak. If their video is not on, they need to raise their virtual hand or unmute and say their name. Choose one person to be air traffic control and if two people want to speak at the same time, the air traffic controller will choose an order. Every attendee must have an opportunity to check in. If an attendee's audio and video is not working, ask them to check in by text.

This is the most basic activity that can help you engage and interact with every attendee. You may see more engagement during your meeting after a check-in and you may see more engagement after your meeting if your meeting was successful.

The following is a collection of best practices.

Hello: Make sure to greet every attendee as they arrive for the meeting. There's nothing worse than arriving in a strange new location and having no one talk to you. Think of yourself as the greeter or welcoming host to your virtual meeting by saying hello.

"A person's name is the sweetest sound": This quote comes from Dale Carnegie's book *How to Win Friends and Influence People.* Use an attendee's name as often as possible. If someone is new, ask if you are pronouncing their name correctly. If you get the pronunciation, make a phonetic note on how to say their name. Make sure you have the correct spelling when you edit or transcribe their name. There's no faster way to disengage someone than to miss a detail like their name. Using an attendee's name is a sure way to engage them, as they will look back to the screen and figure out what's going on.

Chat: If your meeting starts to be bigger than 15 attendees or if you have a lot of presentation material, then you can use chat to engage your guests. Even if you are in the middle of a discussion with an attendee, you can send a quick "Hello" chat to someone who just logged in without disturbing your conversation.

Engage Your Quiet Attendees: One of the most common challenges is getting attendees who have their video or audio off to engage in the meeting. These attendees are quite often shy or introverted. Help create a safe environment for your attendees to contribute. A good practice is to wait longer than is comfortable for you when you ask a group question. Allow the attendees to figure out when they want to answer the question. The reason this will get your quiet attendees to engage is because they are offering to talk when *they* are ready, not when *you* are ready. A professional host shared that he had an attendee who did not want to turn on her camera. The host thanked her for sharing by audio. The host continued the meeting and eventually the attendee offered to answer a question on her own. Later in the meeting, the attendees were tasked with writing in a shared document. For this quiet attendee, it turned out that writing was her passion. This attendee went on to write 75% of a work assignment. The host believed she contributed because she felt safe. Google conducted 18 months of research for high-performing teams and discovered that psychological safety is one of the top five factors. Creating psychological safety in your virtual meetings will help them be more engaging. See Chapter 3 for more on psychological safety.

Log in Early/Stay Late: The most important meeting is the meeting before the meeting and the meeting after the meeting. One of my strategies for being the host of a virtual meeting is to log in 10–30 minutes early and stay logged in for 10–30 minutes after the meeting. This will give you extra time to meet your attendees and get to know them better before everyone is logged in. Also, it will give you time to have extra conversations after an important meeting to clarify and plan. I discovered this secret while working at Microsoft. I was able to have important conversations with busy but important developers, executives, and employees who were too busy to schedule a one-on-one. I got the information I needed and I accelerated many projects and relationships this way.

Create a Checklist: In smaller meetings, from 5 to 15 people, you can ensure that you have engaged every attendee by creating a simple checklist of every attendee and making sure you check off each one as you engage them with a question, a report out, or a chat. Make sure to find a way to end the meeting by attempting to engage everybody at least once.

"Pass": Allow an attendee to say "Pass" if they are called on during a meeting. The key here is to not force someone to engage if they don't want to, and allowing them to pass is a simple way to do that. This means that they don't have anything they'd like to contribute or they would rather use the time for something else, while making it known that you made an attempt to engage with that person.

Let the Inmates Run the Asylum: An incredible strategy to engage your audience is to give control of the meeting over to them. The original concept derived from Edgar Allan Poe's "The System of Dr. Tarr and Professor Fether." Here, it means that you let the attendees run the meeting. If you find ways to hand over control of the meeting to your attendees, they become immediately engaged.

The Association of Talent Development (ATD) states that the top three adult learning theories are:

1. *Adragogy: Tapping into prior experiences.* This means that adult learning attendees arrive already smart in many areas and you should let them share their expertise.
2. *Transformational learning: Revealing perspectives to create aha moments.* This means that you should help create adult learning experiences where attendees can draw their own lessons or *aha* moments. Whatever an attendee decides to get out of an experience is 10 to 100 times more powerful than anything the presenter will ever say.
3. *Experiential learning: Tying reality to create meaning.* This means that you should create adult learning where attendees get to try something themselves and create meaning out of that experience. If you let them do something, they'll engage.

For instance, the activity "A to Z" (see Chapter 8) is a case where after you teach how the activity works, you let the inmates run the asylum, which means that you turn over total control to the attendees. Resist your urges to assist or coach the attendees. Ideally, do nothing. Have a backup plan at key points to give hints without giving a solution away. If you give the solution to the attendees, you rob them of the learning lesson and they will take nothing away, except to give you their problems. If your attendees own the solution, they will also own the learning they derive from the activity.

The Participation Map: When your meeting grows to more than 15 attendees or if you have a more complex meeting, such as a learning meeting, consider using a participation map. A participation map can help you recognize common patterns of problem meetings, such as one or two people dominating the meeting, certain members contributing nothing, and helping shy attendees turn on their camera or engage.

Use our template or make your own. On the left side, write every participant's name, in alphabetical order by first name so they are easy to find. On the top, write your key goals or time marks. For this first participation map, you can use "Logged In, Checked In, Chat, Share, End." When you conduct your meeting, make a checkmark or write a comment anytime someone participates. If someone participates too much, make sure to call on other people. If someone does not participate at all, make sure to check in with them. Remember that you can allow them to "Pass." Checking in with them lets them know they were given an opportunity to contribute as opposed to feeling ignored or left out. You can use a spreadsheet if you have multiple screens or you can print the map if that is more comfortable for you. Inclusion is a powerful engagement tool and it will help engage all your attendees of various personalities and styles. This can be difficult for one person to do, so this is one of the first roles I delegate (see "Never Lead a Meeting Alone").

Engaging Virtual Meetings 1	0:05	0:15	0:25	0:15	0:30	
Participation Map	Air Traffic Control	Good Looks	Shared Document	ENGAGE	Last Word	Q&A
	1:30 PM	1:35 PM	1:50 PM	2:15 PM	2:30 PM	3:00 PM
	1:30 PM	1:35 PM	1:50 PM	2:15 PM	2:30 PM	3:00 PM
	0:00	0:00	0:00	0:00	0:00	0:00
Screen Name	**Air Traffic Control**	**Good Looks**	**Shared Document**	**ENGAGE**	**Last Word**	**Q&A**
Christina Hake - Sacramento, CA - Avery Murphy, LLC	Enjoying weather, SO	Change photos	x	x	Enjoyed	
Debbie Ann Schneider - Queens, NY - Geoteaming	Out of eggs	More lighting	x	x	Learned a lot	
Fatima -, -	Out of almond milk	Add art	x	x	I like the poem	
Maha -, -	Taking online courses	Interesting items	x	x	air traffic control	
Mahanned -, -	No gym	Something	x	x	I needed you 2	
Mahoud -, -	Spending time with	Wear nice	x	x	thank you!	
Maryam -, -			x			
Perry Lam - Hong Kong, HK - LAM Institute	Jeddah, cook for	Add bookshelf	x	x	Participation	
Quoc-Hoan Do - Federal Way, WA - Speaker	Reading books	Put up logo	x	x	I'm improving my	

Source: Used with permission from Microsoft

In this participation map, you can see the attendees' names on the left. The names are sorted by first name so it's easy to find them. On the top of the document, I have the plan for this meeting. I have the Planned Time and the Actual Time, which I fill in with the time I start the activity. During the meeting, I can enter the time I start and it will help me calculate if I'm ahead or behind schedule. The name of every activity is at the top so I know where I am in the agenda. You can see comments made by the attendee in the Air Traffic Control column. All of these notes help the host know if they have engaged everybody. The host can create more engagement by reusing comments that were made earlier.

Go to bit.ly/evmmap to see a professional producer edit a participation map during a meeting.

During my trainings, I show my participation map toward the end of the meeting to show what we have been doing. For most attendees, this is the biggest surprise because they didn't see it coming. This is the biggest takeaway, as almost none of the attendees were using a map before the training.

I've been using participation maps since 1999 to track participation on teleconference-based trainings. The response was enormous then and continues to be now. Many non-engaging meetings are dominated by one person and leave many people out. Use participation maps and you can balance your meeting's engagement.

I find when we're doing our calls, two people are stone rolling the whole meeting. They are going off and nobody gets a word in edgewise. The participation map will be very useful for fixing that.

Christine Wagg, Ontario, Canada

The participation map I absolutely *love*! I can't wait for you to share that!
Julie Rocks, corporate trainer, Costa Mesa, California

You taught me something very important with the participation map. I never saw that coming! That was *tremendously* useful.
Jegatheeswaran Manoharan, Accordia Training & Development, Malaysia

Virtual meetings have a variety of engagement tools. The most important one is you. Be engaging and your meetings will be engaging, too.

Never Lead a Meeting Alone

If you are new to virtual meetings, there are a lot of different elements to creating an engaging meeting. In a face-to-face meeting, you've had years of practice to notice body language, watch for breaks in the conversation, and see when people are engaged or not. In virtual meetings, you need to relearn how to do all this.

The fastest way to make your meetings more engaging is to never lead a meeting alone. This means meeting as a team and delegating key roles, as necessary, to other attendees. This has the side effect of engaging them during the meeting because they have an important role. By meeting as a team, you can focus even more on being the host or presenter of your virtual meeting.

While you don't need to delegate if you have a one-on-one meeting, consider delegating when you have 15 or more attendees or if you have a specialized goal for the meeting, such as training or data review.

Common Roles to Delegate

- Schedule and invitations
- Pre-meeting preparation
- The participation map or checklist
- Chat
- Share
- Scribe
- Speaker handler
- Security
- Post-meeting follow-up

When I launched new online classes in March 2020 in response to the coronavirus pandemic, I did everything myself. I created a new meeting on Zoom. I set up registration. I did marketing on email and social media. I logged in 30 minutes early to greet guests. I started streaming to Facebook LIVE. I muted people who were loud. I ran my own slide deck. I presented and facilitated everything. I engaged people in chat. I held up signs when people were on mute. I kept a participation map to ensure everyone engaged. I stayed on for 30 minutes afterwards to answer questions. I did this for over 20 meetings. And then I suddenly realized, I forgot to hit record. All this work and no post-event marketing value. I was exhausted. I was deflated.

Then, an amazing student named Gil Peretz, the co-founder of PositiveChutzpah.com, gave me this wisdom: never meet alone. Some of my best friends were interested in how I was delivering these meetings. Debbie Ann Schneider and I had already worked together at the top youth camp Global Youth Leadership Summit. Debbie Ann became one of my first producers. First, she tackled the participation map, and as the speaker I was able to focus even more on the attendees. Next, she took over chat engagement and then security and muting/unmuting. I was able to facilitate four programs in a single day by using a team. When I was asked to coach, co-produce, and co-emcee a 200-person four-day conference, we created a team of 36 people to handle one live conference, one Asia watch party, and one EMEA (Europe, the Middle East, Africa) watch party. Never lead a meeting alone. Each team member has a role and they are more engaged as a result. By dividing and delegating roles, you will be a better host and your attendees will feel more attended to because more people are helping them during your virtual meeting.

Good Looks

After you've followed the best steps from the Virtual Presence Primer (see Chapter 2), make sure you look good during your meeting. Center your head to the camera. Position your main screen as close as possible to the video window. When making a key point, take a moment to look directly into the camera.

Donna Cunningham of Seattle Genetics (seattlegenetics.com) drew eyes on a Post-It note and put it next to her camera to remind her to look at the camera as much as she would look at someone in the eyes during her meeting.

Looking good also means sounding good. If possible, meet in a quiet location. If this isn't possible, make sure to mute when you're not speaking. Most systems have a push-to-talk button, like the space bar, to help control your background noise.

One of the most common mistakes is forgetting to unmute if you're going to talk. Make sure to check your mute status before you start speaking. You might have been muted by the host. If you're the host, make sure to give reminders to unmute if you ask someone to speak.

Brad Cochrane, keynote speaker at story1stmarketing.com, was one of the first to use visual signs during meetings. He wouldn't have to unmute. He could just hold up a sign that said Yes or No. I created a collection of useful and fun signs. The most popular sign is "You're On Mute." Here's a link to signs that you can customize: bit.ly/evmsigns.

If you need to step away or take another call, there is no established etiquette. This is a place where your virtual meeting can establish an etiquette. In one successful virtual meeting, the attendee chats BRB or "Be right back" and then steps out. If necessary, they mute their microphone and turn off their camera. When they return, they unmute their microphone and turn on their camera and chat, "I'm back."

Air Traffic Control

One of the top problems with virtual meetings is people talking over each other. Until technology comes out where attendees can talk at the same time, nobody can understand anything when two or more people talk. To maximize your virtual meeting, create systems to make sure that all audio is clear and understood by all attendees. Imagine that your audio channel is like air space and that you want to create air traffic control so you don't have collisions in mid-air. Good air traffic control includes systems so that only one attendee is talking at a time and that someone is in charge of muting attendees who are loud by accident. This can include children, pets, lawnmowers, and other noises that are transmitted to your virtual meeting. If you're having a one-on-one meeting, you won't have to worry about this as much, but as your meeting grows in attendees, the problem grows. Attendees should raise their hand to speak, and if two or more people want to speak, the air traffic control person should choose the order.

To practice, just have every person check in, such as with their name and where they are calling from. Make sure every attendee has the opportunity to check in if you have 25 attendees or fewer.

Air traffic control also means maximizing your audio. If someone has noisy audio, such as moving, wind noise, background noise, leaf blowers, pets, or children, you don't have to say anything. As the host, just mute them and they will figure out how to unmute themselves if they want to say something. You can click their window and click mute or find them in "Participants" and click mute. Clear audio is critical to an engaging virtual meeting.

Go to bit.ly/evmatc to see an example of air traffic control in action with a professional host and producer.

What's the value of air traffic control? KC Frankenberger at Reynolds Community College (reynolds.edu) asked to be air traffic control for a virtual meeting. She noticed that out of all the virtual meetings, the most work got done at this meeting *and* the team got the most work done in the day after the meeting than in any other day over the past two months.

Get Productive with Virtual Tools

Chat and Share are two of your top virtual tools. Chat is a way to communicate by text during the meeting. It's powerful because it's the easiest way to communicate while someone is talking. Share is powerful because it allows you to share anything that you see on your screen. It's the fastest way to have all attendees understand what you're talking about and get on the same page.

Chat

Because only one person at a time can talk effectively in a virtual meeting, chat is the second most powerful engagement tool in virtual meetings.

- After learning air traffic control, show everyone Chat.
- Have everyone chat "Hello" or their favorite hobby.
- Once everybody has chatted, encourage attendees to chat while other people are talking.

Chat engages attendees to focus on the meeting and give immediate feedback without having to wait.

This feature helps the extroverts in the group who think out loud and want to share their thoughts in real time.

Chat also helps introverts, as after consuming audio, video, and chats, they often have the right answer and one of their chats can change the entire meeting.

In a poll I conducted online, 41 out of 41 of my industry professionals said that Chat is required for engaging virtual meetings.

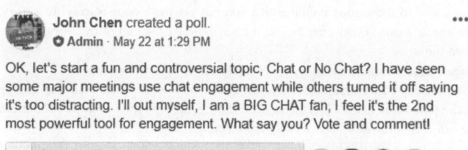

John Chen created a poll.
⬢ Admin · May 22 at 1:29 PM
•••

OK, let's start a fun and controversial topic, Chat or No Chat? I have seen some major meetings use chat engagement while others turned it off saying it's too distracting. I'll out myself, I am a BIG CHAT fan, I feel it's the 2nd most powerful tool for engagement. What say you? Vote and comment!

◉ **Chat**
Added by you

○ **No Chat**
Added by you

+38

One organization turned off Chat because they had a negative experience with it and found it distracting. Further research showed that the attendees on chat were giving feedback that they couldn't hear, the content was pre-recorded, no one was responding to their chat in real time, and the meeting wasn't meeting their expectations. Instead of adding a chat moderator and responding to the feedback, they decided to turn off Chat. Turning off Chat did not solve the problem; it only silenced the feedback to the actual source of the problem. The lesson here is to listen to your attendees' feedback and respond quickly, especially if that feedback is on Chat.

If you have a larger meeting, consider assigning or delegating the responsibility of monitoring the chat to someone on your team. It's their job to welcome people by chat as soon as they log in, ask engaging chat questions, and acknowledge people who chat so they and others feel more comfortable chatting.

If you're attending someone else's virtual meeting, hit up the chat room. It's the fastest way to find out if the organizer or speaker is paying attention to chat. If no one replies, you know that they are not looking at it. For me, that is very non-engaging, the same as if a famous speaker ignored me. Quite often, I find that it's not the speaker I want to network with, it's the people who are replying to my chats.

Share screen: We all need to meet to get work done. Collaboration is one of the most powerful tools for teamwork. The first way to get work done is to create an agenda before the meeting.

Decide how you'll open the meeting, what you want to get done, and how you're going to close the meeting. Plan with people who will be presenting during the meeting. Send out the agenda to everyone before the meeting.

Learning how to share documents and videos is a key skill to getting work done. The following is an example using Zoom.

Click "Share Screen" and choose Screen 1.

Open up a document.

An easy way to show your attendees that you can get work done is to write a story. Write a story one line at a time; every attendee must contribute. At the end of the story, ask if everyone agrees with the story.

Another valuable exercise is to write the agenda for your next meeting.

If you have shared tools, such as Microsoft Office or Google Docs, email the link before the meeting and post a link in the chat during the meeting. Take the time to show your attendees that everyone can edit at the same time during the meeting.

To share a video, click "Share Screen," then click "Share computer sound";[3] choose Screen 1 and click "Share."

Without being face-to-face, Share Screen is one of the best ways to engage your virtual meeting attendees, collaborate, and get something done that everyone agrees with.

End Your Meeting on a High Note

Do you want attendees to want to come back to your meeting? Find a way to end on a high note. You can ask a simple question such as "What did you get out of this meeting?" and ensure that you have enough time for everyone to answer. If you have a large meeting, ask the question in Chat. If you are short on time, ask everyone to use the sign language for applause for the meeting organizer. Ask people to raise their hands next to their head, then shake both hands, which is sign language for applause.[4] You can end your meeting on a high note in under 30 seconds because it's easy to teach, no one has to unmute, and you've taught something new to every attendee.

Another way to ensure that you end on a high note is to play a musical, inspirational, or recap video. The video can be of this group meeting together in the past. It can be a music video with a song that every attendee identifies with. Music has the power to change everybody's mood. The video can be an inspirational video that will leave attendees feeling uplifted before the meeting ends.

You can acknowledge others in the meeting. Acknowledgment doesn't cost anything and it's shown to be a key factor in high-performing teams. A Globoforce research study in 2013 showed that 89% of people are more motivated by being told what they are doing right than by being told what they are doing wrong.[5]

Whatever you do, budget time to close your meeting on a high note.

2 | Preparing for Virtual Meetings

Good Looks—The Virtual Presence Primer

If you want an engaging virtual meeting, look good. Be camera ready. Clean up. Dress as you would for an in-person meeting. Check your teeth and your hair. Make sure everything in your background supports who you are.

Here is a picture of me on my computer hosting a virtual meeting.

What do you see in my background?

What does it mean to you?

What does it tell you about me without me saying anything?

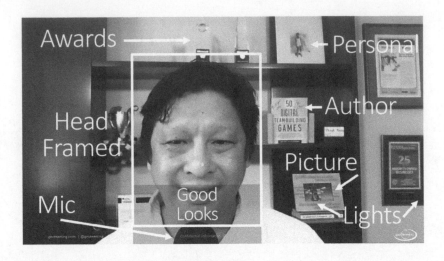

Everything in my background is there for a purpose.

In this example, there are awards, books, pictures, and personal items to tell you something about myself and the company I work for.

I use two LED light panels and a microphone to give my attendees my best presence. Using two lights removes dark shadows and ensures that my face is lit up well. Television studios use this technique to make sure their subjects look good. Bright lighting also helps your attendees see you clearly. If you have very little light, it takes longer for video cameras to collect enough light and an attendee will see a blurry video if you are moving around. This results in the attendee having to use more brain cycles to understand what your video panel is doing, resulting in more video fatigue for your attendees. In the Engaging Virtual Meeting Speaker Checklist (later in this chapter), I give options ranging from $20 to $149 for your setup.

I realized that good looks were important to virtual meetings in 1990. I noticed that even famous people calling on Skype were in their kitchens or other unflattering locations. I felt like it was hurting their hard-earned brands. I took the time to create my first designed-for-Skype office for my friend. He positioned his laptop where it would be for a Skype meeting. He turned Skype on and I evaluated everything I saw on his screen. We removed everything from his back wall, and he painted it a color that matched his brand. Together, we placed three objects to his left and three to his right. These objects were important to him and included his company's logo, an award he won, his favorite photo with a famous person, a picture of his family, and a picture of his favorite hobby.

After 30 days, he called me. During that time, most people didn't say anything about his background in the beginning of the call, but many of them commented at the end of the call that they appreciated his background. Many of them said they were going to improve their backgrounds. Most of all, he said he was statistically closing more business!

In a virtual meeting, your virtual good looks is all you have. Set up your camera or computer where you're going to meet and do everything you can to improve what attendees see in your window. The background of our videoconferences is key to the image we present of ourselves.

My friend Paul Kim saw one of my social media posts and he immediately changed his office to this. What do you see?

Paul is the chief revenue officer of Launch Consulting. He meets with a lot of top executives and he wanted to communicate the feeling of a newsroom when his clients met with him.

Paul cleaned up, shaved, is in his suit with no tie, and has his Rolex on. He's telling me that he's ready for business and he's successful.

He put a chessboard in his office, telling me that he's strategic and thinking ahead. Others may think that he likes chess or might be a chess collector.

He put CSPAN in his background, telling me that he's keeping up with the latest news and financials.

He set out books, specifically *Do One Thing Every Day That Scares You*, which tells me he is a calculated risk-taker and willing to innovate. By the way, I looked this book up and it currently costs $1,012.90 in paperback because it's out of print.

Paul has his notepad and his phone with no case, telling me he's a minimalist.

He has his journal, telling me that he likes to keep notes and values reflection.

What's most striking is what Paul does *not* have in his window—a computer. Just by putting his computer further back, Paul gives the illusion that he is not on a computer like everybody else; he's giving the feeling that you are sitting in his office. As the chief revenue officer, he knows the one thing he needs most is trust and he is using his window to create an experience just like his old face-to-face culture.

This is one of the best and most creative virtual presences I have seen in my lifetime.

Here's a memorable example of "bad looks," or what not to do, from my friend Cynthia Clay, president of NetSpeed Learning Solutions (https://netspeedlearning.com), which helps people to be online instructors:

My best/worst virtual meeting was our staff retreat. We invited a guest speaker to do some virtual team building with our virtual team. She was on camera leading some activities. After an hour, we decided to take a break and she asked me how to freeze her camera. I explained, and, thinking she had paused her camera, she stood up and turned around. At that point, we realized that she was wearing only a lacy pair of Victoria Secret underwear on her lower half. She proceeded to bend over to straighten up items on the desk behind her. Whoa, we could all not unsee that. That birthed our memorable virtual meeting motto: Always wear pants!

Even *USA Today* knows that "What's behind you on that Zoom call reveals even more than what you say."[1]

Do you want to see the latest in virtual presence? See https://twitter.com/ratemyskyperoom. They rate famous and not-so-famous rooms with witty commentary and a score from −10 to 10.

Room Rater @ratemyskyperoom · Jun 5

The chair gets a 8 by itself. @TaikaWaititi reading James and the Giant Peach is 10/10.

💬 8　　　　🔁 21　　　　♡ 750　　　⬆

Think about the best ways to improve your virtual presence (or the best ways to avoid disaster) as you learn about the Engaging Virtual Meeting Speaker Checklist.

The Engaging Virtual Meeting Speaker Checklist

Complete this checklist to be one of the top 20% of all engaging virtual speakers:

- Computer, tablet, or phone: Make sure you have a computer, tablet, or phone that allows you to connect to your meeting. Place it on a stable surface. Use the fastest, most powerful computer you have, as that will let you do more while you are meeting. Reboot your device before a big series of meetings.
- Network: Find the fastest stable connection.
  - A fast network is important so that your video and audio is clear and your attendees see and hear you clearly.
  - Most programs require .5–3.0 Mbps (megabits per second) upload (sending to other attendees) and download (receiving from other attendees) speeds.
  - Test: Use SpeedTest[2] to find your real speed. Currently, I have a 71 Mbps download speed and an 18 Mbps upload speed, which is faster than recommended.
  - Direct-connect Ethernet using a cable to your internet.
  - Wi-Fi: Get as close to the Wi-Fi router as possible.
  - Upgrade your internet speed if necessary (if your attendees tell you that they can't see or hear you).

- Software: Update to the latest version.
- Multiple screens: Two or more.
  - Monitors: If you can connect two or more screens to your computers, do it. Studies show you can get a 20–30% increase from two monitors.[3] I use seven.
  - Computers, tablets, and phones: You can also use other computers, tablets, and phones as additional monitors. This can help watch multiple chats, look up items during a call, watch email, and prepare information to share.
    - On Zoom, you can show up to 49 people on one screen if your computer processor can handle it.[4]
- Speakers/headphones
  - Use the "Test Speaker & Microphone" feature of your app.
  - Find high-quality speakers.
    - I personally use speakers because I can virtually meet for a longer period of time without headphones. It looks and feels more natural.
    - I use the Edifier Exclaim Bi-Amped 2.0 Speaker System (e10) and Polk Audio's Command Bar for loud karaoke.
  - Find high-quality headphones.
    - If you use headphones, make sure they are comfortable and loud enough for your meetings. I personally use Apple's headphones and Polk Audio's Noise-Canceling UltraFocus 8000. Look for top noise-canceling headphones online.[5]
- Mic
  - When you move to virtual, all you have is your voice and video. Here's what you need to make your voice come through crisp and clear on your virtual meetings.
  - Use the "Test Speaker & Microphone" feature of your app.
  - Find the highest-quality microphone.
    - I personally stand by IK's iRig Mic HD 2 at $79–$129.[6] I have had multiple people tell me that I sounded the best after listening to multiple speakers in a day.
    - One *Wall Street Journal* article with professional voice actor Jon Bailey recommends the Yeti at $130 and the Snowball Ice at $50,[7] while *Laptop Mag* found this most reliable, cheap microphone at $20.[8]
    - You can plug most of these microphones into a USB connection on your computer, then select the microphone from the audio settings.
  - Echo
    - If you have echo, look for two or more devices that are connected to audio and are close to each other. Remove all but one by selecting "Leave Computer Audio."
  - Background noise: Find a *quiet* location and minimize background noise such as pets, children, TVs, housemates, lawnmowers, and so forth.
  - Jon Bailey also recommends that you pick a room with soft, sound-absorbing material such as couches, rugs, and blankets. If you want to take it up a level, you can install affordable acoustic foam.

- KRISP: This is a noise-canceling application for PC, Mac, Apple, and Droid. It can remove noise from children, pets, restaurants, and so on.[9]
- Camera
  - Built-in: Use the camera built into your computer, tablet, or phone.
  - Clean: Clean your camera lens.[10]
  - Quality: Get the best camera possible.
    - Search for "top webcam"; best cameras are constantly improving.
  - Position: The camera should be approximately an arm's length away at eye level.
  - Frame: Move the camera to frame your head in the center.
    - Do *not* point your camera too high and show only your eyes.
    - Do *not* have your camera too low and point up your nose.
    - Settings: You can lock your autofocus and improve your look through exposure with a $.99 app, Webcam Systems Settings on a PC,[11] or the Mactaris Webcam Settings app for Mac.[12]
- Background
  - Clean: Remove extra items from your background.
  - Brand: Add your branding, such as your company's logo or personal awards.
  - Personal: Add a personal item to help build rapport.
  - Virtual background
    - If you are using a virtual background, make sure it works and is appropriate for your meeting.
- Lighting: I recommend two LED panels as they look great at any time of day.
  - Put the lights to the left and right of your face to eliminate shadows.
  - Use natural light. Face a window that light is coming through; know what shadows come through at every time of day.
  - Use existing lights. I would remove the lampshade and put the light behind my computer's camera, lighting my face.
  - Do *not* point your camera into a light; you will become a black silhouette.
- Good looks
  - Be camera ready.
  - Dress appropriately.
  - Change your onscreen name to a friendly name tag such as First Last, City, State, Company.
    - Example: John Chen, Seattle, WA, Geoteaming
- Ice water: Hydrate! If you are presenting, you and your voice need to be in top form. Have at least 32 ounces of ice-cold water, says Roger Love, top voice coach, whose clients include Anthony Robbins and Suze Orman.
- Clock: Look for a clock on your computer or move a clock directly below your center monitor, as some videoconferencing apps do not allow you to see your clock. This will help you to always know the time and make decisions based on the amount of time remaining for your meeting.

- Agenda: Create an agenda for your meeting. Allocate time to estimate how long you have for each section. Best practice is to make this a sharable document using Microsoft's OneDrive or Google Docs. Give access to all meeting presenters so they always have the latest version of the agenda.
  - Open: What will you do to open the meeting that helps your goals?
  - Middle: How will you design the middle of the meeting to meet your goals?
  - Close: How can we close this meeting with all members agreeing on the same goal?
- Dry run: Always meet before the meeting with all key members involved, including the meeting leader, the speakers, and the producer. Quickly test your agenda, transitions, and technology from audio and video to sharing documents and videos. Make changes to your agenda as needed.
- Backup plan: Make a plan for what to do if any of your technology fails. Make sure you have the telephone call-in number, a charged phone, and a backup battery.
- Security: Meet safe
  - Prevent Zoombombing (see Chapter 6) and unwanted visitors.
  - Passwords
  - Registration
  - Waiting room/lobby
  - Turn screen sharing off.
    - As host, know how to Share Screen to stop others from sharing their disruptive screen.
  - Remove disruptive or uninvited attendees.
    - Ensure that they can't come back.
- Present: Always be present and bring your A-game online.
  - Remove distractions.
  - Don't text or email.
  - Focus.
  - Be prepared.

Engaging Virtual Meeting Speaker Checklist

- Computer, tablet, or phone: Reboot
- Network: Test speed
- Software: Upgrade
- Multiple screens: Two or more
- Speakers/headphones: Attendees sound good
- Mic: You sound good
- Camera: Pointing in the right direction
- Lighting: You look bright
- Good looks: You look good
- Background: You look good
- Ice water: Hydrate

- Clock: Meet on time
- Agenda: What are we doing?
- Dry run: Rehearse
- Backup plan: Plan B, C, and D
- Security: Meet safe
- Present: Be your best online

Go to bit.ly/evmspeaker for the latest, downloadable copy of the checklist.

3 | Psychological Safety: How to Get the Quiet Attendees (and everyone else) to Engage

Google conducted groundbreaking research on what makes a team effective. Their research indicates that five factors are important for team and meeting performance. They are:

1. **Psychological Safety**
Team members feel safe to take risks and be vulnerable in front of each other.

2. **Dependability**
Team members get things done on time and meet Google's high bar for excellence.

3. **Structure & Clarity**
Team members have clear roles, plans, and goals.

4. **Meaning**
Work is personally important to team members.

5. **Impact**
Team members think their work matters and creates change.

Let's focus on #1, psychological safety. Psychological safety is the invisible factor that helps your meeting become engaging. In every meeting, everything I do is to help create psychological safety for attendees I have never met and who have never met me.

Attendees do not engage if they do not feel psychologically safe. Your quiet attendees may be introverted, shy, challenged by being on camera, or for many other reasons. One way to know you are beginning to create psychological safety is that your quiet attendees take one new step. For instance, they contribute by audio. They choose to turn their camera on. They contribute to the meeting by chat. It is critical that the quiet attendee chooses to contribute, not that you called them out to do it. Attendee choice is a key factor for psychological safety. Most attendees like to have choice and be in control of their input.

One way to get your quiet attendees to engage more is to acknowledge or thank them. You do not need to draw unnecessary attention. For example, just a "Thank you (name) for contributing" will do. By acknowledging, there is significant research that says this reinforcement will get you more of the behavior you want.

To have a psychologically safe meeting, attendees need to be able to contribute. If you have an expressive and extroverted attendee who is taking all the airtime, you will need to moderate. A common complaint I hear is that one or two people are taking all the airtime during a meeting. To redirect, you can ask to hear from someone else. If necessary, ask the talkative attendee to choose someone else to hear from. If you have a very stubborn talkative attendee, you can say that their audio is having problems, so you're going to go on to the next person and come back. This is a technique another facilitator showed me from the early days of cell phones. The key is to not completely shut down the talkative attendee, just moderate the meeting so every attendee has a chance to engage.

The following are ways that you can create more psychological safety.

- Be organized: Attendees can sense if you planned and are organized for your meeting. If you're at ease, they're at ease.
- Be prepared: Being ready for anything gives the attendee the sense that they are taken care of. Knowing that they don't have to take care of other tasks, like muting people, means they can focus more attention to your meeting. Make sure to do research on your attendees. Be ready to demonstrate that you prepared for the meeting.
- Come in a ready state: I've always said that if you are nervous, your attendees will be nervous. If you are ready, your attendees will be ready. You can be technically prepared for a meeting, but if you show up in the wrong mental state, it can affect your entire meeting. How you show up to your meeting is critical to your attendees' psychological safety and your meeting's result. Even if you've had a challenging situation before your meeting, find a way, such as deep breathing, to collect yourself before you log in.
- Welcome: Welcome attendees as soon as they arrive so they know that this is a safe and welcoming environment. For instance, I presented to 40 attendees from Saudi Arabia. I made sure

to say "Asalamu alaykom" ("hello" in Arabic) at the beginning of my presentation. While I do not speak fluent Arabic, they appreciated that I welcomed them in their own language.

- Acknowledge: Take steps to listen and acknowledge what attendees are saying. If you can't understand, ask the attendee to repeat. Learn the phrase, "So what I think I hear you say is . . ."
- Be open-minded: Even if you don't agree with an attendee, find a way to have an open viewpoint by acknowledging and not judging what they said. A quick way to disengage an attendee is to tell them they are wrong. Instead, as the host, find a way to be open to new ideas and ask questions to learn more. If the attendee's idea is not accepted, let the other attendees give that feedback.

- Allow and celebrate mistakes: When coronavirus hit in March 2020, it was the world's largest disruption. People were making mistakes all the time because everything was new. Finally, I got tired of people saying "I'm sorry." I created a "No sorry zone." I just let people know that it was okay, they don't have to say they're sorry around me because we're all doing the best we can. My friend, Cathey Armillas (http://catheyarmillas.com), made me this graphic, which I published on social media and got a lot of positive feedback.
- Engage all: Psychological safety is created when everyone is treated equally and fairly. I make sure to give every attendee the opportunity to talk no matter how they logged into the meeting. This prevents the meeting from being dominated by one or two attendees.
- Choice: Choice creates psychological safety because it puts attendees in control. During check-ins or openers, I allow people to participate when they're ready. This small distinction is a big help as attendees realize that I will wait and they are in control. This means that the host needs to be comfortable with silence at the right times. The other way to create choice is to present and give multiple choices for attendees to engage. For instance, I allow attendees to say "Pass" if they don't want to contribute. I make sure to present quickly for extroverts and slowly for introverts at different times.

- Make a conscious choice about recording: For most meetings, turning off live streaming and recording will create more psychological safety, as people know that they can say more—almost anything, if there is also a rule of confidentiality. If you detect there is a problem with psychological safety and you're recording, consider turning recording off and altering the discussion to talk about the real problem. In another meeting, a professional program manager encountered two teams who were fighting with each other. She turned on the record button and the announcement that the meeting was being recorded played for every attendee. The two teams reconsidered their words and the meeting got back on track. Decide how recording and not recording can benefit your meeting.

- Authenticity: There's nothing you can do to create authenticity. You need to be authentic. You need to be comfortable with yourself. You need to be comfortable hosting your meeting. You need to believe what you're saying and doing. You need to be telling your truth. This authenticity of allowing yourself to be yourself gives others psychological safety to show up and be themselves.

- Believe: If you believe you can create psychological safety and make a connection with someone halfway around the world, you can. I can tell you that I've been able to form friendships and do great work virtually because I believe it's possible.

When you have psychological safety, you should see positive results in your virtual meetings. Attendees begin to engage in ways that benefit your meeting more. Attendees start to exhibit positive behaviors that they didn't do before. Attendees are excited to come back. Attendees share personal stories that help deepen the relationships of the attendees with each other. Attendees have the courage to do things that are uncomfortable for them, like lead a presentation. Attendees create solutions that everyone follows up on when there is psychological safety. There is value for creating psychological safety and it's worth learning how to create it in a new arena such as a virtual meeting.

Zoe Euster, a project manager, applied psychological safety to her open mic virtual meeting. This was a meeting where people who don't usually perform, perform poetry, music, or whatever they'd like. It takes courage, as public speaking is the number-one fear that most people have. Read her results as she applies psychological safety to her virtual meeting:

When the coronavirus hit, I had very little experience with online events. In March 2020, I met John and was introduced to his online workshops. John taught me a lot in the first two months in training as a producer for the Engaging Virtual Meeting Workshops. I eagerly applied all I learned to my own event, a Zoom literary open mic called Words of Hope. Like his meetings, we started with intros and check-ins. The 15 attendees started to connect right away.

The spirit of psychological safety rang true through the whole event. Some of the pieces people read were very vulnerable. The readers were acknowledged and celebrated for their bravery. One person who had not written anything shared some thoughts. She had collected a list from her friends on social media about what hope meant to them. As she read, the audience engaged through nodding and deep listening.

Even though many of the folks present had never met before, a feeling of community grew. Everyone engaged at least once, whether they shared their own writing or spoke up to praise the work of someone else. The meeting had air traffic control. People didn't talk over each other. It went smoothly because people really listened to each other and reacted accordingly.

Using Chat helped build the sense of community. People messaged their socials, email address, and examples of their work for folks to read. I liked how they connected during the event in Chat but remained engaged with the performances. As host, I could moderate the chat during the performances.

I spoke with a good friend who has been to several of my live performances over the years. She said that the online open mic was one of the best events of mine that she has been to. Much of that is thanks to what I have learned from John about creating online spaces where people feel comfortable and engaged. People at the event liked it so much they want to do more online open mics!

Source: Zoe Euster, Project Manager (linkedin.com/in/zoeeuster)

4 | Managing Participants

Learning how to manage participants is a key step in an engaging meeting. Learning how to mute people who have background noise or turning on and off video is a key role of a host that helps remove unnecessary distractions from your virtual meetings. In addition, the participants feature gives multiple ways for attendees to communicate with you.

Mute and Unmute Audio and Video

Zoom
Step 1: Click "Participants."

Step 2: You can mute and unmute participants by hovering the mouse over their name and clicking "Mute" or "Unmute."

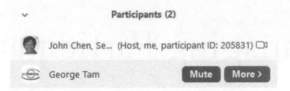

This feature also allows the host to turn off video.

Step 1: Click "Participants."
Step 2: Hover over the participant's name and click "More."
Step 3: Click "Stop Video."

You can ask a participant to turn on their video.

Step 1: Click "Participants."
Step 2: Hover over the participant's name and click "More."
Step 3: Click "Ask to Start Video."

Step 4: The participant will see a dialog box that gives them the choice to "Start My Video" or "Later," meaning they will start their video later.

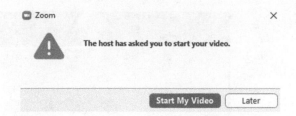

Microsoft Teams

Step 1: Click "Show Participants."

Step 2: Find the person and click the microphone to mute or unmute.

You can ask participants to turn on or off their camera.
To turn off your camera:
Step 1: Find the toolbar and click "Turn camera off."

To turn on your camera:
Step 1: Find the toolbar and click "Turn camera on."

Microsoft Teams makes it easy to look up someone from your company directly and ask if they can join your meeting on the fly. This is a useful feature if you discover you need the approval of another person to go forward with your decision.

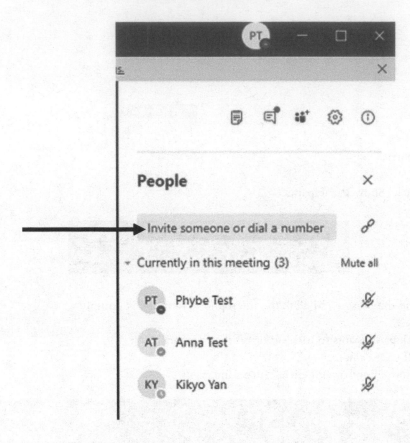

Make Host

If you are the host of a meeting, you can delegate the role of host to another participant. This feature is useful if you are the organizer of the meeting but want someone else to be the producer or take all other roles during the meeting. Making someone host will give them the ability to mute, unmute, rename, create breakout sessions, and designate the co-host role to other participants. See your virtual meeting platform for a complete list of features. This is also useful if you need to leave the meeting but want the meeting to keep going. Make someone the host and then leave the meeting, making sure you don't end the meeting for all. Once you give someone host role, you cannot take it back. The new host needs to make you host to get this ability back.

Step 1: Click "Participants."
Step 2: Hover over the participant's name and click "More."
Step 3: Click "Make Host."

Make Co-Host

If you are the host of a meeting, you can delegate the role of co-host to one or more participants and still maintain overall control of the meeting. Co-hosts can mute, unmute, rename, or record, but they can't create breakout rooms and make someone else a co-host. Co-hosting is one of the most valuable ways to never lead a meeting alone. As a host, you maintain your ability to control the meeting, including removing the co-host role from someone. See your virtual platform for the latest set of features.

Step 1: Click "Participants."
Step 2: Hover over the participant's name and click "More."
Step 3: Click "Make Co-Host."

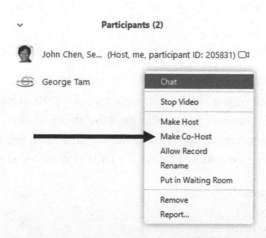

Rename

As the host, you have the ability to rename a participant. If this is a new virtual meeting, you can greet someone and ask them their name. You can follow with, "Where are you calling from?" You can rename this participant with their name and location. Like a "My Name is . . ." nametag, this helps your meeting be more engaging by displaying a participant's name, which allows other participants to get to know the attendee by their name.

Step 1: Click "Participants."
Step 2: Hover over the participant's name and click "More."
Step 3: Click "Rename."

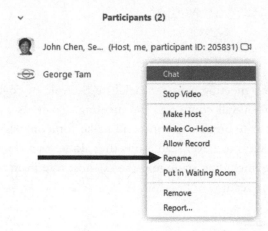

See "Virtual Meeting Nametag Openers" in Chapter 7 for more ideas on how to use Rename in creative and effective ways.

Mute All

Have you ever tried to start your meeting and you couldn't get all of the participants to stop talking? Well, now you can if you are the host. You have the ability to turn everybody's microphones off all at once. You can announce you are starting the meeting, then mute everybody and, if necessary, unmute the host and any speakers. This is very helpful with presentations.

Step 1: Click "Participants."
Step 2: Click "Mute All."
Step 3 (optional): Unmute the host and speakers.

Unmute All

Would you like to end your meeting with applause from your entire group? Would you like everyone to thank your guest speaker? Then you need to Unmute All, which will turn on everybody's microphones. This can give the feeling of a big meeting by hearing a collection of voices.

Step 1: Click "Participants."
Step 2: Click "..."
Step 3: Click "Ask All to Unmute"

Case Study: When You Think You're on Mute and You're Not

Cathey Armillas was leading a meeting when one of her attendees did something surprising when she thought she was on mute:

The funniest thing I've ever witnessed was a person who thought she was on mute and was not.

Here's the scene: I'm running a meeting for a client's leadership team and there are about 15 or so leaders on the call. One lady, who I'll call Karin, was known within the company as the sweetest, most soft-spoken person you'll ever meet. Karin was an up-and-coming star in the company. She knew her job well and was working hard to make her way up the leadership ladder. Karin has two young kids who were home during this particular online meeting. We were in a very intense brainstorming session. Lots of great energy was flowing and ideas were popping. In the background of Karin's camera, you could see one of her kids come into the room. She's a pro with online tools and so she muted herself and you could see her having a conversation with her son and she started waving her hand toward the door in the room as if she was shooing him away. Then, as she started to turn back to the camera, and the rest of the team, she must have unmuted herself. Her son reentered the room and she pulled her head off screen so you couldn't see her head anymore and all of us hear this: "I SAID DON'T BOTHER ME UNLESS IT'S AN EMERGENCY. AND ALMONDS ARE NOT AN EMERGENCY!"

She turned back into the camera frame and saw all of us with shocked looks on our faces. Her face flushed bright red as she said in a super-soft voice, "Oh, I thought I was on mute." We all died laughing. She was completely embarrassed. To this day, the team references her line when something isn't an emergency as "almonds are not an emergency!"

Don't be a Karin. Know when you're not on mute.

Source: Cathey Armillas, catheyarmillas.com

Mute/Unmute Participants on Entry

Have you ever had a productive meeting and a participant, logging in late, was driving in their car while playing their music? You can now avoid hearing this, as you can set your participant's sound when they log in. If you want to mute participants when they log in:

Step 1: Click "Participants."
Step 2: Click "..."
Step 3: Check "Mute Participants upon Entry."

There are times that you want your participants' microphones on by default. At the beginning of the meeting, you may prefer to have microphones on so when someone logs on, they can reply immediately to your greeting. To turn microphones on by default:

Step 1: Click "Participants."
Step 2: Click "..."
Step 3: Uncheck "Mute Participants on Entry."

Disallow/Allow Participants to Unmute Themselves

Have you ever had a meeting that was so unruly that participants continued to unmute themselves and talk out of order and over each other? This can be very important if you have a speaker or a collection of speakers for a presentation. Any nonspeaker attendee noise, like someone coughing loudly in your meeting or unwanted attendees coming in to protest your meeting, becomes distracting. You can control this during your meeting to ensure that you have the engagement you want. To disallow participants to unmute themselves:

Step 1: Click "Participants."
Step 2: Click "…"
Step 3: Uncheck "Allow Participants to Unmute Themselves."

Most participants want control. If you are having a meeting instead of a presentation, then the default is to give control of muting and unmuting to the participant. Another example is if after a speaker finishes, there is a question-and-answer period; you can give control back to the participants to unmute themselves to ask a question. Here's how to allow participants to unmute themselves:

Step 1: Click "Participants."
Step 2: Click "…"
Step 3: Check "Allow Participants to Unmute Themselves."

All of these are small details that can help your meeting be more engaging by minimizing distractions and focusing on the task you are attempting to complete.

You can look up all the latest participant features on Zoom or your virtual meeting platform.[1]

Remove

Have you ever had an unwanted visitor enter your virtual meeting? They might not be authorized to be there. They might be exhibiting disruptive behavior. You can remove this attendee to keep your meeting productive and engaging.

To remove an attendee:

Step 1: Click "Participants."

Step 2: Click "More" next to the participant's name.
Step 3: Click "Remove."

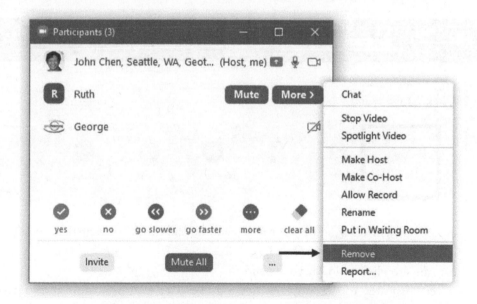

This will remove the participant from your meeting. It is set by default that a removed participant can't reenter the same meeting.

If you have a repeat offender, you can click "Report . . .," which will send a report to your virtual platform. If enough people have reported a user, the virtual platform will revoke their account.

Raise Hand

Do you have participants who don't turn on their video cameras? Do you have more than a screenful of participants? Are you looking for an easy way to find out who wants to ask a question or contribute to the meeting?

Then consider using Raise Hand as your meeting's preferred way of engaging and helping air traffic control. Clicking "Raise Hand" will raise a virtual hand that the host can easily see. The host can engage with all of the participants who have their hands up and the host can lower a hand after the participant has contributed. You can also take informal polls using the Raise Hand feature. Teach "Raise Hand" at the beginning of your meeting and continue to use it throughout your meetings so your participants can get used to using this feature and feel engaged.

To "Raise Hand":

Step 1: Click "Participants."

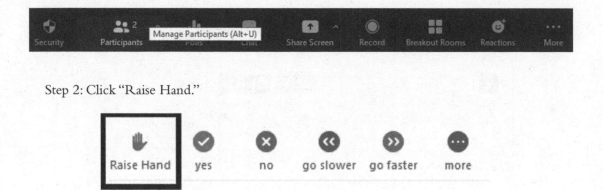

Step 2: Click "Raise Hand."

Your raised hand will show up on your video and on the host's "Participants" window.

You can click again to lower your hand.

Your host can also click to lower your hand.

This is a very easy way to ask people something like "Can you hear me?" and to have them raise their hand if they have a question.

Microsoft Teams

In Microsoft Teams, it's even easier to raise hands.

Step 1: Click "Raise your hand" on the toolbar.

You will move to the top of the list of participants so it's easy for every participant to see your raised hand when there is a big audience. The host can lower your hand after your question is answered. You can lower your hand if your question has already been answered or you no longer want to contribute.

If you train your group to all raise their hands, the host can click "Clear all" or "Lower all hands" to lower all hands.

Yes/No

Yes/No can be used for voting or fast two-option polling for your group. The host can see the number for each vote in real time and report that result back to the group. This can help with quick decision making or taking official votes on decisions.

To use Yes/No:

Step 1: Click "Participants."

Step 2: Click the green checkmark for Yes and the red X for No.

To teach your participants how to use Yes/No, you can start with an easy question such as "Can you hear me?" Add the hand motion of putting your hand to your ear so your participants should be able to understand that you are asking "Can you hear me?" even if the audio isn't working.

To finish teaching this tool, ask your participants to chat questions that can be answered Yes/No. As the host, you see a count of Yes and No and can share that count with the participants. You can encourage people who haven't replied to select one to make sure you get 100% participation.

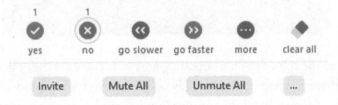

Go Slower/Go Faster

Did you ever wish you could tell your instructor or presenter to go faster or slower? Well, now you can. If you have a meeting that could benefit from feedback from the participants, then consider using the Go Slower and Go Faster buttons. My friend took a video editing course that did not use Go Slower and Go Faster in which the instructor proceeded to teach a feature that he had never seen before. He could not get it to work as the instructor showed it and by the time he figured it out, he had already missed 25 minutes of instruction. A Go Slower button here could have increased the instructor's effectiveness greatly.

To use Go Slower/Go Faster:

Step 1: Click "Participants."

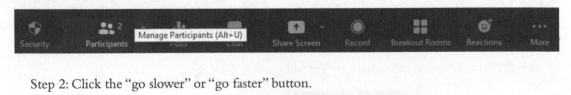

Step 2: Click the "go slower" or "go faster" button.

If you are the host, you need to pay attention to these buttons on your Manage Participants control and respond to your participants when they start clicking the buttons. You can ask a question to check to see what part is too fast or too slow. An easy exercise to teach your participants this feature is to read a paragraph of a book. Start off reading it too fast, watch for most attendees to say "go slower," then slow down to a snail's pace; then, when most participants say "go faster," speed up until you see most of the "go faster"s go away.

Dislike/Like

Do you need a way find out if your participants like or dislike a topic? Teach them the dislike and like buttons. For a simple two-way question, I would use Yes/No or even a hand raise on the screen if that's faster. You can attach more meaning by using like and dislike through the virtual meeting as a way to express your mood or your thoughts about the current topic.

To dislike or like:

Step 1: Click "Participants."

Step 2: Click "more."
Step 3: Click the thumbs-down for "dislike" and the thumbs-up for "like."

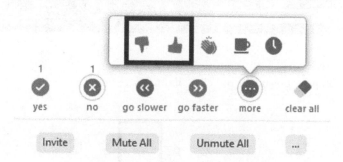

As the host, you can get a count of how many thumbs-ups and thumbs-downs you have.

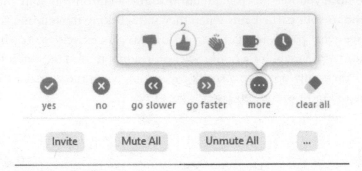

Note: This is different than the Reactions->Thumbs Up, so if you show both or your participants know both, be clear about which one you are using. I recommend using the Reactions->Thumbs Up before Dislike/Like because it's easier for attendees to access it.

Clap

Do your participants have their video turned off? Do your participants have their audio muted? Do you want to signify applause for a large audience? Consider using Clap. Clap will put a clap icon next to an attendee's name in the "Participants" screen. Anyone can see the icon in the "Participants" screen and can see if the majority of people are clapping.

To Clap:

Step 1: Click "Participants."

Step 2: Click "more."
Step 3: Click the hands applauding or "clap" icon.

> *Note:* This is different than Reactions->Applause, so if you show both or your participants know both, be clear about which one you are using; otherwise, you will have to keep track of both locations and it will take more effort if you need to merge the "Clap" and the "Applause" results together.

Need a Break

Have you ever had a speaker go too long on a topic? Has a meeting been so intense that you needed a break? Do you need a bio break now? Consider adopting the "need a break" icon into your meeting. Show this at the beginning of your meeting and now your participants have a way to communicate to you that they need a break. They just need to click the "need a break" icon and when you see a good collection of these icons, allow for a 10- to 15-minute break if you want to maintain high engagement.

To have your participants tell you that they need a break:

Step 1: Click "Participants."

Step 2: Click "more."
Step 3: Click the "need a break" coffee cup icon.

If you're the host and you show how to use this icon, make sure you follow up and listen to your participants. Engagement is a two-way street and if you accidentally make it a one-way street, such as if your participants offer you feedback and you as the host ignore it, then your participants are much less likely to offer you future feedback.

Away

Do you need to take a phone call? Do you need to run to the restroom? Do you need to attend to your children or pets for a moment? Find a way to communicate that to your other attendees, especially if you are responsible for a portion of the meeting or if you're presenting. There is no consistent etiquette yet for all virtual meetings but you can establish one for your meeting. You could mute your microphone, click your "away" icon, and then leave your video on so everyone can see that you are not at your computer. Muting your microphone means that any conversations you need to have or accidental background noise will not be heard in your meeting. Clicking the away icon will tell people that you left and not to call on you. Leaving your video on will confirm that you're gone or you have returned and if you're available or still taking care of something such as a phone call.

To turn on "away":

Step 1: Click "Participants."

Step 2: Click "more."
Step 3: Click the "away" clock icon.

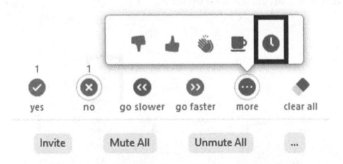

Think of this as the virtual way of stepping out of a meeting for a phone call. Proper etiquette usually says to not take calls during important meetings, but if you must do so during a face-to-face meeting, then have your phone ringer on silent, motion that you need to take a call, walk out of the meeting room, and then take your call. All of these steps are taken to cause the least amount of disruption to your meeting. The host of your meeting should notice and not call on you or schedule around your presentation until you get back.

Clear All

Did you just ask 100 people to vote Yes or No? Did everyone in your meeting just clap? Did everyone in your meeting ask for a break and now you're on break? These are all perfect opportunities to "Clear All." "Clear All" removes all the participants' icons such as Yes, No, go slower, go faster, and more.

To Clear All:

Step 1: Click "Participants."

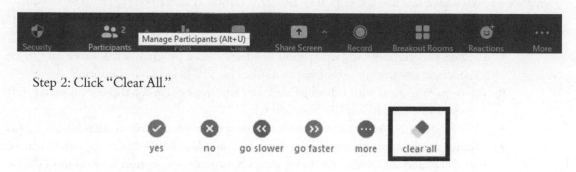

Step 2: Click "Clear All."

This feature is only available to hosts and co-hosts. This is a quick way to clear all the responses from everybody. You can use this to clear all the responses before you ask for new ones.

★★★

Learning all the tools to manage participants is what makes a great, interactive digital event. Joan Eisenstodt of Eisenstodt Associates is a meeting veteran. She is a legend in conference programs, contract negotiations, and diversity and inclusion in meetings. Joan reminds us that every attendee has different needs and great meeting design learns how to address these needs.

I'm an aural learner . . . someone who likes to talk out issues. It is almost the only way I learn and understand concepts—by saying what I think is being said and having a conversation about what applies. I'm also a strong Introvert (see MBTI[2]) who "wants to be alone."

Webinars generally are difficult for me to deliver and in which to participate. Yet many are used to them because so many meetings are delivered by "sages on stages" without more than the aisle mic for "Q&A at the end," which is not remotely interactive.

I write to contribute to this long-needed book because of what John Chen does so well in physical meetings and digitally to engage people. As I write, I'm a participant in a Zoom presentation that (a) doesn't list the participants; (b) doesn't allow us to see the other participants' faces if they want to be seen; (c) only allows general discussion to the presenter and (d) though I asked in the chat for all to introduce themselves, only two others have replied. I do not know how many of us are here.

Let me tell you about one of my best physical meeting experiences: a large area was set behind the production and main stage with comfy seating clusters where I sat with a colleague. My aural-learning self could talk during the sessions presented from the main stage to discuss what we heard without disturbing the speaker. Twitter was another way to engage with those who were "out front" and wanted to discuss the content.

What's best for digital is what's best for physical meetings:

- Provide expectations for participation in advance. As a program starts, make sure to let attendees know that it's acceptable to not be "seen" if being seen is optional.
- Allow participation with others in attendance in some form for those who prefer it. If it needs to be limited, explain how and why.
- Have a question asker/moderator to keep the speaker connected to attendee questions.
- Ensure participation is inclusive for those who are deaf, hard of hearing, blind, or have low vision, and who prefer not to be seen. Captioning is an option now on most digital platforms.
- Describe the slides—not read the words—and describe images for all who are unable to see.
- Encourage engagement in whatever way is possible.
- Provide slides, notes, and resources ahead of the program. For those like me who take notes instead of frantically writing what's being shown and said, encourage printing on post-consumer or other non-paper materials (I like Ecopaper as a source). Those of us who like taking notes or writing thoughts can do so with the presentation so that we don't have to madly listen, take notes, and engage at the same time.
- Use language appropriate to the audience—and please, avoid calling everyone "guys"— it is not generic.

Source: Joan Eisenstodt, eisenstodt.com

5 | Virtual Engagement Tools

There are a lot of engagement features built into every video platform. The best ones and how to use them are discussed here. As of June 2020, the top popular videoconferencing apps are Zoom, Microsoft Teams, RingCentral, and GoToMeeting.[1] The one constant in technology is change, so this list can change rapidly. The good news is that you can find similar features on whatever your favorite platform is.

"You cannot mandate productivity, you must provide the tools to let people become their best."

—*Steve Jobs*

Only use the right tools for the right job. Often, the right tool is the one your participants already know rather than a new one. Please understand, you don't have to use any or all of these tools. As the host, it's useful to know about these tools so you can help solve challenges and keep the meeting engaging by using the correct tool during your meeting.

"The (person) who moves a mountain begins by carrying away small stones."

—*Confucius*

As you think about tools, use the metaphor of small stones as your virtual meeting tools. Introduce your virtual meeting tools one at a time instead of introducing a mountain of them at the same time. Applying adult learning theory, if your participants experience success with a new tool, they are more likely to use it and are more likely to want to learn the next tool. Think about staging your tools. *Do not* introduce all of your virtual engagement tools at once. For new participants, this is overwhelming and threatening and they will consider not coming back. Instead show one or two tools after you feel your participants have mastered the existing tools they know. Invest time and introduce each tool in a unique, possibly fun and nonwork way before using it for real work. Engage your audience and find out if they like the tool. Just because you like it doesn't mean they will. Find someone who is good at using the tool. For instance, one of your participants might be an artist, so doing freehand annotations could be their skill. In your staging, have a strategy reminding yourself that your goal is to be engaging and to get work done.

You can join the Engaging Virtual Meetings Facebook group at bit.ly/evmfb for free to keep up with the latest platforms and virtual tools.

Chat

Chat is the second most engaging virtual tool and I addressed it in Chapter 1 as part of Get Productive with Virtual Tools. Let's go into further detail with Chat and how you can use it in your meetings.

The most common problem with virtual meetings is that only one person can talk at a time. As soon as your meetings get to five people or more, you most likely can't say something when you want to say it, like you would in a face-to-face meeting. Chat solves that.

Just click "chat" and type in a message and everyone attending can see. I suggest you introduce chat after you engage and interact with every participant using audio and video. The best way to introduce chat is to have everyone chat something like their name or location. As the host, make sure everybody has chatted something. If they haven't chatted, make sure you ask them to chat and, if necessary, help them find the chat feature on their computer, tablet, or phone.

To chat:

On a PC or Mac computer:

Step 1: Click "Chat."

On an iPad or iPhone or Droid phone or tablet:

> Step 1: Tap "More. . ."
> Step 2: Tap "Chat."

If a participant is on a phone or tablet, the chat window covers some or all of their screen, so they will have a harder time watching chat all the time. They do get a notification with every new chat, but they will be slower to reply by chat.

Private Chat

Remember when you could have sidebar conversations in a meeting? You could whisper to the person next to you about the meeting and not disturb the actual meeting. If you do that in a virtual meeting, every participant hears you at the same volume as the speaker; it is very distracting and could be embarrassing, depending on what you are saying.

Private chat is the sidebar conversation. Private chat is the ability to send a message to one participant that no one else can see.

To "private chat":

> Step 1: Open your chat window.
> Step 2: Select To: and choose a participant.
> Step 3: Type a message and hit enter.

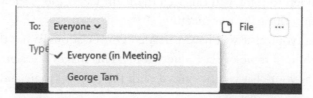

Be very careful to double-check who you are sending to if you are sending sensitive information. If you private chat someone or someone private chats you, most virtual meetings will default to private chat back to that person. That's great, except when you want to chat to everyone. A common mistake is to send a private chat to a participant when you meant to send it to everybody.

Microsoft Teams
To chat:

Step 1: Click "Show conversation."

Step 2: Write a message and press Enter.

Microsoft Teams has a robust chat feature that includes font editing such as size and color; a standard, important (marked as important), and urgent feature (chatting someone will notify them every 2 minutes for 20 minutes); chatting files; emojis (emotion icons such as happy and sad), GIFs (moving pictures); stickers; and any Microsoft app such as Microsoft Forms to send a survey in the chat.

If you have a large screen or multiple screens, you can follow chat in a separate Teams window or in an internet browser using http://teams.microsoft.com to find your chat. This will give you the advantage of being able to see your meeting, your participants (for hand raising or muting), and your chat window at the same time. This can give you the ability to respond quickly if you are paying attention to all of the windows. I suggest you have a scanning routine. Much like lifeguards are taught to scan from left to right, you can scan the main video, the participant window, and the chat window consistently through your meeting.

In Microsoft Teams, your chat will have threaded conversations. What this means is that you have the choice to reply to a topic or start a new topic. This makes it easier for all participants to follow a conversation, as your chat will be shown with the original topic and easier to understand as you can read the replies in order.

Breakouts

Breakouts are the third most valuable virtual meeting engagement tool behind audio/video and chat. The key reason breakout rooms are engaging is that they change speaking and engagement dynamics. By putting participants into smaller groups, more people can talk, and some people who are not comfortable asking questions in a large group are more likely to participate in a small group. One benefit of more people being able to talk means that your meeting can be more engaging.

You must turn this feature on before you can use it. Here's how to turn on Breakout Rooms in Zoom:

Step 1: Log in to your account on zoom.us.

Sign In

Email Address

john@geoteaming.com

Password

•••••••••   Forgot password?

Zoom is protected by reCAPTCHA and the Privacy Policy and Terms of Service apply.

Sign In

☑ Stay signed in   New to Zoom? Sign Up Free

Step 2: Go to the "Admin" section and click "Account Management."
Step 3: Click "Account Settings."

ADMIN

> User Management

> Room Management

∨ Account Management

Account Profile

→ Account Settings

Step 4: Click "In Meeting (advanced)," turn on "Breakout Rooms."
Step 5: Check the "Allow host to assign participants to breakout rooms when scheduling" box.

Breakout room

Allow host to split meeting participants into separate, smaller rooms

✅ Allow host to assign participants to breakout rooms when scheduling [V.]

If this feature is not available to you, it can be turned off at the company level. Ask your company's IT department if it's turned off and whether they will consider turning it on.

The next time you start a meeting, you'll see the Breakout Rooms button.

When you have three or more people in your meeting, you can create a breakout room.[2] Automatic assignments will randomly and evenly assign participants to breakout rooms. This feature is great if you did not plan ahead or if you are looking for random networking.

To create a breakout room using Automatic assignment:

Step 1: Click the "Breakout Rooms" button.

Step 2: Click the number of rooms you want.
Step 3: Click "Automatically."
Step 4: Click "Create Breakout Rooms."

Step 5: Click "Open All Rooms."

Step 6: Participants will receive a message to join their breakout rooms.

Step 7 (optional): As the host, you have the capability of joining any room. It is a good practice to check that each room has participants in it and that they understand what they should be doing. To join a breakout room, click "Join" next to the Breakout Session.

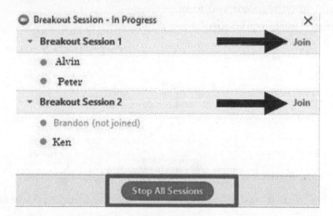

Step 8 (optional): Click "Broadcast a message to all" and enter a message to send to all. *Tip:* Have your messages ready, copy and paste a message, and then click "Broadcast" at the specified time. See the example below for a suggested format for broadcast messages.

Step 9: Click "Close All Rooms" and participants will return to the main meeting.

To create a breakout room using manual assignment:

Step 1: Click the "Breakout Rooms" button.

Step 2: Click "Manually."
Step 3: Click the number of rooms you want.
Step 4: Click "Create Breakout Rooms."

Step 5: Click "Assign" next to each breakout room and check who you'd like to assign to that room.

Step 6: Click "Open All Rooms."

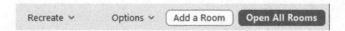

Step 7: Participants will receive a message to join their breakout rooms.

Step 8 (optional): As the host, you have the capability of joining any room. Again, it is a good practice to check that each room has participants in it and that they understand what they should be doing. To join a breakout room, click "Join" next to the Breakout Session.

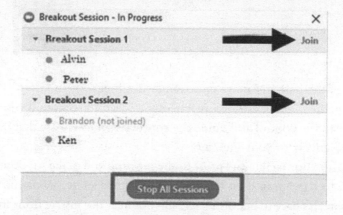

Step 9 (optional): Click "Broadcast a message to all" and enter a message to send to all. *Tip:* Have your messages ready, copy and paste a message, and then click "Broadcast" at the specified time. See the example below for a suggested format for broadcast messages.

Step 10: Click "Close All Rooms" and participants will return to the main meeting.

You can randomly assign people to rooms or you can assign people to specific rooms.

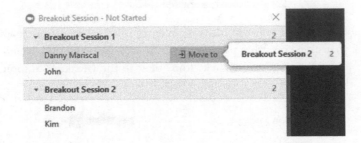

Here are some of the best and more creative uses for breakout rooms.

In a learning meeting, one of our best practices is to have a breakout room facilitator who can help monitor the air traffic control and guide the conversation to ensure that it's engaging and can be reported back effectively to your meeting.

You can meet with your facilitators prior to the meeting and make sure they know the agenda and what you'd like to happen in each breakout room. Since some people may not have been in breakout rooms before, it's easy to get distracted and not hear the instructions from the host. Assign one facilitator to every room. Next, assign other participants to the rooms.

Another best practice is to pre-write breakout messages. We find 6 minutes for a 60-minute meeting is a good breakout time to start with; it's not too long and not too short. You should put two to six people in a standard breakout where they are addressing a question or a topic. The goal of the breakout is for one member to report back to the main meeting for 30 or 60 seconds. The guidelines for the breakout meeting are that every participant gets an opportunity to contribute and you have a speaker ready by the end. For a 6-minute breakout, here are example messages to discuss engaging virtual meetings:

Welcome to your breakout room; you have 6 minutes to discuss what makes a virtual meeting engaging.
There are 4 minutes remaining—remember to give each person at least one chance to talk.
There are 2 minutes remaining—remember to select one person to report back in 60 seconds.
There is 1 minute remaining—close up your conversation by the end of the 60-second timer.
Now click the "Close Breakout Rooms" button.

New uses for breakout rooms are developing every day. Here is a clever way to give participants thinking time. Create breakout rooms of one person each and send people off to the breakout room to contemplate a question or their learning. This benefits those who like to analyze or need quiet time to process information, such as introverts. Jimbo Clark at Innogreat (innogreat .com) was the first person I saw to use this.

Here is Zoom's current guide to managing breakout rooms.[3] Please know that this technology is rapidly changing, so make sure to test out breakout rooms before you attempt to use them in a meeting.

Microsoft Teams Breakout Rooms

To create breakout rooms in Microsoft Teams:

Step 1: Create one or more meetings in your Microsoft Teams calendar.
Step 2: Copy the links for each of the meetings.

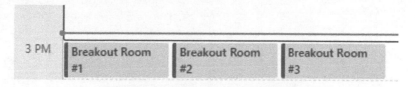

Step 3: During your Teams meeting, chat the links to the breakout rooms.

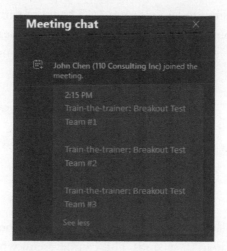

Step 4: Give clear instructions of who should click which link. For example, first names starting with A through I click Link #1, first names starting with J through O click Link #2, and first names starting with P through Z click Link #3.

Step 5: Tell every participant to click the telephone "Hang Up" button when they are done with their breakout to return to the main room.

While there are fewer steps than Zoom, Teams currently has less control. This means that an attendee can go to the wrong room and it's easier to get "lost in space," meaning stuck in a room and not able to return to the general session. One best practice is to have a breakout room facilitator and make sure they are the first person to get to a room to greet people as they enter the breakout room. The breakout room facilitator should also be the last person in the room to help anyone hang up from the room and return to the correct location. The features in Microsoft Teams are changing. You can read the Microsoft Teams blog for their latest updates.[4]

Reactions

Applause

Let's say you're having a medium to large meeting (15 or more participants) where most participants will spend their time on mute because you have a special speaker. You can ask for applause for the speaker using Reactions. This has the benefit of you and the speaker seeing the applause at the same time on the screen.

Click "Reactions->Applause" to show applause. This will show an applause icon in your video window for approximately 10 seconds. This can be useful when your audio is muted and/or your video is turned off.

Thumbs Up

You're holding a meeting and again most participants are on mute. If you want to confirm that they can hear you or that they can hear the audio from your shared video, ask them to use Reactions to give you a thumbs up. You can pause or talk to someone who doesn't have their thumbs up until you fix all the technical problems.

Click "Reactions->Thumbs Up" to show approval in your video window for 10 seconds. This can be useful when your audio is muted and/or your video is turned off.

On the diversity and inclusion front, you can customize the color of your reaction skin tone to match yours or to represent you differently.

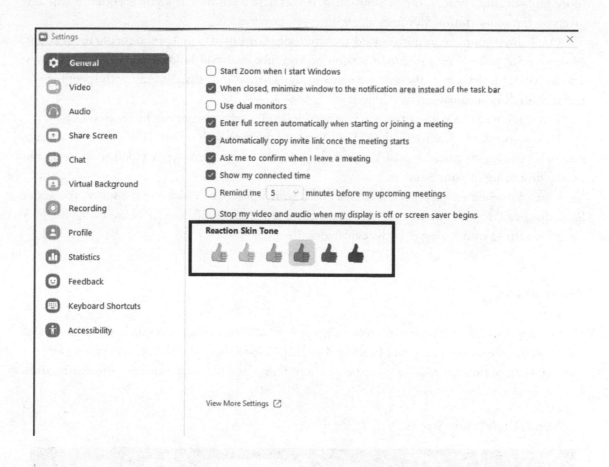

Record

Did you ever want your meeting recorded? Was it too much to set up multiple cameras and microphones? Did you want to share your meeting with someone who couldn't attend?

Zoom, Teams, and most virtual meeting platforms have a record feature. It's as simple as clicking one button. You can record to your computer or you can record to the cloud, an online storage location that can be shared easily.

If you record to the cloud, you will get a link to a video after the meeting. You can send that link to any participant to share.

On Zoom, you can set the recording to record different views such as active speaker, gallery, and presentation mode (speaker plus shared screen). If you are editing your video, this gives you more high-quality choices to edit your video. If you have a Zoom corporate account, it can also give you the transcription automatically with every saved video.

On Teams, your recording is saved to Microsoft Streams if you have a corporate account. Microsoft Streams is like an internal version of YouTube that will hold all of your videos, allow you to protect it from out-of-company viewers, and allow you to share it only with specific people; it also offers automatic transcription.

If you recorded to your computer, you need to find a way to share the file with others.

Recording allows you to use the video you create to share with others. This is a way to engage others by sharing on social media. You can also take the time to edit your video to increase the production value of your content.

One of the best examples is The Actors Fund, which produced a video of the song "You Can't Stop the Beat" to raise money for this charity. You'll see masterful editing of over 100 people's virtual meetings into a song at bit.ly/evmactors.

Share Video

Sharing a video can be a powerful way to engage your audience. Cisco's research says that 80% of the content consumed online will be video by 2021.[5] Videos have the ability to explain a lot in a short amount of time, to educate while being entertaining, and to visually engage your participants.

To share a video:

Step 1: Click "Share Screen."

Step 2: Check "Optimize Screen Sharing for Video Clip." This will also check "Share computer sound." A common mistake is to forget to check "Share computer sound," so double-check it.

Step 3: Click "Share."

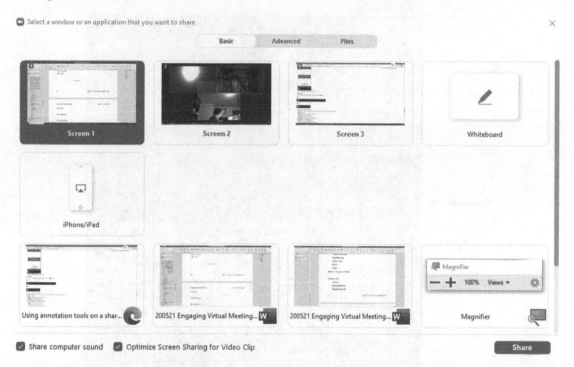

Step 4: Click "Play" on your video. If this is the first time you're playing a video, play 10–15 seconds, pause the video, and ask if your participants can hear the video. If they can, click "Play" again.

Step 5 (optional): Your audio can echo when you are sharing a video, so click "Mute" to turn off your microphone.

Step 6 (optional): If you want to see the reactions of your participants, click "More" and then click "Show Video Panel." Note that your participants' video panel will block the other participants' view of the playing video, so drag it to another screen or make sure the video panel window is in a place that is not blocking an important part of the playing video.

Step 7 (optional): Click "Unmute" when your video is done.
Step 8: Click "Stop Share."

You may choose to play a short video to create energy and make a point to your participants. You may choose to play a longer video such as an educational keynote and use virtual tools such as chat to have a discussion while you and your participants watch the video. Videos can be a powerful engagement tool when you pick and present the right video for your participants.

Share Whiteboard

The whiteboard is a good place for your participants to collaborate. Like chat, the whiteboard is a place where your participants can collaborate at the same time. It is visual so it can help you represent complex ideas quickly. For most participants, this is a new feature, so make sure to take time for your participants to learn about this tool before attempting to do work with it.

To share a whiteboard:

Step 1: Click "Share Screen."

Step 2: Click "Whiteboard"
Step 3: Click "Share."

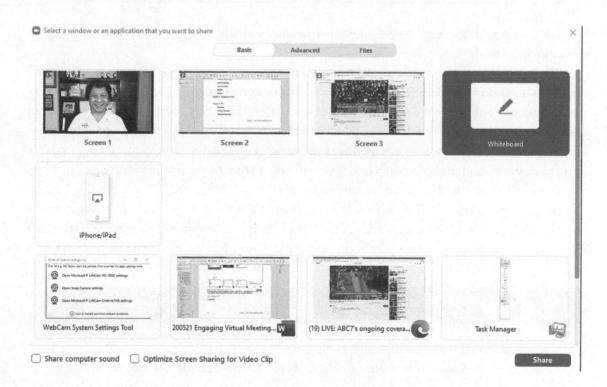

The default tool is the pen. You and every participant can draw on the whiteboard.

See Chapter 16 for how to use additional advanced virtual engagement tools, including all the annotation tools.

One of the easiest ways to learn how to use this tool is to play Pictionary. The organizer private chats a word to the drawer. The drawer proceeds to draw something to get the other participants to guess the drawn word in 60 seconds or less without talking or using any gestures. You can ensure that by turning off the drawer's audio and video. Take turns with each participant being the drawer. Now, in the future, you can use the whiteboard as a virtual meeting tool to help visualize ideas, brainstorm, and plan. You can click "Save" to save a copy of the image you create.

You can see an example on bit.ly/evmpictionary.

Do you ever brainstorm with Post-It notes? You can teach how to use the whiteboard by completing a brainstorming exercise. Click the "Text" tool, click on the whiteboard, and start typing. Have the participants add one or more text boxes with ideas on it. When the host says stop, you can move the text boxes to group them together into like ideas.

If you want to save your whiteboard, click "Save."

Click "Show in folder" if you want to know where your whiteboard is saved.

Ask the drawer to click "Stop Share."

As the host, you can click "Share Screen" to take control back and quickly click "Stop Share" to return to the gallery view.

Share iPhone/iPad

You can share your iPhone or iPad screen. If you are showing an app, you can show exactly how it looks and works to your participants, which can help if your app only works on the iPhone or iPad. This can help in making a decision to buy an app or how to use an app for an upcoming meeting. This is also a fast way to show photos or videos that are only on your phone.

This is a multi-step process. Make sure to test and practice this before you attempt to use it during your virtual meeting.

Step 1: Click "Share Screen."

Step 2: Click "iPhone/iPad."

Step 3: Click "Share."

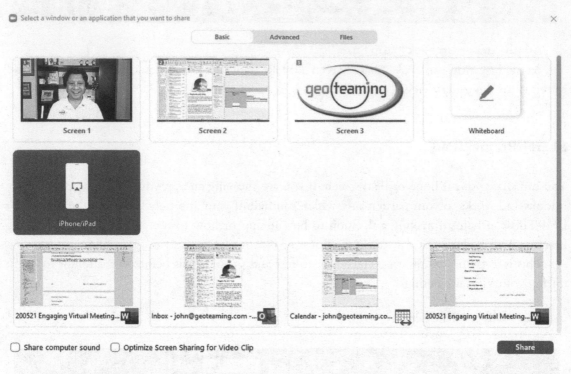

Step 4 (optional): If this is the first time sharing your iPhone, you will click "Install" on the plugin.

Step 5: Make sure your iPhone is on and that you are connected to the same network as the computer.

On your iPhone or iPad:

1. Connect to Wi-Fi network **Please connect to the same network as this PC.**

2. Tap ⧉ **Screen Mirroring**
   How to find it: swipe down from the top right corner of the screen
   On iOS 11 or earlier, swipe up from the bottom of the screen

3. Choose **Zoom-John Chen**
   Don't see it? Restart your device

Step 6: On your iPhone or iPad, swipe up and tap the "Screen Mirroring" button.

Step 7: Tap on the name of your device, usually Zoom–(device name).

Step 8: Go to your device and go to the app that you want to share. Ask your participants if they can see your screen.

Step 9: Click "Stop Share."

You can use this feature for creative uses. If you want the equivalent of an overhead projector or a second camera, you can share your device's camera. You can have it mounted on a tripod or other device to stabilize the camera. Look for new uses for this feature and use it if it works for your virtual meeting.

For a video to demonstrate this, see bit.ly/evmshareiphone.

Polling

Polling is a very engaging tool with which you can engage a large number of participants in a very short amount of time. Polling can also work for smaller groups. Once the numbers exceed 25 people, polling becomes a preferred tool as it can engage everyone quickly.

To use Polling, you need to turn this feature on:

Step 1: Log in to your account on zoom.us.

Sign In

Email Address

john@geoteaming.com

Password

••••••••••   Forgot password?

Zoom is protected by reCAPTCHA and the Privacy Policy and Terms of Service apply.

Sign In

☑ Stay signed in   New to Zoom? Sign Up Free

Step 2: Go to "Admin->Account Settings->Polling."

ADMIN

› **User Management**

› **Room Management**

⌄ **Account Management**

Account Profile

→ Account Settings

Step 3: Turn on Polling.

Polling

Add 'Polls' to the meeting controls. This allows the host to survey the attendees. 🗹

To set up a poll for a meeting:

Step 1: Log in to your account on zoom.us.

Step 2a: If you want to reuse polls, set up polls for your Personal Meeting Room and use your Personal Meeting Room for any meeting you want to poll. Go to "Personal->Meetings->Personal Meeting Room."

Step 2b: If you want to set up a poll for just one meeting, go to "Personal->Meetings->Upcoming Meetings" and select the meeting you want to poll.

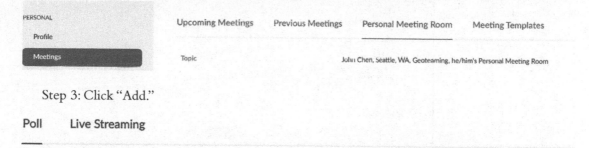

Step 3: Click "Add."

Poll   Live Streaming

You have created 3 polls for this meeting.   Add

Step 4: Enter a title for this poll.

Step 5: Check the box if you want your poll to be anonymous. If you leave the box unchecked, it will generate a report you can download that has the username, email address, date, and time they submitted their answer, the poll question, and what the user answered.

Step 6: Enter your question for this poll.

Step 7: Choose single choice or multiple choice.

Step 8: Enter an answer. Repeat one to nine more times.

Step 9: Click "Save."

Edit Poll 2   ✕

When do you think we'll be able to go out?

☑ Anonymous? ⓘ

1.
   When do you think we'll be able to go out? Defined as the
   entire US open and back to pre-Corona style business?

   ⦿ Single Choice   ○ Multiple Choice

   June 2020

   September 2020

   December 2020

   March 2021

   June 2021

   September 2021

   December 2021

   March 2022

   June 2022

   Later than June 2022

                                                             Delete

                      + Add a Question

                                       [Save] [Cancel]

To run your poll during your meeting:

Step 1: Click "Polls." A common mistake is to make the poll in the wrong meeting, So if your poll
is not there, go back to the previous step and confirm which meeting you put your poll in. A
good practice is to rehearse your poll by starting the link for your meeting and testing your poll
with another participant.

Step 2: Select your poll. If you have more than one poll, click the ⬛ and select the poll you
want to start.

Step 3: Click "Launch Polling."

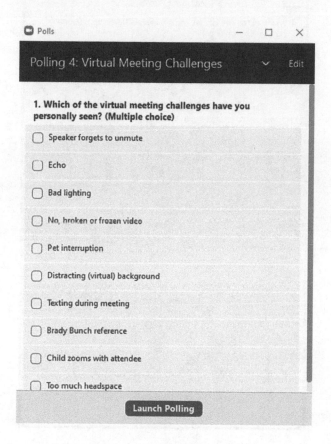

Step 4: Ask your participants if they can see the poll. This is what the poll looks like to a participant. A best practice is to read the poll aloud, including the choices. This is helpful for those who may not be able to read the screen. It also takes time for people to see the poll, make a decision, make their selections, and click "Submit." You can see how many of the participants have responded to the poll, which will help you decide when to end the poll.

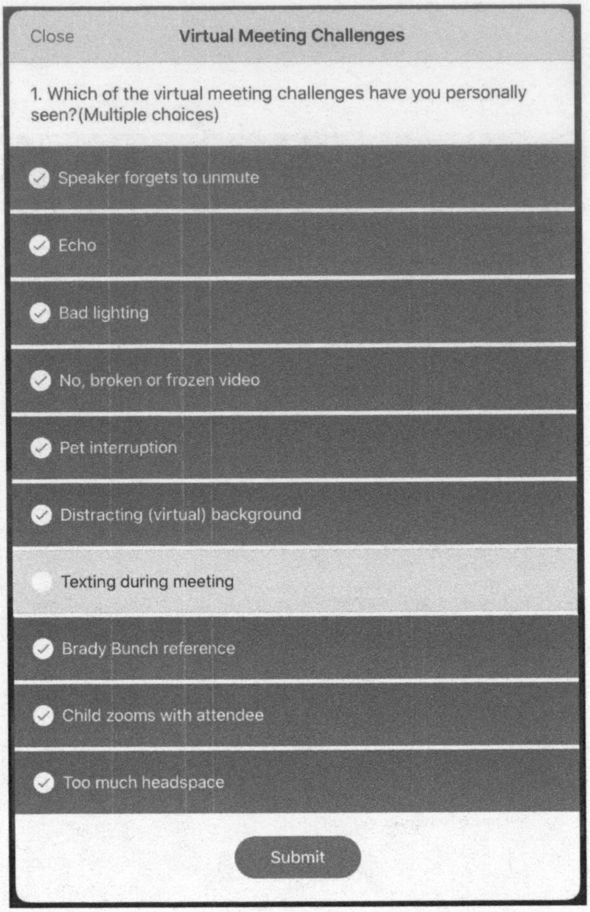

| Close | **Virtual Meeting Challenges** |

1. Which of the virtual meeting challenges have you personally seen?(Multiple choices)

- ✓ Speaker forgets to unmute
- ✓ Echo
- ✓ Bad lighting
- ✓ No, broken or frozen video
- ✓ Pet interruption
- ✓ Distracting (virtual) background
- ○ Texting during meeting
- ✓ Brady Bunch reference
- ✓ Child zooms with attendee
- ✓ Too much headspace

Submit

Step 5: End the poll by clicking "End Polling."

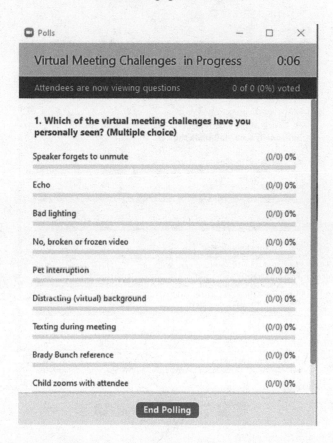

Step 6 (optional): Click "Share Results." One of the engaging features of polling is that you can instantly share the results with your participants. It's natural for participants to want to see the results of the poll and how it relates to how they personally voted. You can engage your participants by asking what they see in these poll results. This can also help you make decisions, as you can see what your participants want to do.

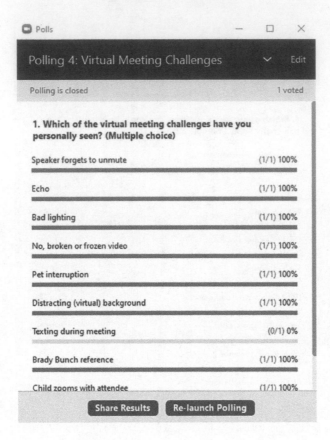

Step 7: Click "Stop Share Results" to complete your poll. If you want to run two or more polls back to back, click "Re-launch Polling" and choose another poll. Go back to Step 3.

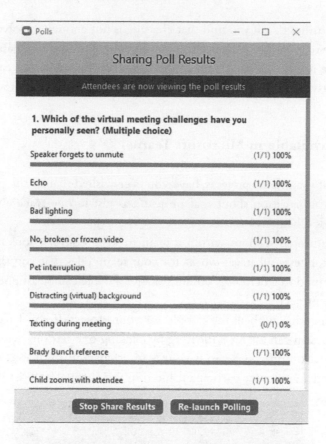

Company-Wide Chat (only available in Microsoft Teams)

While Zoom currently has the most videoconference features, Microsoft Teams excels in integration with Office 365 and other third-party applications. Microsoft Teams brings together a collection of collaboration tools that allow large groups to work together and share more information in an organized way.

Have you ever wanted to chat with any teammate, whether they were around the world or in a different area of the same building? Many virtual platforms' chat is limited only to the people logged in. Microsoft Team's chat works with anyone on your company's system. It's private to the company, so you don't have to worry about the security and challenges of open social media systems like Facebook, Twitter, and Instagram. The real value is in getting answers almost instantly. Microsoft Teams' chat is faster than email and if the other person is online, they can respond instantly.

Another key feature is that if you find that chatting is not enough to solve your problem, then you can instantly invite the other person into your meeting. Just like being able to ask someone to join your conference room, this is even faster and more convenient as you can ask anyone to join your meeting instantly, no matter where they are in the world, assuming they are up and online.

Channels (only available in Microsoft Teams)

Instead of emails that span many projects, have you ever wished that all the people, conversations, files, and important information about that project was just in one place? Now you can have it with Microsoft Teams Channels.

Channels are dedicated sections within a team to keep conversations organized by specific topics, projects, disciplines—whatever works for your team. Files that you share in a channel (on the "Files" tab) are stored in Microsoft's online storage.[6] People can be assigned to a channel as the people involved in a project.

You can call a meeting with all the people for your project. If you have already defined the people for a channel, you can ask for a meeting by clicking one button, "Meet." This is a way you can increase collaboration on your team if your team is currently available. You can schedule the meeting in the calendar and every participant listed in the channel will get the invite.

Click "Teams" and you'll see a list of channels. For a project, there is a general channel and then you can add more as subprojects.

Every channel has a collection of people who are involved with the project and will get notified if anything changes. You can have different levels of security so everyone on a project can see the general channel, but only some people will see a confidential channel.

General has key features such as posts, files, wiki (a website that allows for collaborative editing of its content and structure by its users), and any of the Office 365 apps like OneNote, Word, and Excel. What this means is that you can create a big collection of a wide variety of resources for your project that includes Microsoft as well as over 500 programs from other developers.

For instance, when we were planning for a 200-person conference, we had 36 people from around the world who were helping to deliver the conference. We had a Teams channel for all 36 people. It featured the RunTheShow Excel document that locations around the world needed to use. It also had every survey used, every infographic used in the presentations, every slide deck for the presentations, and every video that was recorded and used for playback later. Any change was instantly seen by anyone around the world who was in that channel. Ultimately, it led to an engaging meeting for the 200 attendees because the 36 people worked so well together using Microsoft Teams Channels.

Teams Apps (only available in Microsoft Teams)

A key feature of Teams is the ability to create an app that works with Microsoft Teams. Let's say your project uses Quizlet, a program that allows you to create quizzes to learn new material and share them with other participants. Instead of sharing a link that takes you outside to another program, you can add your Quizlet using a Teams app and it will be available in Microsoft Teams. There are over 500 apps as of this writing for analytics, artificial intelligence, collaboration, and more. If you are a Microsoft Teams user, take the time to learn this feature and look for solutions that already exist instead of creating something yourself.

During your virtual meeting, you can chat the link to your Quizlet app and have every participant take your quiz to find out if they retained the information from the last meeting. Because there are many apps, with more apps being added every day, new virtual tools are becoming available to your virtual meetings to help you get your job done.

There is even a Zoom Teams app, which means you can use both the collaboration features of Teams and the videoconferencing of Zoom in the same application. Some companies have chosen to do this to get the best features of Zoom and Microsoft Teams.

6 | Security

One of the hidden keys to an engaging virtual meeting is security. Security includes the challenges of securing your meeting data, especially if it is confidential or sensitive to the phenomenon of Zoombombing,[1] which is the unwanted intrusion into a videoconference call by an individual or group, causing disruption. There's nothing more disengaging than having a company secret stolen or having unwanted visitors during your meeting.

Your meetings will be much more secure than most Zoom meetings if you incorporate these three practices: (1) Use a password to protect and enable access to your meeting; (2) Do not post the link on social media; and (3) Enable the "Waiting Room" feature and dedicate a person to let invited people into your meeting.

Look up guides and articles on the best security practices for your virtual meeting platform.[2,3] Many of your settings may be set by your company as part of their IT security policies. If features such as Turn Screen Sharing Off or the Waiting Room are not available, ask your IT department if they can be turned on for your meeting. If the content of your meeting is confidential and requires a high level of security, you should research all of the security features available for the platform you are using. Then, use any and all security features possible!

Here is an example of my first Zoombomber. Unfortunately, they were able to share their screen and audio with my meeting attendees. I quickly regained control by taking back control of the shared screen and removing the user: bit.ly/evmzoombomb.

To help facilitators avoid this issue, I created a master class in Zoombombing. In this class, we used a variety of techniques, including disabling the "share screen" feature.

However, we let in all of the attendees in the waiting room at once. This is not recommended! We fended off over a dozen Zoombombers. Warning: strong language is in this video: bit.ly/evm-zoombombmc.

Require Passwords

In the beginning, many Zoom users were just concerned with attendees getting into their virtual meetings. Many changed their Zoom meeting ID to their phone number. They published their link to the meeting widely if they were advertising an open class. It worked, as many people were able to join the class easily. During the 2020 coronavirus pandemic, over 340 million people moved online and started to create new problems. Uninvited and disturbing visitors started showing up at virtual meetings. Security suddenly became a top issue and the first security measure is to protect your virtual meeting with a password.

To require a password for your Personal Meeting ID:

Step 1: Log in to your account on zoom.us.

Sign In

Email Address

john@geoteaming.com

Password

•••••••••• Forgot password?

Zoom is protected by reCAPTCHA and the Privacy Policy and Terms of Service apply.

Sign In

☑ Stay signed in   New to Zoom? Sign Up Free

Step 2: Go to "Personal->Settings->Meeting:
Turn on "Require a password for Personal Meeting ID (PMI)."

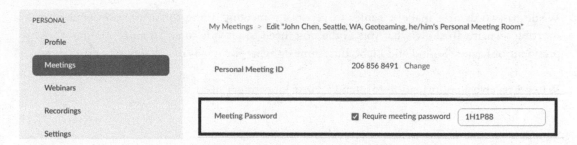

To require a password when scheduling new meetings:

Step 1: Log in to your account on zoom.us.
Step 2: Go to "Admin->Account Management->Account Settings->Schedule Meeting."
Step 3: Turn on "Require password when scheduling new meetings."

Require a password when scheduling new meetings

A password will be generated when scheduling a meeting and participants require the password to join the meeting. The Personal Meeting ID (PMI) meetings are not included.

Require a password for meetings which have already been scheduled ⑦

You can make it easier while making it secure. You can customize the meeting ID of your personal meeting room; a clever, but not as secure, trick is to use your phone number.

You can customize your password for your Personal Meeting ID to something related to you or your business.

You can create an easier-to-type link after you create a secure link. When you get the link to your meeting ID with the password associated with it, it might look like something like this:

https://zoom.us/j/5555551212?pwd=eEJmU0cvwwfUWUwraEM1TFBmTUdCZz09

This makes it secure, but difficult to type in.

To make it easier to join your meetings, buy a new URL like http://zoomwithjohn.com or create a redirection[4] from a page on your website to your Zoom link. A good example link is http://company.com/zoom. Remember, every time you share this link it could become not secure if someone shares it inappropriately.

To keep your Personal Meeting ID link safe, create a new meeting link if you host a large public meeting. You can advertise this link on more marketing resources like social media. Like a burner phone or a cheap phone, you use your meeting ID once and then dispose of your meeting code after the meeting, so if you do encounter trouble, a future meeting won't be interrupted.

Microsoft Teams automatically generates passwords for all of their meetings and does much of their security as part of their overall network security. This means you need to be logged in to your company account to get access to your virtual meetings. Also, most of the security is taken care of for you by logging in to your company account.

While passwords may make it harder to get into a meeting, using them increases your virtual meeting security. To show what you, as the host, need to provide to an attendee, Bonnie Lackey, president of Lackey Sound and Light, Inc., sums up what she needs in a meeting confirmation:

When I receive a confirmation to attend a virtual meeting, I need:

a. A link to the meeting
b. A telephone number where I can call in
c. The meeting number
d. The code number

Why don't I just use the link? You all can laugh, however, I started on the internet with Compuserve before many of you were born (1985). It was purchased by AOL. I still use AOL for my personal email. AOL's search engine doesn't support Zoom or many of the other online services. I have to copy the link and put it in a different search engine. Why do I sometimes attend by telephone? I attend by telephone sometimes because I need to use my computer to continue working while listening. Thank you!

Source: Bonnie Lackey, President, Lackey Sound and Light, Inc., http://bonnielackey.com

Turn Screen Sharing Off

A common Zoombombing strategy is to use screen sharing to take over the screen and show inappropriate videos, pictures, or text. You can turn this feature off by default and then enable it only when you know you have trusted attendees in your meeting.

To turn off screen sharing for all meetings:

Step 1: Log in to your account on zoom.us.

Sign In

Email Address

john@geoteaming.com

Password

••••••••   Forgot password?

Zoom is protected by reCAPTCHA and the Privacy Policy and Terms of Service apply.

Sign In

☑ Stay signed in   New to Zoom? Sign Up Free

Step 2: Go to Admin->Account Management->Account Settings->In Meeting (Basic)->Screen Sharing."

Step 3: Turn screen sharing on, then in the "Who can share?" section, click "Host Only."

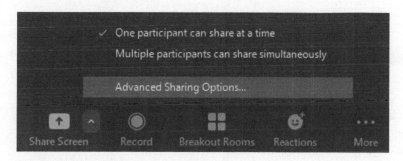

In a meeting, if you want an attendee to be able to share their screen:

Step 1: Click the up arrow next to "Share Screen."

Step 2: Click "Advanced Sharing Options. . ."

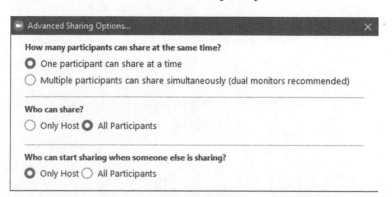

Step 3: In the "Who can share?" section, click "All participants."

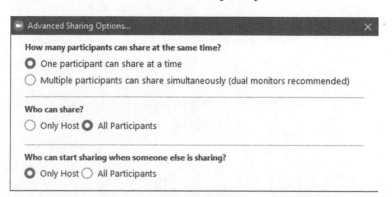

Step 4: Click the "X" on the top right of the box.

Step 5: Ask your attendee to share their screen; they should now have it enabled.

For additional security and to prevent Zoombombing later in your meeting, you can turn this option back to "Only Host" after your attendee shares their screen.

Enable the Waiting Room

If you have an open public event, I strongly recommend using the waiting room and assigning one person to admitting people in. It's like the velvet rope outside a nightclub, with your assigned bouncer carefully monitoring who gets let in.

To turn on the waiting room for your Personal Meeting ID:

Step 1: Log in to your account on zoom.us.

Step 2: Go to "Personal->Meetings->Personal Meeting Room."

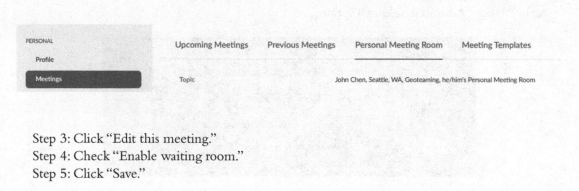

Step 3: Click "Edit this meeting."

Step 4: Check "Enable waiting room."

Step 5: Click "Save."

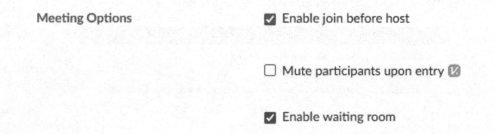

To turn on the waiting room for all of your meetings:

Step 1: Log in to your account on zoom.us.
Step 2: Go to "Admin->Account Management->Account Settings."

Step 3: Click "In Meeting (Advanced)."

Schedule Meeting

In Meeting (Basic)

➤ **In Meeting (Advanced)**

Email Notification

Admin Options

Step 4: Scroll down and turn on "Waiting room."
Step 5: Choose which participants to place in the waiting room. If you don't know which option, choose "Everyone."

Waiting room

When participants join a meeting, place them in a waiting room and require the host to admit them individually. Enabling the waiting room automatically disables the setting for allowing participants to join before host.

Choose which participants to place in the waiting room:

◉ Everyone

◯ Users not in your account

◯ Users who are not in your account and not part of your whitelisted domains

Customize the title, logo, and description ✎

You can customize the title, logo, and description of your waiting room. This is another place where you can customize your virtual meeting platform. Use this branding opportunity to further improve your company image or add a marketing opportunity. Here is an example of our waiting room.

Customize the waiting room UI

Meeting ID : 888-888-888

Let's have an engaging virtual meeting. ✎

{ Your Meeting Topic }

Your meeting will start in a moment. Take this moment and think about your most engaging virtual meeting. What did it have? What did they do? What did you do? Could you share your most engaging virtual meeting practice during this meeting? I look forward to personally meeting you!   ✎ 🗑

Logo should be in GIF/JPG/PNG format. The file size cannot exceed 1MB
Logo minimum width or height is 60px and cannot exceed 400px

[Close]

The value of your waiting room comes when you start your meeting. As the host, you are in charge of the waiting room. I suggest you train someone to be your co-host and handle the waiting room.

To admit an attendee who is waiting in the waiting room:

Step 1: Click "Participants."

Step 2: Find the attendee you want to let in and click "Admit."

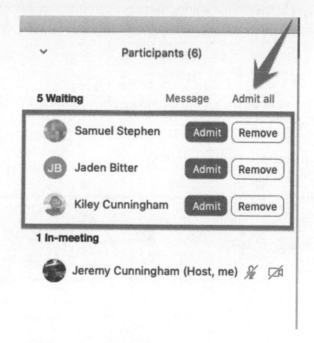

Step 3: If you do not know this person, take a moment to see that person enter your meeting and see if they are an expected attendee. If they are not, see Chapter 4 on how to remove an attendee.

Step 4: Go back to step 2 and repeat.

If you recognize everyone in the waiting room, you can reduce their waiting time by clicking "Admit all."

If you are still getting ready or if you're not ready to admit attendees to your meeting, you can send them a message to let them know you are getting ready for their meeting:

Step 1: Click "Message."

Step 2: Type a message and press Enter.

Your message will look like this to an attendee in the waiting room:

Meeting Messages

From Host to Everyone (in Waiting Room):
Thank you for waiting, we'll let you enter in just a
few minutes.

By default, the waiting room is turned on for new meetings. When you log in, click "Participants" and at the top will be a list of people waiting to be admitted. Just click the button to let them in. If you delegate this role to someone else, just wait for them to log in, click "Participants," and click "Make Co-Host" next to their name.

You can send messages by chat to the waiting room, but unfortunately, attendees can't reply. You can turn this feature on using the Security button in the toolbar if you find you need it during a meeting.

Microsoft Teams

Microsoft Teams has a Lobby, which is the holding place for their meeting.
To turn on the "Lobby":

Step 1: Schedule a meeting in Microsoft Teams.
Step 2: Click "Meeting Options."

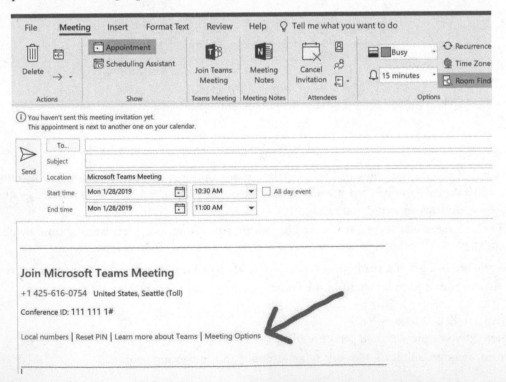

Step 3: Select "Everyone in Company" in Who can bypass the lobby?
Step 4: Click Save.

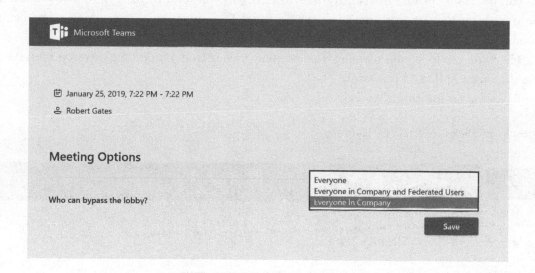

Using the waiting room takes practice if you do not know all of the people coming in. I suggest practicing with others before the meeting. One suggestion is to have people log in up to 30 minutes early so you can take more time to let people in. You can let people you know in more quickly. If you have one or more people you don't know, you can let them in one at a time, and you or someone else can watch that person and mute them or remove them if they don't belong in your meeting.

Require Registration

One way to further protect your meeting is through registration. This means that attendees need to register information, including their email, before getting a link to the meeting. You can also decide whether you want automatic approval or manual approval so you can approve each person who registered and deny people you are not expecting.

You can add branding, such as a banner and a logo, to your registration page.

See https://support.zoom.us/hc/en-us/articles/211579443-Registration-for-Meetings for how Zoom's registration works.

Lock Your Meeting

Are you discussing private or sensitive information? Do you want to make sure that you are not disturbed by new attendees entering your meeting? Do you want your meeting to be behind closed and locked doors?

Then you can lock your meeting. This prevents anyone from joining the meeting, even if they have the meeting ID and password.

To lock your meeting:

Step 1: Click the "Security" button.

Step 2: Click "Lock Meeting."

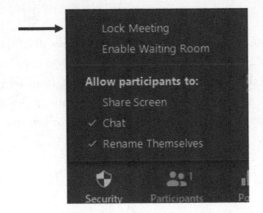

You can use the "Lock Meeting" security feature in combination with "Remove" to ensure that an unwanted attendee can't get back in. You can turn this off if you are ready to have other attendees join the meeting, such as if you are done discussing confidential information.

Control Your Meeting's Chat

Chat is the second most engaging tool in virtual meetings, but sometimes you may want to turn it off. Perhaps you have a speaker who wants no distractions. Maybe you have a security concern. Maybe your attendees are not having a productive conversation on chat or maybe they are chatting inappropriate messages. These are times that turning off chat will make your meeting more productive.

To turn off chat:

Step 1: Click "Chat."
Step 2: Click "More."
Step 3: Check "Allow attendees to chat with: No one."

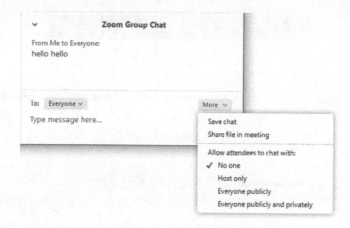

This will turn off chat for all attendees in your meeting. You can turn it back on at a later part of your meeting. Learning how to control chat will help your meetings stay on task.

Secure File Transfer

You can add more security by preventing attendees from trading files through chat by file transfer. I prefer to leave this feature on, as attendees have sent useful graphics and pictures to each other through chat. Some Zoombombers use the file transfer to send inappropriate pictures and files, so you may want to turn file transfer off before or during the meeting.

To turn off secure file transfer:

Step 1: Log in to your account on zoom.us.

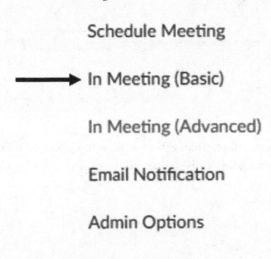

Step 2: Go to "Admin->Account Management->Account Settings->In Meeting (Basic)."

Schedule Meeting

➤ **In Meeting (Basic)**

In Meeting (Advanced)

Email Notification

Admin Options

Step 3: Scroll down to "File transfer" and turn it off.

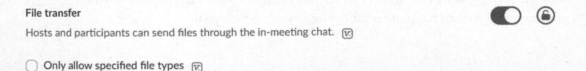

File transfer
Hosts and participants can send files through the in-meeting chat. 🔟

⚪ Only allow specified file types 🔟

How important is virtual meeting security? It's more important than you may think. A 2014 Forrester report found that trade secrets are shared in as many as 1 in 5 online meetings. That is potentially millions of meetings where valuable information could be compromised.

While Zoombombings are cretinous, they are nowhere near as nefarious as someone tuning in to your call and simply taking notes. One hacker who joins a random meeting at the right time might be able to gain leverage against that organization.

Using the right combination of security to protect your meetings will keep your meetings productive while preventing losses to your company's important assets.

PART 2

Openers, Games, and Activities for Communication, Morale, and Trust

7 | Openers

Openers are pivotal. Starting a meeting with an effective opener (or an opening game/activity) allows every attendee to feel welcomed and engaged right from the start of the meeting. If the host uses the same kind of opener at the beginning of every meeting, a sense of rhythm and routine is created. Rhythm and routine lead to stability and comfort, which improves team dynamics in the long run.

"Go slow to go fast" is a good mantra for openers. To set your expectations as a meeting host, you should expect to spend more time on creating openers the first time you use them. You'll find that, with practice, you can create openers that take less time, allowing your team to knock out an opener and get to work quickly. Most of all, you'll find that taking time to add openers to your meetings will eventually make your meetings more productive.

Why Use Openers?

The purpose of an opener is to make sure everyone is focused on the meeting and not their email, text messages, or social media.

Michelle Cummings, owner of Training Wheels and a proponent of using openers, says that openers are crucial because there must be connection before content.

Think back to when you were in grade school. Whenever a teacher would say, "Find a partner," who would you immediately want to partner with? Your best friend, of course! One of the main reasons for this is because your best friend usually falls into the category of your comfort zone. When you feel comfortable with someone, you can be your authentic, true self. Now apply that concept to your team meetings. The more comfortable we are with others, the more we will be our authentic, true selves. People need to have some level of connection before they will feel comfortable sharing their thoughts, emotions, or ideas. Individuals will naturally hold back unless they feel a certain level of comfort with the environment or the other people in the room. And when we feel comfortable with others, we will organically start to connect with the intent, meaning, or purpose of your content.

Getting individuals to connect with one or two other people in the room can have a profound impact on their engagement level. It helps to break the ice and loosen people up to talking. If you are a trainer and you have ever asked a question at the beginning of your session and received blank stares as your answer, you have probably not warmed up the room. Allowing people to have a quick conversation with another person welcomes them into the "sharing" space. Until then, it may still feel a little cold, and some individuals will not want to be the first person to speak up.

I first heard the phrase "connection before content" after my husband attended a workshop put on by Peter Block. I connected instantly with the phrase and I audibly let out a "Yaaassssss, what an amazing phrase!" One, it's a cool alliteration, and who doesn't love that. But two, it gave me a good catchphrase to use with participants that now immediately diffuses the eye-rolling in the room when I announce that we are going to start out with an icebreaker activity. (Almost!) There is something disarming about the phrase that gives purpose and meaning for why we make time for connection before we dive into business. We need to create space and time to connect before we dive into content so people feel a certain level of trust with others in the room. Inviting people to share simple tidbits of their likes, dislikes, and other interesting facts allows for a certain level of vulnerability with one another, which in turn increases our capacity to be authentic with each other. And if we're doing that when answering an icebreaker question, we are likely going to transfer that same behavior when we are talking about business strategies, resolving conflict, or confronting behaviors that need to be changed.

I use a phrase in group work, "pairing and sharing," as deeper connections and conversations generally happen in pairs or trios. Many people will feel intimidated and guarded if they are put on the spot when asked a question in front of their peers.

Pairing and sharing with one or two other people sitting near you first creates time and space for each participant to answer the question, not just one person talking while the rest of the group listens. It also allows for some brainstorming and perspective building to happen before it is discussed in the larger group.

Several years ago, I created a set of question cards I called Comfort Zone Wheelies. At the time, I had a client ask me to help their team members get to know one another on a deeper level, and to somehow get below the surface-level sharing that was routinely happening. I decided to color-code different icebreaker questions based on level of risk, and, like any good parent, I decided to test them out on my teenage children first.

On Sunday evenings my family of four holds a scrum meeting. The term *scrum* (short for scrummage) stems from rugby, and involves both teams, with heads down, packing into a huddle. The corporate world has adopted this phrase, and in basic terms it means a game plan. You can find numerous articles for how to lead an effective scrum meeting for your team with a quick Google search. We adapted this phrase for our family scrum meeting, and it is basically a game plan for the week . . . who has assignments or projects due, what kind of workload my husband and I have, whether we are traveling, who needs a ride, whether we have visitors, etc., as well as an established time we connect as a family. Toward the end of last semester when there were lots of assignments due and a few grades needed to be raised, you could tell that the boys were starting to dread the scrum meeting. When conversations around capability vs. effort, accountability, and follow-through were more dominant, we didn't always leave the scrum meeting on a high note. For one meeting, I decided we needed to start out with something a little more fun before we dug deeper into the harder conversations. I broke out the Comfort Zone Wheelies as an icebreaker for our meeting. In this deck, the questions are color-coded by level of risk: green questions are lower-risk questions, yellow questions are medium-risk questions, and red questions are higher-risk questions. I put them into three piles, and each of us started with a green question, then moved to a yellow, then finished up with a red. I wasn't really sure how it would go, but figured it was worth a try.

What happened next was something I didn't expect. I've always been a very involved parent. I feel like I know my kids very well and that our relationships are solid and deep. That night we sat for an hour asking each other these questions, and I learned more about my kids and my husband in that hour than I had in years prior. We now use them every week, and we have had more in-depth conversations in the last few months than we have had their entire lives. I feel like I know them so much better now than I did before, but the reverse is true as well. They also know me so much better as a person and a parent than they did before. We're having real conversations about tough stuff that does not naturally come up in normal conversation. . ."Hey Dawson, want to hear about the time I struggled most in life?" They now know examples of what is hard in life for me, when I made mistakes and what I would do differently if I could turn back time, what stretches me outside my comfort zone, and how I've changed in the last five years.

Overall, these question cards have strengthened us as a family in ways I cannot describe.

Here are a few examples to get you started:

Green Questions:

- Who is your greatest hero?
- Name your ideal car.
- Where is one place you'd like to go that you haven't been?
- What's one thing you wish you knew how to do?
- What was your best birthday?

Yellow Questions:

- When have you felt your biggest adrenaline rush?
- What is one dream you have yet to accomplish?
- What are three things you value most about a person?
- If you could tell your former self one thing right now, what would it be?
- What's the greatest risk you've ever taken?

Red Questions:

- What was the worst phase of your life?
- What is one thing that people misunderstand about you?
- What is something a past relationship taught you?
- What is the greatest struggle you have overcome?
- Describe something that takes courage for you to do.

I love it when I create a new tool that ends up being a huge gift back to myself. If you have any kind of relationship where you would like to know the other person better, I would encourage you to pick up a set of these cards. If you want to make a set of these cards on your own, use different-colored index cards or write the questions with different-colored pens.

In the virtual world, it's even more critical to help keep people connected when individuals may feel more isolated and less a part of your team. Reserving a mere 10 minutes at the beginning of your sessions can help reduce any barriers that may be between people, create more empathy and understanding of others' behaviors, and help clarify a sense of purpose for those you share a workspace with. Leaders who are able to be vulnerable with their teams and share some of their failures help make them more approachable and relatable. Creating time and space for connection before content will strengthen your teams in ways you cannot even imagine.

Source: Michelle Cumming, Owner Training Wheels, Retrieved from (trainingwheels.com)

Open with a Check-in Question

Opening with a check-in question is one of the easiest ways to create engagement in your meeting and create connection as everyone learns about who is attending the meeting. You learn something about each person at the meeting from their answer to the check-in question.

Have every person check in with an answer to a question. If the group is new, make sure they add information such as their name, their location, the company they work at, or their role at the company.

Following is a collection of check-in ideas.

Check-in

Goals: Show how checking in with every attendee can make your meeting more engaging. Ensure that every attendee's audio and/or video is working. Find out how every attendee is doing.

Time: 5–30 minutes
Participants: 2–25
Technology: Audio, video, chat
Category: Opener

Game Summary: Have every attendee check in by saying their name, (optional) location and the answer to one of the questions below.

Rules: Attendees must raise their hand to speak. If their video is not on, they need to raise their virtual hand or unmute and say their name. Choose one person to be air traffic control and if two people want to speak at the same time, the air traffic controller will choose an order. Every attendee must have an opportunity to check in. If an attendee's audio and video is not working, ask them to check in by text.

(Optional) You may want to use a timer if you have a lot of people or a limited amount of time.

Here is a collection of check-in questions:

What's the best thing that happened to you this week?
What's your best work achievement since we last met?
What are you working on now?
What challenges are you facing?
What's something that nobody knows about you?
What are you excited about?
What are you passionate about?
How do you know _____?
What are you watching?
What are you reading?
What are you doing this weekend?
What's your favorite restaurant and why?
What's the most recent news story you read?
What's a picture on your cell phone you can share? Can you tell us the story?
If you could be any character in a book, movie, or TV show, who would you choose and why?

(Continued)

What's your biggest fear?
What's your biggest regret?
Who is one of your role models and why?
Is there a charitable cause you support?
What do you like about working here?
If you had to describe your style so I could work better with you, what would you tell me?
How are you feeling about today's meeting?
On a scale of 1 to 10, how ready are you for today's meeting?
What's your goal?

There are many other great examples online if you need even more variety for opening questions.

One of my favorite check-in questions was, "What's your goal?" This was a key strategy I used during my 10 years at Microsoft. I made sure everybody knew what the goal of the meeting was. When everybody agreed, it helped me deal with tangents. When someone disagreed, we took time to redefine the meeting, saving valuable time instead of discovering that later.

Did you know that ClearCompany conducted research and found that only 5.9% of companies communicate goals daily? Here is a tip that will put you in the top 5.9% of all companies: send one email a day to your work team with the goals your team is working on. You could add updates to the goals. You could complete your email with the goals your team completed to celebrate. You'll immediately be in the top 5.9% of all companies!

One-Word Check-ins

Strapped for time? Turn the check-in question activity into a one-word response activity. Modify any of the sample questions so that attendees can answer the question with one word. This reduces the time to 30 seconds or less per attendee. Here are a few examples of questions that can be answered with one word:

How do you feel?
What are you looking forward to?
What's one word we need to succeed?
What's one word to describe your last week?
On a scale of 1 to 10, how do you feel?

One-Word Check-ins with Pen and Paper

Another visual and effective modification is to have attendees write down their one-word answer on paper. If you're looking for an interactive exercise that will engage everyone in an online meeting of any size and have an enormous impact, this is a great one to use. Cathey Armillas, author of "How to Rock a TED Talk," used this in her training:

The facilitator simply asks a question that everyone answers with a single word. Each person will write down the word and hold it up as a physical visual to share with the entire group. The visual is powerful because all at once, everyone in the meeting gets to see all the other answers. Many times, there are a lot of the same answers and other times there is a common theme that is present. Most of the time, there will be a few really creative answers that stand out. The facilitator can quickly read off the answers and have fresh content to use on the spot.

The first time I ever used this, I was running a marketing workshop for Hong Kong University and I asked the students this question: "In one word, please create a campaign that describes what we need to get through this global pandemic." There were about 50 students online and the answers were powerful: hope, love, breathe, friendship, togetherness, smile, look, nature, and many more.

The facilitator steps are:

1. Ask participants to bring index cards and a thick pen, like a Sharpie.
2. Ask the participants a question (keep it simple) that will elicit a one-word answer.
3. Have the participants write out a one-word answer on a piece of paper (or, preferably, on an index card) with a dark marker.
4. Have the participants hold up their answer to their camera all at once so that everyone can see all the answers. Have them hold it up long enough for everyone to read all the answers.
5. The facilitator should read aloud some of the answers while saying the name of the person who shared the answer.

The greatest power in this activity is the moment when everyone is sharing their answer and seeing everyone else's answer. It's engaging and it creates a sense of connection with everyone in the meeting. The number of people in the meeting won't affect the outcome—in fact, just the opposite. The more people who participate, the more visually stunning this exercise becomes.

(Continued)

It's best when the facilitator asks everyone ahead of time to bring a thick marker and index cards to the call. If that isn't possible, it's easy to ask everyone to write something out on any paper they have laying around. A thick marker on index cards is best to use because it's easy to read. This creates a nice visual that works better than polling or typing something in the chat box. There is something special about seeing a bunch of single words written out in different handwriting and styles all at once.

This is an exercise you can do several times throughout a meeting. You can even have fun with it and create variations. For example, you could make a game out of it where the participants have to guess the answer to something; they write down their answer and get to see everyone else's before they find out the correct one.

Either way, keep this in your bag of engagement tools. It's simple, it's easy, it's fast, and people love it.

Cathey Armillas, top TED speaker coach, creator of the "How to Rock a TED Talk" program (catheyarmillas.com)

I have used this opener and have seen other hosts use it. It continues to get good feedback as people enjoy the process of writing one word and seeing each other's response. One additional tip is to turn off your virtual background before holding up your card or to hold your card up in front of your face or shirt so it can be seen by others.

Challenging Childhood Story

Patrick Lencioni, author of *The Five Dysfunctions of a Team*, suggests that you check in with something challenging in participants' childhood. Take 20 minutes and have each teammate tell something challenging from their childhood. This simple exercise always gets people to see each other in a new way, even among executives. In one story, a not trusting micromanaging CFO told a story of growing up broke and doing anything to not be broke again. Everyone looked at the CFO in a new way after this opener.

Video Openers

These video openers are fast, easy, and super-engaging because they just use the video function of your virtual meeting. They use very little instruction, take one minute or less, and are very easy for attendees to participate in.

Video Openers

Goals: Test that video is working for attendees. Create rapport with all attendees. Increase energy for meeting.

Time: 1–10 minutes
Participants: 2–Max
Technology: Video, audio
Category: Opener

Game Summary: Give a response to the question in your video using your body.

Rules: If an attendee's video is off, pretend that the attendee is following along. If an attendee isn't following along, say their name and encourage them to participate. Each video opener takes about 30 seconds, so you can do up to 10 of them in 5 minutes.

Thumbs Up, Thumbs Down, Thumbs Middle

This is a quick opener that also lets the host know if everybody is ready for the meeting. Ask attendees if they are ready.

Thumbs up is yes.

Thumbs down is no.

Thumbs middle is that you don't entirely agree, but you agree to go along for the group.

If you have any thumbs down, ask the attendee what would have to happen for them to be a thumbs middle or thumbs up.

When you and the attendee can change the question or proposal so it would be acceptable to both, ask every attendee to vote with their thumbs again.

You can use this again later in your meeting as a voting system to make decisions. I suggest if you have any thumbs down that you change your decisions until you get at least all thumbs middle or thumbs up. If you get all thumbs middle or thumbs up, the likelihood of your attendees following through with their decision should be very high.

(Continued)

1–10

This is a quick opener that can poll your attendees quickly about a topic using only their video. It takes less than a minute and you can do more than one question to gain more information from your participants.

You would say something like, "I would like to get all of the attendees' status before we start our meeting. When I ask a question, just hold up your fingers between 1 and 10 with 10 being the best. Please hold them up until I am done reading all your numbers."

Suggested questions are:

How are you feeling now?
How ready are you for this meeting?
How excited are you for our guest speaker?
How many virtual meetings have you been on today?
How excited are you about our project?

While attendees hold up a number between 1 and 10, call off their names and their number to acknowledge them. Ask them to lower their hands when you're done.

Brady Bunch

Almost everyone (even Millennials) knows the iconic open to the 70s hit *The Brady Bunch*. Shots of Mom, Dad, the kids, and even Alice are in a checkerboard format across the TV screen, and all the characters are looking around, happily waving at the person in the boxes above and below them. The gallery view of a video call looks a lot like that opening scene!

A fun opener I like to do is to ask each attendee to try and re-create this scene by looking directly all around, as if someone is actually above, below, or next to them. If you are recording, you can edit the *Brady Bunch* theme song with your video as a fun morale booster for a future meeting.

Here are the instructions:

Doesn't this videoconference look like the opening scene in *The Brady Bunch*? This was a TV show that had an opening scene with 9 people in boxes looking at each other. Let's take 10 seconds and re-create this by looking up, down, left, right, and any diagonal.
10 (look a direction), 9 (look a different direction), 8, 7, 6, 5, 4, 3, 2, and back to center, 1. Thank you for participating.
You can encourage an attendee at 9 and below if they are not moving their head.

Strike a Pose

A fun opener is to have your attendees all pose at the same time. This can be as simple as showing a mood to remind attendees how important body language is. It can be more complex or fun by striking an unusual or theatrical pose.

Here are the instructions:

Do you remember Madonna's song "Vogue"? Have you ever seen a fashion show where a model strikes a pose at the end of a runway? Have you ever made an expression to show the mood you're in? What do they all have in common? They asked you to strike a pose.
On the count of 3, strike any pose that you'd like and hold it until I say okay. 1, 2, 3.

This activity is useful to add energy or levity to your meeting. You can pair it with "Breakouts" by asking attendees to strike a pose when they return from their breakout rooms. You attendees will laugh when they see all the different poses the attendees are in as they "teleport" back into the main meeting.

Matching and Mirroring Openers

Generally, people like people like themselves.
Joseph Deitch, author of *Elevate: An Essential Guide to Life*

Matching and mirroring operates on the principle that people like people who are like themselves. These are easy openers that only use video and can take 1–3 minutes. You can use just one or combine 2 to 10 of these openers. You can sequence the openers, such as lower-energy or easier openers followed by openers that have more energy or that are more complex.

Behavioral research shows that matching and mirroring—copying other people's body language, mannerisms, and repeating their words—helps build trust and establishes rapport. This benefit can help your meeting attendees get into sync or rapport at the beginning of the meeting and help the results of your meeting by the end.

Here is a story of how powerful matching and mirroring can be.

I was at a training program showing how matching and mirroring is a valuable meeting skill. When I learned this skill, we were divided into teams of three. One person, Helen, was asked to strongly imagine an emotionally intense experience. I was the second person and I attempted to match that person's body position, breathing, and muscle tension as much as possible. The third person, Alan, coached me on how to move or change to match the first person exactly.

After five minutes of getting into and holding this position, I imagined that she was in a white building with stained glass, she was kneeling up front and was contemplating a big decision.

After the exercise, she disclosed she was in her white church in Georgia with stained glass, kneeling and praying in the front row. She was trying to decide if she was going to stay in her marriage.

Reminder: I had just met Helen and had no idea of what she was imagining. Needless to say, we were all blown away as I was able to connect with her in a meaningful way even though I had just met her.

The point of the exercise is that the correct use of matching and mirroring is one of many ways to help build strong connections between team members in a short amount of time. While you may not see somebody's experience, you can get your attendees to feel more connected and engaged with each other.

Matching and Mirroring Openers

Goals: Test that video is working for attendees. Create rapport with all attendees. Increase energy for meeting.

Time: 1–10 minutes
Participants: 2–Max
Technology: Video, audio
Category: Opener

Game Summary: Follow what the leader is doing.

Rules: If an attendee's video is off, pretend that the attendee is following along. If an attendee isn't following along, say their name and encourage them to participate. Each video opener takes about 1 minute, so you can do up to 10 of them in 5 minutes.

Here's how to lead Matching and Mirroring:

Let's do an easy opener. Behavioral research shows that matching and mirroring helps build trust and establishes rapport, even when we're not in the same room. Let's try it—just follow what I do.

Follow the instructions below for different examples of matching and mirroring. You can customize matching and mirroring to fit your group. For instance, I had a group from India that enjoyed greeting each other by putting their hands together in a prayer pose and saying "Namaste." I used that in their matching and mirroring and they engaged quickly with the meeting.

Tips: Encourage people to follow what you do. You can call out by name if you are watching their video. You can encourage people not on video to follow along; you can joke in a playful way that you can see them. You can use some or all of these. It's ideal that you teach gestures that you are going to use again later in the meeting (like Thumbs Up if you can see my slides).

Head Nod

Let's start with an easy one. Just nod your head up and down. Like you understand what I'm saying. Like you agree with what I'm saying.

Thumbs Up

Now, let's say that if you can hear what I'm saying, give me two thumbs up. Thank you (name), hey (name) can you give me a thumbs up please?

Thumbs Down

Now, let's say you disagree or you're unhappy with something or you can't hear me. Give me two thumbs down, boo, thumbs down.

Mind Blown

Let's say that something you hear or learn in this meeting is amazing. Just put both of your hands into fists on the side of your head and on 3, just blow your mind. Go from closed hands to open hands; you can even make the noise like something is blowing up.

Jimbo Clark from InnoGreat (innogreat.com) was the first to show me this during one of his program openers.

(Continued)

High Five

We can't do this because we're not together, but put your right hand up, yes, put your hand up, and high five your camera!

Fist Bump

Now, take your left hand, make a fist, and fist bump the camera.

Credited to Ben Kenyon, founder of Great Day Squad (instagram.com/GreatDaySquad); he likes to call them "knucks" and "strong knucks."

Applause

Let's pretend I gave a great keynote, everyone applaud—yes, clap, thank you!

Sign Language Applause

Now, most of time we are on mute, so we can't hear your applause. So, let me show you how to applaud in sign language. Put your hands up next to your head and shake your hands! This is applause in sign language. Use this any time you'd like to applaud.[1]

Walk Like an Egyptian

Do you remember an 80s band that sang about an ancient civilization? Yes, everybody walk like an Egyptian in one direction. And now switch. And back to me.

You can use any of the latest dance crazes; the best dances are ones that are upper body–focused like the song "Watch Me" (Whip/Nae Nae) or "YMCA."

Click bit.ly/evmwalk to see an example of how to walk like an Egyptian.

Dance to the Beat of a Different Drummer

This is a high-energy matching and mirroring opener. You or someone you choose can lead the first dance and every other attendee must follow. You can create a rule that when the song changes, you change to another leader. Make sure all the attendees know what the order of leaders is and that they can clearly hear when the song changes.

Here is how you lead this activity:

I'm going to play a collection of songs.

I (or someone else) will start as the leader.

Everybody else needs to follow what the leader does.

When the song changes, we'll change leaders. I'll say "Switch" to remind you.

The order of leaders is (name), (name), (name), (name), and (name).

Does anybody have any questions?

Then I'll play the first song.

You can use one minute of different songs to signal when to switch leaders for more variety. This can lead to hilarious dance moves and a lot of energy.

Try this video with the most popular songs of 2017 in one minute: bit.ly/evm1min.

Breathe

Breathing together is an easy way to use matching and mirroring to get your attendees in sync. Breathing can focus your attendees. Breathing is a way to calm or center the energy created from previous matching and mirroring.

Put one hand on your heart and one hand on your stomach and take three slow breaths with me.

Credited to Isabel Allen, founder of Isabel Allen Yoga http://www.isabel.yoga.

You can use other breathing patterns, such as a four-count breathing in and a four-count breathing out.

Stretch

Open the meeting with a few easy stretches by matching one person leading the stretches. Tilt your head left and right. Shrug your shoulders up and down. Stretch your left and right arm across your chest. If the attendee has been on more than one meeting in a day, this is a

(Continued)

welcome and pleasant physical break in the day. It will have the hidden benefit of getting all your attendees in sync at the beginning of the meeting.

Here's a link to a video showing many of the video openers in action: bit.ly/evmmatching.

Create Your Own

Now that you understand matching and mirroring openers, it's very easy to create your own. Look for gestures that reflect your community, For instance, the East Indian group mentioned earlier that was meeting said "Namaste," put their hands in a prayer position, and bowed. A teenage group that was meeting virtually used the "Dab" motion, which is dropping their head into the bent crook of a slanted, upwardly angled arm while raising the opposite arm out straight in a parallel direction, similar to sneezing into the inside of their elbow.[2] I suggest ordering your openers from easy to more dramatic or energetic openers. You can help engage and interact with every attendee by opening and closing your meetings in the same way. Matching and mirroring openers are one of the easiest ways to achieve that goal.

Virtual Meeting Nametag Openers

An easy and useful opener is to log in up to 30 minutes early for your meeting and while people come in, take time to ask them where they are from and what company they work for. As the host, you can rename them by right-clicking on their video and selecting "Rename."

Another way to ask for this information is during registration. You can prepare the information and quickly cut and paste it as people log in.

Like a name tag, this helps attendees network as they can see where each of the others are from and who they work for, helping to create new connections as they log in.

Virtual Meeting Nametag Openers

Goals: Teach attendees how to use the rename feature. Increase networking by providing an easy way to know everybody's name and useful information such as where they live and where they work.

Time: 1–5 minutes
Participants: 2–Max
Technology: Video, audio, rename
Category: Opener

Game Summary: Ask every attendee to rename themselves using a format of your choice.

Rules: Show attendees where their rename function is located. If an attendee needs help, you can ask them to chat what their nametag should say. Any host or co-host can help an attendee rename their name.

Recommended Name Tag

I recommend and use Name, Location, Company. This is the most common information people want to know and allows them to start networking with each other easily.

Example: "John Chen, Seattle, WA, Geoteaming"

Pronouns

Many organizations now value pronouns like he/him. The ACLU (American Civil Liberties Union) of Northern California said, "The pronoun line on the nametag helps create a more inclusive space that will facilitate people being referred to respectfully and gives us the

(Continued)

opportunity to talk to people about pronouns and the importance of not making assumptions about people's identities."[3]

You can add these to your name so attendees don't have to ask you what pronoun you prefer to use.

Example: "John Chen, Seattle, WA, Geoteaming, he/him"

Assessments

If you have taken any behavior or personality assessment such as Myers Briggs, DiSC, or True Colors, you can add those to your name. This will remind attendees what your style is and what they can do to help work with you better. For instance, I could add ENTJ to the end of my profile and you would know that I'm an extrovert.

Example: "John Chen, Seattle, WA, Geoteaming, ENTJ"

One Word

Ask attendees to describe themselves in one word. Ask attendees to write their favorite band. Ask attendees to write their favorite movie. Ask attendees to describe themselves as an animal.

Examples: "John Chen, Queen"; "John Chen, *The Matrix* (and it's more than you think)"; "John Chen, dolphin"

Mood

You can add your mood to the end of your name to help others understand where you're coming from. Happy, mad, sad, hangry can help others understand how you're feeling.

Examples: "John Chen, hangry"; "John Chen, I need a cookie"; "John Chen, happy for sun"

Superhero Names

Ben Kenyon, Portland Trailblazers performance coach and founder of Great Day Squad (insta-gram.com/GreatDaySquad), loves to ask his group to choose a Superhero name. This helps shift their identities, helps them follow through on performance commitments they make, and it's fun.

Examples: "Flash, Carlin Isles"; "Bearded Beast, Ben Kenyon"

Beverage

At a happy hour, you write what your beverage is. This can help networking, as you learn something about the people by what they are drinking, and help create topics of conversation.

Example: "John Chen, Seattle, WA, Manhattan"

Chat Openers

Another method of conducting openers is to ask your attendees to type out something in the chat feature of the video calling platform. Chat openers are recommended for meetings of more than 25 participants, when you have limited time or when many attendees may not be able to use their audio, such as if they are in loud environments. You can use similar ideas from the verbal one-word openers; they are different here as your attendees reply by chat. Instead of having to use air traffic control, attendees can chat at the same time. One tip is to have the host read one or more of the chats, making sure to use the attendee's name and thanking them for their input. Here are some opening activities that are specifically geared toward chatting.

Chat Openers

Goals: Teach attendees where the chat feature is. Get to know each other and find out something about every attendee.

Time: 1–5 minutes
Participants: 2–Max
Technology: Chat
Category: Opener

(Continued)

Game Summary: Ask every attendee to chat an answer to a question.

Rules: Use the attendee list as a checklist and make sure every attendee has chatted. You can ask an attendee to chat if they haven't yet. Choose one or more of the questions below.

Tip: When giving a suggestion for a chat, make sure to give a choice if an attendee is uncomfortable sharing what you ask for. You can just ask that they chat anything because you want to make sure every attendee can chat, which will be important for the next thing we are doing in this meeting. This can guarantee that everyone knows where chat is and that it works for them.

Location

One way to help your attendees make connections is to get them talking about places. Here are some examples of opening questions, which you can ask your attendees to answer within the meeting chat:

Where do you work?
Where do you live?
Where did you grow up?
What is your favorite location in the world?
Where do you want to travel to?

These are all great networking topics that can help connect attendees to others, which engages them.

Social Media

Ask people to share their LinkedIn profile or Facebook, Instagram, Twitter, TikTok, or other social media link. This allows people to network and choose who to connect with. Most virtual platforms will turn "http://geoteaming.com" into a clickable link, making it even easier for attendees to network. I have made many LinkedIn connections this way, which have led to meetings and sometimes to business.

Conversation Starters

A great way to open a meeting is to ask a powerful question or conversation starter, such as:

What is the last book you read?
What's a win that you're celebrating this week?
What's holding you back in your current project?

Here is a link to 250 conversation starters (bit.ly/evm250) and you can easily search online for more.

Video

Since 80% of the content attendees are consuming is video, you can ask what the last video is they watched. It might be the latest pop culture TV show or movie or it could be an educational TED talk. You can learn something about every attendee by their choice.

What's the last video you watched?

Quotes

According to neurobiologist Mary Helen Immordino-Yang, the reason certain stories make you feel strongly about them is that they stimulate activity in the very parts of the brain that make your heart beat, make you breathe when you are asleep, and make your blood pressure stay within normal limits. Likewise, quotes or words of wisdom can have a similar impact.[4]

Asking your attendees about their favorite quote will give you insight to who inspires them and how they think. The quotes can also inspire other attendees with their power.

What is a quote that you live your life by?
What is a quote that's important to you?
What's your favorite quote?

Why are meeting openers important? Ann Chastain at Michigan State University said it best: "Meeting openers are activities that help people feel welcome and comfortable in discussion with others and help to focus on the purpose or content of the meeting, according to 'Developing Community Leadership, a guide for MSU Extension,' Michigan State University Extension LeadNet and Community Development AoE Team, 2005."[5]

When you choose the right meeting opener for your group, you should find your meeting to be more engaging, more inclusive, and help get more work done.

8 | Activities for Communication, Morale, and Trust

After you've mastered the basics of virtual meetings, you'll run into the familiar meeting problems of inefficient communication, low morale, and not trusting your attendees. You knew many of the rules of communication, morale, and trust in your face-to-face meetings. The challenge is that the rules for these in a virtual meeting are different. You and your attendees need new rules.

A virtual meeting activity is a good way to learn a new virtual tool, raise morale by having fun, and increase trust in your attendees. A good virtual meeting activity addresses your attendees' key issues, is easy for your attendees to learn, is engaging enough to get your attendees to buy in to the outcome of your activity, and is able to be completed in the time you have available.

"Yes, and . . ."—Accept Attendees' Ideas and Improve Communication

Goals: Get every attendee to participate. Reduce negativity in your meeting. Improve brainstorming and creativity. Demonstrate a winning technique from top teams.

Have you ever shared an idea in a meeting and immediately have it shot down? Are you wondering why nobody is saying anything when you ask for input? Do you wish you had a brainstorm where every idea got better and better?

"Yes, and . . ." is a concept that is at the core of improvisation. It comes from the concept of accepting anything an attendee says. Even if you don't agree, you can say Yes (I heard you), and (insert your point of view). As simple as this practice is, it turns out to be one of the seven factors of winning teams during our 23-plus years of professional team building. Teams that say "Yes, and . . ." to each other during a competitive team-building program win.

Time: 1–10 minutes
Participants: 2–25; you can use breakout rooms if you have more people
Technology: Audio, video
Category: Communication

Game Summary: The first person says a statement of one to three sentences. The next person says "Yes, and . . ." and finds a way to build on the previous statement.

Rules: Choose someone to be air traffic control. This person will create an order if two or more people raise their hand at the same time.

Remind attendees to start their statement with "Yes, and . . ."

Choose people who haven't already gone.

End the game when everybody has participated (or you can use an optional time limit).

Use the attendee list as a checklist if necessary and make sure every attendee has said "Yes, and . . . ."

The Association for Talent Development, one of the top training associations in the world, agrees that the "Yes, and . . ." approach can work when working with difficult attendees or clients.[1]

You can also do this exercise with "No, but . . ." and ask how attendees feel after each round. Attendees frequently say that "No, but . . ." feels negating and makes it harder to brainstorm, be creative, or take a risk.

Three-Headed Consultant—Communicating One Word at a Time

Goals: Increase listening skills. Increase collaboration. Have fun.

Have you ever had three people who couldn't work together, who would fight with each other or discount each other's words? Here's one way that could help them listen and work with each other.

Time: 1–10 minutes
Participants: 2–25; you can use breakout rooms for larger groups
Technology: Video, audio
Category: Communication, collaboration, improvisation

Game Summary: Ask three attendees to become a three-headed consultant. Have other attendees ask the three-headed consultant a question. The three-headed consultant can answer the question but with only one word at a time.

Rules: Create an order for the three-headed consultant to answer the questions; determine who will go first, second, and third. Remind the consultant to use only one word at a time. The three-headed consultant can say "period" to end their response.

Great three-headed consultants listen to each other and build on an idea even if it's not theirs. Terrible three-headed consultants don't listen to what the previous person said and say words that don't make any sense.

If the consultant is terrible, you can ask what would have to happen to become a better consultant and see if they can try that for the next question until they start working better together. Best answers include listening for the direction the consultant is going in, saying a word that sets up the next response, and responding quickly. Many top improvisation experts say, "The more you think, the worse it gets." When you create a three-headed consultant, you'll find a natural flow that balances listening, setup, and quick responses. You'll find that this can help your meeting with an activity that increases the listening, engagement, and flow of your attendees.

A to Z—Teaching Why Your Meeting Needs a System

Goals: Chat from A to Z as fast as possible. Show that high-performing meetings must have a system like Air Traffic Control. Show how easy it is to step on each other's toes in virtual meetings.

Do you have a meeting where people are confused? Are you having to redo work? Do you have to throw away work because two or more people did it?

What your virtual meeting attendees need is rhythm. Rhythm is a new set of rules for your attendees to get work done. A to Z is the perfect activity to have your attendees realize this for themselves. This activity can be followed by the group discussing and agreeing on a new rhythm or set of meeting rules that will help their future meetings get more work done.

Time: 5–30 minutes
Participants: 4–12; you can use breakout rooms if you have more participants
Technology: Chat
Category: Improving performance
Instructions: Your goal is to chat the letters A to Z as fast as possible.
Every attendee can only chat one letter.
Each attendee cannot chat twice in a row.
If you repeat a letter or chat a letter out of order, you must start over.
You cannot talk while chatting from A to Z.
If you repeat or chat a letter out of order, you can talk until someone chats A to start.
(optional) Every attendee must chat at least one letter.

Tips: At five minutes, if your attendees are still struggling, ask if they would like to see the rules again. If they say yes, show the rules again and highlight the rule showing when they can talk.

Debrief: To help your attendees get their lessons from this experience, you can ask:

What? What happened during A to Z? How did your attendees tackle this challenge?
So what? So what did you learn about virtual meetings?
Now what? Now what will you do differently at your next virtual meeting based on this activity?

Variation: You can repeat this initiative up to two more times and time each iteration. You can give two to five minutes of planning time before you start the stopwatch. Write down the times for each completion and calculate the percentage increase or decrease in time. Usually a team can reduce their time 20–80% just through team process!

Case Study: I ran A to Z over 40 times in 2020. The fastest time it was completed was 50.3 seconds. The slowest time was 10:35.0 and it was completed by the *only* team that didn't establish a system with each other. All the groups broke into two major groups:

1. 90% Chatting A to Z using the alphabetized first names of every attendee as the order
2. 10% Chatting A to Z using only two people bouncing back and forth

The majority of groups started chatting A either without asking questions or chatting A while I was only halfway through the instructions. This is what I call "fire, ready, aim," where the attendees attempt to solve the problem before they really understand it.

Only twice (less than 5%) did a leader emerge and make a system before they attempted A to Z. If you wanted an example of why we need more virtual leadership, here is a prime statistic.

I used this initiative for a day of training for anyone who volunteered for an organization to help them be better leaders. In the first two rounds, one team clearly showed their skills by being first with the fastest time. In the third round, a new team that was almost *last* jumped to *first!* They were able to reduce their time in half and come in with the fastest time. When I interviewed them afterwards, they said the secret of their success was taking a risk on a new process that could create a big jump in speed. They thought about it in the second round, but they were too afraid that it wouldn't work and they would come in last. In the last round, they decided that they didn't want to play not to lose—they wanted to play to win. They practiced the new technique to prove that it worked and when it came to the actual time trial, they *nailed* it! What they learned is that you can make small incremental improvements, but to make a quantum leap in performance, sometimes you need to abandon your previous process and invent a new and better one. And the rewards of winning made it all worthwhile. All this came from typing A to Z, which shows how a very simple initiative becomes a great activity with great learning.

Go to bit.ly/evmatoz to see an example of A to Z.

Alpha Names—A Networking Activity to Learn Everyone's Name

Goals: Chat all the attendees' names in alphabetical order.

Is this the first time your attendees are meeting? Do you want them to learn each other's names and see how they are going to work together at the same time?

(Continued)

This text or chat initiative looks deceptively simple, but without a leader, it can become challenging. Also, it's an easy way to learn everybody's name and learn something about their team style in a short amount of time. With this initiative, a facilitator can learn about the team's default style and process.

Time: 10–20 minutes
Participants: 4–20; for more people you can use breakout rooms
Technology: Chat
Category: Opener

Instructions: We're going to get a chance to meet each other and see how fast you can work as a team. Chat all of your first names in alphabetical order. If you get one out of order, you need to start again from the beginning. You can only use chat to communicate. I have a stopwatch to time you. Any questions?

Tips: Use a stopwatch with a "lap" timer. Tap "lap" every time the attendees start over. Tap "stop" at the end and use the last lap time.

The fastest method I've seen used is to have your name pretyped in your chat and know what order the team needs to go in, hitting Enter as soon as you see the name before you.

Debrief: Who was the leader in the group? How did you decide on a process? What did you do when you failed? How can you do it even faster?

Variations: Allow the teams to do this two or three times to increase their speed. If their names are displayed on the app they're using, it can make it too easy and you can have them chat A–Z in alphabetical order instead.

Case Study: We used this activity with one particularly dysfunctional team of 10. They asked no questions before they started, they spent no time on process, and they just started working by trial and error. Joe typed his name, then Beth typed her name, and they had to start all over. They would get three or four names done, then someone would go out of order. Next, they got through five or six and someone chimed in with a suggestion, making them start all over. In the debrief, this team realized that a clear team leader would have helped them and nobody wanted that role. In addition, they realized that if they had used their planning time, they could have asked more questions, would have agreed on their plan, and then would have executed it. This was a big parallel to how they were working as an online team. They were doing redundant work at multiple sites and not taking the time to plan who was doing what before starting a project.

Last Team Texting—Sharing Valuable Information

Goals: To get as many wins as possible as a group.

This is a fast activity that shows how trusting and sharing valuable information with your team can create more success.

Time: 10–30 minutes
Participants: Two per team; unlimited teams
Technology: Chat
Category: Trust
Setup: Divide into teams of two, where one person is A and the other is B. Make sure each team has a way to communicate by private chat. Have the Power to Win Every Time information ready to share.
Instructions to the Audience: You get a win when you text the other person a 0, making you the winner.
The A's will start by texting 13 to the B's.
The B's can subtract 1, 2, or 3 from the number and text it back during each turn.
A's and B's take turns until someone can text 0 to the other person to win.
Play three rounds. Take turns starting.
When you are done, group chat how many times you won.
Tips: After playing three rounds, private chat the Power to Win Every Time information to the team with the worst record and then let them play three more rounds.

Power to Win Every Time

1. Always text 8.
2. Always text 4.
3. Always text 0 for the win.
4. If you go second, you can always win if you subtract 1 and text 12.

See how many more wins you get overall.

(Continued)

The key is to look and see if the team with the Power to Win Every Time information shared it. If they did, ask why. If they didn't, ask why.

You can revisit the goal, which is to get as many wins as possible as a group. Now, ask them again what they think they should do.

If you have time, you can play three more rounds; you should get 100% of the wins possible.

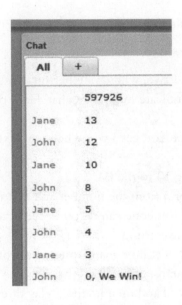

Case Study: Sam Sikes was taught this activity when he was on a break at a workshop. He said it helped him convince a company's decision maker that he might have valuable information that he should trust and share with their people about how to work better as teams. After watching his team and himself play this game, he went on to share this valuable information and make a significant impact on the company.

Source: Sam Sikes, "Knowledge Is Power," in *Executive Marbles* (Learning Unlimited Corporation, 1998) p. 104.

PechaKucha (peh-chak-cha)—Present in Just 6 Minutes 40 Seconds

Goals: Present more information in less time.

Are you tired of presentations that are too long? Just like how TED talks changed the format for keynotes, PechaKucha has changed the format for presentations. PechaKucha allows you to show 20 slides for 20 seconds each for a total of 6 minutes and 40 seconds. Your attendees will learn how to communicate more effectively by learning how to transmit the maximum amount of information in a limited time.

Time: 6 minutes 40 seconds–120 minutes
Participants: 1–64; unlimited for audience, presentations of 1–8 people each
Technology: PowerPoint or other presentation software, virtual meeting platform with Share Screen or projector
Category: Communication, creativity, teamwork, presentation

Instructions: What is PechaKucha? This video at bit.ly/evmpecha gives you an overview. This is a great way to present a new topic, talk about a new offering, or teach a company concept. Also, the byproduct of this presentation is that it's very easy to click record and the video can be shared as best practices or information. This rapid-fire format is perfect for attention deficit audiences and "death by PowerPoint," the poor use of presentation software. Results can range from hilarious to pure genius. You (and your team) must create 20 slides that advance every 20 seconds and present them.

Tip: Send the PechaKucha template (bit.ly/pechatemplate) to every team leader.

Case Study: Mahak Chand, Matthew Gusavson, and Michele Knabbe, students at the Stony Brook University in the College of Leadership and Service, used PechaKucha to present their case study on how their team used Web 2.0 technology to overcome virtual distance. The three of them worked together as a team to select slides, do voiceovers, compile them, and upload it as a video, all while living in three different places! They used a shared website and even created shared team values, used Facebook to share with each other, ooVoo to create three-way videoconferences, and Twitter to stay connected and get feedback from other classmates. This is pretty impressive to show in a 400-second video!

Definition of PechaKucha: bit.ly/evmpechakucha
Daniel Pink describes what a PechaKucha is: bit.ly/evmdanielpink
National Speakers Association Texas president does a PechaKucha on PechaKucha bit.ly/evmpechansa
PechaKucha Template: bit.ly/evmpechatemplate
The three students who worked together: bit.ly/evm3students

PowerPoint Karaoke—Improving Improvisation

Goals: Learn how to improve your improvisation by presenting a PowerPoint slidedeck without ever seeing it.

Have you ever had something not go as planned during your meeting? Do you wish you could handle that with ease? Then, practice your improvisation skills by presenting slide decks you've never seen before. Billed as the "Newest Form of Corporate Embarrassment" by trendhunter.com, this is a great initiative for improvisation and how to work with unexpected challenges. Most of all, this team-building event is fun and funny; most likely, you'll be in tears at least once during this event.

Time: 30–120 minutes
Participants: 1–120; unlimited for audience
Technology: Share Screen, PowerPoint, Google Slides or other presentation software
Category: Communication, creativity, teamwork, presentation

Instructions: You can use the PowerPoint decks we provide or you can instruct the attendees to build a 12-slide presentation ahead of time and send it to the organizer. You know what karaoke is, right? People who sing a song over music. Well, this is PowerPoint karaoke, where you present a slide deck you've never seen before. Before you present, you will be assigned a random slide deck. You will need to present your slide deck in five minutes or less. Points will be given for flow, gesture, jargon, credibility, and, of course, getting through all the slides.

Tips: If you use judges, you can have the judges give commentary after every presentation. Use a timer, if necessary, to keep your presenters on time. You can have one presenter or multiple presenters if you are working on getting teams to present.

Debrief: What roles or tactics did you use in designing the slides? How did you do in dealing with an unknown presentation from another person? Did you feel supported or set up to fail? What did you learn about dealing with unexpected challenges?

Case Study: We used PowerPoint Karaoke as part of the Northwest Event Show. During this event, it was great to watch what attendees put together as slides. Some slide decks were cohesive and helped the speaker with their presentation. Other teams put together very random slides next to each other, knocking the presenter for a loop each time they advanced the slide. What was impressive was that the best presenters were able to take a difficult slide deck and make them fantastic (0:22 of video, see the Gyrotronic cycle with Fred), while one challenged presenter just read each slide on a slide deck about how to give a PowerPoint presentation and, of course, what it said not to do: read a slide word for word (3:35 of video)!

PowerPoint Karaoke: bit.ly/evmpowerpoint
SXSW BattleDecks: bit.ly/evmsxsw
20 Random PowerPoint Decks: bit.ly/evmppkaraoke

Blind Tangrams—Do Not Assume in Your Communication

Goals: To discover communication assumptions and improve communication.

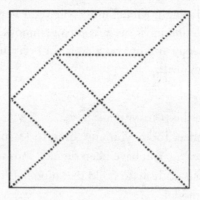

This is a great initiative to increase verbal communication. It's especially useful when some attendees are unable to turn on their cameras since it provides a way to engage them. Attendees will develop skills of asking questions to test assumptions of other attendees, which will lead to fewer production and process mistakes in the future.

Time: 30–60 minutes
Participants: Teams of 2; use breakout rooms for more attendees
Technology: Audio, video, breakouts
Category: Communication

Setup: Divide your attendees into teams of two; label one attendee A and the other B. Send all the A's a link to a completed tangram, such as bit.ly/evmtangram.
Search "tangrams" and click images to find a model you want.

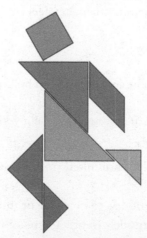

(Continued)

There are two options for B's:

1. Analog—Before the meeting starts, send them a link to a Tangram Model bit.ly/evmtangrammodel. Tell the attendees to print it out and cut out the pieces before the meeting.
2. Digital—Send them a Tangram Model using Microsoft PowerPoint or Google Drawings. There is a downloadable model at bit.ly/evmtangrampowerpoint or bit.ly/evmtangramdrawings. Download a copy and upload a copy for every team to your own server. Chat the B's a link to the document.

Start your virtual meeting.

Set up the breakouts with the pairs you assigned.

Instructions to the Audience: Today you are going to learn about the assumptions each attendee has over a virtual meeting. You have been divided into teams of 2. A's have a Tangram model and will give instructions on how to build that model. B's have the pieces of a Tangram and will attempt to build A's model.

After you're done, make sure you turn off all cameras.

Send attendees to their breakouts; suggested timing is 10 minutes.

When they return, ask them to turn on their cameras and see who solved the puzzle.

A great visual is for A's to show their models, then have B's show what they built.

You can lead a debrief to get the key lessons.

Tips: If you want to increase difficulty and the depth of the lesson of making assumptions, you can send a color version of this tangram to A, like bit.ly/evmtangrama. You can send a color version of the tangram with different colors to B, like bit.ly/evmtangramb. This will be an additional challenge as A's may ask about an orange triangle and B's will not know that it is a different-sized orange triangle.

Debrief: You can ask questions before and after the pictures are revealed.

What was easy in working with your other attendee?
What was challenging?
What assumptions did you discover?
How did you discover them?
On a scale of 1–10, how confident are you that you built the correct model?
What did you learn from this?
What will you do differently in the future in working with a virtual team?

This exercise can be paired with instructions on how to ask better questions.[2]

Variations: You can give attendees unlimited time if you want to give them higher odds of success.

You can change the different models to be easier or more complex.

You can change the different models to fit a theme of your meeting.

Case Study: This game was originally a favorite of one of my managers at Microsoft, who went on to be the general manager for the Microsoft Dynamics division. He originally ran this initiative live and back-to-back with another manager. Out of all the training, this is one of his most remembered and used training moments. We replicated this same game at Boeing with six managers, using email. They generated 150 emails in about 20 minutes where we could track the teams' different progress at different times. One manager realized that he got stuck calling a triangle by a certain color and the other person had that triangle but in a different size as all the pieces were different colors than the model. Both of them failed the task and they were highly frustrated at the end. It had a huge impact on his communication style as a manager. And he still remembers that learning lesson today: to not make assumptions when working with his teammates and to ask questions about his assumptions before he believes them to be true. He's now the manager of over 1,400 people in a division with over $1 billion in revenue!

Broken Squares—Giving Is Better Than Getting for Engaging Meetings

Goals: Get attendees to realize that giving more information is better than just receiving for solving problems and collaborating.

Five teammates work together to put five triangles together with a fixed set of rules. This is a classic team-building event called Broken Squares that is updated for virtual meetings using Google Slides or Microsoft PowerPoint. The key lesson with this game is that the more you share, the faster the meeting will achieve their goals. Conversely, if you hoard your pieces or your single solution, you can hold up the entire meeting.

Time: 20–40 minutes
Participants: 4–5 per team; use breakouts for more attendees
Technology: Share Screen, Microsoft PowerPoint, or Google Slides
Category: Collaboration

Setup: Go to bit.ly/evmsquaresdrawing for a Google Drawing template or bit.ly/evmsquarespowerpoint for a Microsoft PowerPoint template. Download a copy and save one copy for every team to your server so it can be shared. Get a link to the shared document.

Instructions to the Audience: Please connect to "Broken Squares" through the link I just chatted to you. Let me know when all five of your teammates are there and can move a piece. Each teammate selects an area where your three parts are—there are three spots on the top and two on the bottom. Your goal is to put together five squares, one in front of each of you. Here are the rules:

1. You may use only the pieces provided.
2. No member may speak, gesture, or text to another member in any way throughout the activity.
3. Members may not ask another member for a piece, take a piece from another member, or signal in any way that another person is to give them a piece.
4. Members may give pieces to other members.
5. Members may not place their puzzle pieces in the center area for other team members to take.

Any questions? Okay, remember, no talking, and GO!

Make sure attendees have the ability to share their screen.

You can Mute All and not allow attendees to unmute. You can send teams to breakout rooms. You can move from breakout room to breakout room to see how the groups are doing or you can assign one observer to every room to help enforce the rules.

Debrief: Your job is part observer and part judge. As a judge, make sure that each participant is observing the rules. It is okay for a member to give away all the pieces to their puzzle, even if they have already formed a square. In fact, it's usually a good sign for a team.

As an observer, look for the following:

- How willing were members to give away pieces of the puzzle or completed squares?
- Did anyone finish their puzzle and then withdraw themselves from the group problem solving? If so, how did it affect the rest of the team? This behavior shows a silo mentality of getting one's own work done and not looking at the team goal. It can also prevent an entire team solution as this one participant may be using a vital part of someone else's square.
- Did dominant individuals emerge or did everyone seem to participate equally and share leadership?
- Did you see frustration? If so, how? How did it affect the group?

The key lesson to learn from this exercise is that attendees need to share with each other. Sharing resources, sharing information, and sharing relationships are good examples of how to make more engaging meetings.

Case Study: Broken Squares was used at a retreat for an association board. In this case, there were three teams of five people each. The first team took a moment to get going, but the key was that team members completed a square and then gave the entire square to a teammate who was struggling. That teammate reciprocated by giving all the pieces to the person who was rapidly solving the squares. This team accidentally created four squares out of the parts, but the facilitator clarified that the goal had to be five squares. So, the team went back to working on the solution and completed five squares in just 4½ minutes. According to the facilitator, this was one of the fastest times to date and it came from the best problem-solving people giving away their work, as well as the challenged people being open to accepting help and giving their pieces away to others. The second team completed the exercise in about 9 minutes and the last team took over 17 minutes to complete it. While watching this table, they felt more and more pressure about being late and being observed by 10 other people. In addition, people with completed squares were not giving their work to others, leaving the challenged people to figure it out on their own, and they were not making much progress. In the debrief, there were a variety of comments, but the key lessons of sharing when ahead and accepting help when behind were learned by all in the group. This led to a more productive board retreat and, more importantly, an environment of asking for help when behind in goals and chipping in if you were ahead on your projects. The improved environment resulted in this board achieving many of their year's goals.

Trust Grid—Mapping and Improving Trust

Goals: Measure and increase attendee trust, start conversation about how to build and increase attendee trust.

Team members rate their level of trust with their other teammates and a facilitator helps draws conclusions and actions from the results. Trust Grid is a great way to visually measure a team's overall trust as well as look at trust challenges within the team.

Time: 10–60 minutes
Participants: 2–1,000

(Continued)

Technology: Share Screen, Google Forms or Microsoft Forms

Category: Trust

Setup: Open Microsoft Forms (forms.microsoft.com) or Google Forms (forms.google.com). Forms are an easy way to obtain structured information. Make sure to set the form for Anonymous to ensure that people can truthfully answer without repercussions. Enter the title "Trust Grid" and add "How much do you trust each Attendee? 5 is the highest, 1 is the lowest" to the description. Then, add a question for each Attendee with their name and a rating, such as 5 stars. Click Share and get a link to the form.

Instructions to the Audience: Let's find out how much trust we have on this team. Here is a link to a form. On a scale of 1 to 5 with 1 being "I don't trust you at all" to 5 being "I trust you with my life," I want you to rate your level of trust with other teammates. Your results will be anonymous.

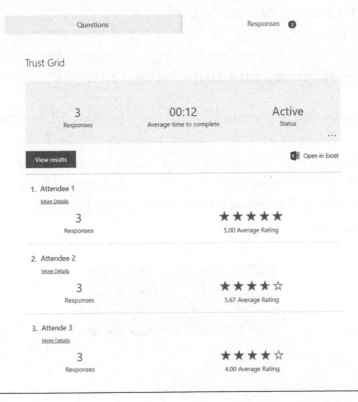

Give a rating to every attendee, then click "Submit." When you're done, I will ask you questions about what has to happen for you to trust another attendee.

Debrief:

What is the overall score?

Which team member is most trusted and why? Which team member is least trusted and why?

What would have to happen to have a number go up?

What relationships are the strongest and most trusted? What relationships could be strengthened?

Know that a low number can be challenging and that you need to be prepared to handle a sensitive situation. If it's very low, you may not want to show the results until the next meeting. If you are not a conflict expert, ask for the help of a professional facilitator, as you can reduce trust instead of build it if this is not handled well.

Tips: Do this at the beginning of a team training and then at the end of the training and see if you can achieve higher numbers by the end of the training. Attendees can be competitive, so make sure to reiterate that this is an average of all attendees and to look at qualities of high-trusted attendees and listen to other attendees about what has to happen to increase trust.

Case Study: During a competitive and collaborative team-building event, we did a Trust Grid between five different teams at the beginning of the event. Then, after a simulation where teams have to find their balance between competition and collaboration, we asked them to do the Trust Grid again. What we didn't tell them is that one third of their score would be based on how high the other teams trusted them. Teams that employed overly aggressive tactics to achieve a high score were rated low in trust, especially if they had to break a deal with another team to achieve that high score. Teams that worked with other teams, shared information, and helped them succeed during the activity achieved high trust scores. This was meant to be a metaphor for this overly aggressive technology company. They discovered that while being competitive can help you with a short-term goal, it can hurt you with the long-term goal if you need to work with other teams in the future. This Trust Grid opened a big conversation about trust between teams and at the end, all teams agreed to be more collaborative so they could join together to take market share from their biggest competitor.

The Johari Window—Discover Attendee Blind Spots

Goals: Find out what attendees think about you versus what you think about yourself.

This personality awareness can help individual attendees learn more about how the other attendees view them and can help build team awareness of strengths and weaknesses. This is a great initiative to do with newly forming teams or as a precursor to finding out how to increase team effectiveness by picking best roles for the team.

Time: 10–30 minutes
Participants: 1–15 or more by making multiple teams and using breakouts
Technology: Audio, video, chat, Share Screen
Category: Trust

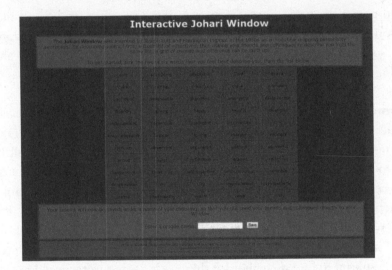

Setup: Chat http://kevan.org/johari to your attendees. Each attendee chooses five words that best describe them. Enter a unique name and click "Save." Copy and save the link so you can always get back to your results. Copy and paste the link into the chat window to have other attendees contribute to your Johari Window. Now, have every attendee contribute to all the other attendees' profiles. To maximize your meeting time, you can do all of the online assessments prior to the meeting, then review the results together during your meeting.

Instructions to the Audience: The Johari Window was invented by Joseph Luft and Harrington Ingham in the 1950s as a model for mapping personality awareness. By describing yourself from a fixed list of adjectives, then asking your friends and colleagues to describe you from the same list, a grid of overlap and difference can be built up. You'll learn of your

Arena (the traits known to you and others), your Blind Spots (the traits not known to you but known by others), your Facades (the traits known to you but not known by others), and the Unknown (the traits not known by you or others).

You'll start by selecting five to six words that best describe you and entering your unique name. Once you've completed that, you can click through the attendee links and choose five to six words that describe them. Take only two minutes per attendee to choose their five or six words and then signal me when you're done. Then, we can review each attendee's results.

As each attendee is reviewed, they can choose a goal to increase or decrease the size of a pane. For instance, if you choose to reduce your Blind Spot, seek feedback from the group and choose an action to utilize that trait (that others know about you, but that you are unaware of) in a future meeting.

One goal your group can look to achieve is to have an Arena window that has all of your original traits. The only way to do that is to share more about yourself. In this sharing, you should see an increase of trust in the group.

By going through this process, you should learn more about the other attendees and help the attendees put people into their best roles and increase trust as you learn more about each other.

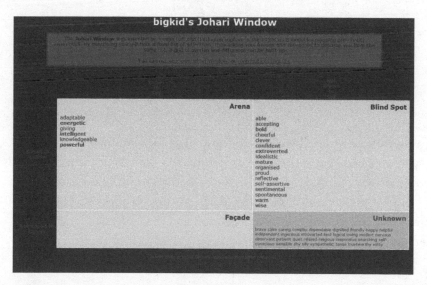

Case Study: On one of our own team-building retreats, one of our facilitators, Tim O'Malley, introduced this tool to us. One of my personal results was that while I was able to get one of my top three traits (Intelligent) into the Arena, my other top two traits

(Continued)

(Confident and Extroverted) were in my Blind Spot. I created the goal of reducing my Blind Spot and I looked to use the traits of Confident and Extroverted in our next team-led project. As the leader of the group, I did not know that my confidence was a key trait that I could use to move a project forward. Also, I knew I was Extroverted and, while I use this trait a lot, I also looked to purposefully talk less during some team meetings to make sure other voices could be heard. Our next team project moved more smoothly than in the past by taking these actions.

1 CACHE—Make Decisions Faster and Stick Longer

Goals: Have your attendees create a faster and more inclusive process for making decisions.

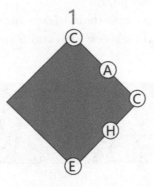

Do you want to engage all your attendees in decisions you make?
Have you ever had your team make a decision and unmake it right afterwards?
Do you ever wish that you could use your meetings to make decisions faster?
Then you should try the 1 CACHE decision-making process. This is a 30-plus-year tested system that helps companies like Microsoft and the National Park Service make decisions faster and make those decisions stick.

Time: 5–60 minutes, depending on the decision to be made and the attendees
Participants: 2–25
Technology: Audio, video
Category: Decision making, consensus
Instructions: Follow these six steps the next time your meeting must result in a decision:

Step 1: One Leader

Choose one leader to lead the process. This is not a directive leader; this is a facilitative leader whose role is to follow this process and make sure everyone agrees at the end.

Step 2: Clear Goal

State the clear goal for this decision. Check that everyone is in agreement with the goal. A thumbs up (agree), down (do not agree), or middle (I agree to go along with the group) vote is an easy way to check that everyone agrees. If someone does not agree, modify the goal until 100% of the attendees agree.

Step 3: All Brainstorm

The leader needs to ensure and keep track that every attendee has at least one chance to talk and add ideas for the decision. The leader should not let attendees cut or criticize ideas; they can let them know to just hold those ideas for the next step.

Step 4: Cut Ideas

The leader should start cutting ideas by suggesting the idea(s) that have the highest odds of success *and* the highest odds for being accepted by the attendees. Other attendees can also now chime in on cutting ideas that they don't think will work. Cutting ideas helps attendees who naturally think counter to the group as well as avoiding ideas that might waste attendees' time.

Step 5: Hear the Solution

The leader now recounts what they think the decision is. Attendees can clarify the decision. The leader now takes a public or private vote. If anyone disagrees, ask for modifications that would allow them to go along with the group or agree. Continue this process until 100% of the attendees agree to go along with the decision.

Step 6: Execute the Plan

The attendees now execute the decision they made.

(Continued)

Tips: Often, I see decisions made in meetings that not everyone buys into and then one or more people sabotage the decision after the meeting as the group attempts to follow through on the decision. I think the worst outcome for a meeting decision is when one person dictates a decision, everybody adjusts their plans for that decision, and then that one person changes their mind on the decision without discussing the impact on everyone else. This creates resentment, distrust, and disengaging in future meetings.

While making a decision this way may take longer than a leader just making a decision and telling everyone, I have seen that a meeting using the 1 CACHE system makes better decisions using the experience and engagement of the attendees. The attendees are more likely to follow through on the decision because they all had a chance to vote on it and all accepted the idea enough to follow through with it.

Debrief: You can compare this decision to previous decisions your attendees have made. If they like the process, keep it. If they want to modify the process, consider accepting the change if the original goal of making decisions faster and making those decisions stick is kept.

Case Study: I was consulting with a software company that was making a new email program. When an email was sent to 10 people, the server "fell over" and didn't return control to the user for 24 hours. The server had a "slight performance problem," which was a vast understatement. The general manager assembled a "performance" team that was asked to go fix this problem. The performance team executed their first approach. They asked for all the performance data from every team. Every team produced performance data that said they were fast for what they were designed for. The performance team needed to take a different approach. They went to the server lead developer and found out he was creating a giant log of everything that was happening. The performance team wrote a customized app that highlighted all of the communication happening between the client and the server. For a simple action of reading an email, it took 43 round trips to the server. This is the equivalent of having 43 dollar bills, picking one up, driving to the bank, writing a deposit slip, depositing the dollar, and driving home, and then doing it 42 more times.

Armed with this information and the 1 CACHE decision-making system, the performance team called a meeting with the leaders from the eight different components. The performance team chose one leader to represent them. This is what the leader said:

The clear goal is that we need to improve performance or we will never ship our product. We are clear it's not just one component that is the problem. Here is the communication between the client and the server. We will never know enough about each of your components to achieve the performance we want. Performance is now all of our problem.

The performance team waited while every team lead read through the communication. Finally, after the longest two minutes of the performance team's lives, every team lead started brainstorming. They asked if they could share information. They asked if they could defer giving the results until later. They found ways to eliminate waste. Toward the end of the meeting, the performance leader cut the ideas until the ideas with the best chance of improving performance were agreed upon. Over the next weeks, they were able to reduce the 43 round trips to the server by half as they started reading two emails every trip. These changes drastically improved the performance of the server where testing proved it could now host 10,000 users/server. The process earned the company two US patents and the server has sold over 200 million client licenses. Making important decisions faster and making them stick with a large team can be critical to your company's success.

9 | Collab—Work Well with Others

Collaboration is the process of two or more people or organizations working together to complete a task or achieve a goal. Collaboration is similar to cooperation. Most collaboration requires leadership, although the form of leadership can be social within a decentralized and egalitarian group. Teams that work collaboratively often access greater resources, recognition, and rewards when facing competition for finite resources.[1]

Team building is a misnomer. In the presence of two or more teams, teams will naturally work together. In my 20-plus years of professional team building, collaboration (or collab, as the cool kids like to say) is the great opportunity of increasing results. Over my 20 years of working in this field, I have discovered the law of 80, 19, and 1. When groups are given the goal to score more points than other groups *and* to work with each other to achieve a larger goal, 80% of the groups go completely competitive, not collaborating with anyone; 19% collaborate with at least one team to achieve slightly higher results; only 1% collaborate with other groups at the highest level to score a maximum amount of points. If you can get your meeting to collaborate, you will immediately move into the top 20% of all meetings.

The activities in this chapter are designed to show your attendees how to collab. They are the most tried and true from 35 years of research and experience.

Simultaneous Editing—Creating a Case Study

Goals: Have attendees create a case study by editing a document at the same time.

Does it take forever for your meeting to create a document? Do you wish you could snap your fingers and get it done? Do you want to tap all the knowledge in your meeting quickly?

The infinite monkey theorem states that a monkey hitting keys at random on a typewriter keyboard for an infinite amount of time will almost surely type any given text, such as the complete works of William Shakespeare.[2]

Your meeting is certainly smarter than a monkey. Collaboration tools have progressed rapidly. Google Docs can currently support 100 simultaneous editors.[3] Microsoft Word can currently support 99 simultaneous editors.[4] Use this power to get more work done.

Give your attendees the task of creating a case study in a limited amount of time and they will learn how to collaborate with each other and produce more work in the same amount of time.

Time: 10 minutes–2 hours
Participants: 2–99 per team; unlimited teams
Technology: Share Screen, Microsoft Word, Google Docs, or other applications that allow simultaneous editing
Category: Collaboration

Setup: Case studies are a great way to tap and apply the knowledge of a large group while engaging them in something that has a real work product at the end. This activity can be used for large events with multiple teams as a way to show new collaboration.

Prepare the case study template and upload to a shared location such as Google Docs or Microsoft OneDrive. Click "share" and get a link to the document. If you have more than one group, upload one document for every group. Use breakouts to separate attendees into groups and have a breakout leader chat the link that allows the group to edit their document.

Instructions to the Audience: Today we are going to work collaboratively to create a case study. You will have a limited amount of time to divide up the work, discuss options, make decisions, and write the report. The link to your case study is in the chat. At the end of this case study, we'll have each team present a summary of their case study.

Tips: Record and save the video and chat from each group to use for future debriefing and learning.

Have one person represent the client of the case study and allow participants to ask the client clarifying questions.

The client can also add new information at key times during the case study to either help progress or add additional challenges.

Be prepared to facilitate success and failure.

Debrief: Allow the group to find their own way. Only interject if you think the group really needs help in working together or needs a suggestion to get through a block. Asking questions as opposed to directing the group is the preferred method for attempting to help the attendees:

What were you thinking in the first planning minutes?
How were conflicts resolved? Did a leader emerge?
When did your group work at its best?
What is a highlight of the results that you'll use back at work?

Case Study: Adrian Segar, author of *Conferences That Work*, blogged about Choate Rosemary School's Joel Backon, who used this unique initiative at edACCESS 2010, a conference for the association of information technology at small independent schools. Joel did the prework in defining and uploading the case study materials where the goal was to reduce educational costs. Then, he set the stage for 40 people, who were meeting live, to work virtually for 90 minutes. While many people felt like they could never finish in the first 20 minutes, the group selected a spreadsheet to focus their work on in Google Docs and the majority of people worked on this spreadsheet. The spreadsheet had multiple tabs and was clearly able to document a 60% educational cost savings for their case study. With 30 minutes to go, a Google Doc of the summary was created and the team of 40 was able to complete their assignment in just 90 minutes. This was an incredible example of teamwork with 40 participants under a tight deadline. The case study shows the power of online collaboration when harnessed correctly. Think about what applications could be used for your virtual meetings as a way to increase engagement.

Go to bit.ly/evmconf to read more about this case study.

Towers of Hanoi—Build a Tower, Build a Team

Goals: Improve your attendees' collaboration and problem solving.

Is your team having problems working together to solve problems? Towers of Hanoi is an exercise where a team of attendees must work together to transfer a tower of items from one location to another. This simple team building brings out communication and trust issues quickly and is a fast way to determine where your team is in terms of team dynamics.

Time: 20–60 minutes
Participants: 2–8 per team; use breakouts for additional teams
Technology: Share Screen, breakouts
Category: Problem solving, collaboration

Setup: Chat bit.ly/evmtower and ask one attendee per team to click on the link. Have the attendee share their screen. If you have more than one team, assign a team leader to each team, share the link, and put them into their own breakout room after you give instructions.

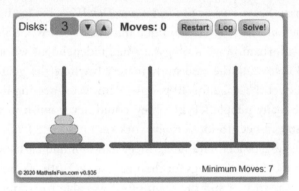

Instructions to the Audience: Your team goal is to move the tower of this stack of disks from one location to another in the least number of moves.

Assign at least one disk to each of your attendees.

You can assign more than one disk to an attendee after every attendee has a disk.

Only move that disk when the attendee asks to move it.

You can only move one disc at a time and you can only put a smaller disk on top of a larger disk in one of the three provided spaces.

Tips: You can use more or less disks to increase or decrease the complexity. 4 disks = 15 moves, 5 disks = 31 moves, 6 disks = 63 moves. Key themes from this team building game are problem solving, communication, sharing of ideas, leadership, and analytical thinking. You can place other metaphors on this event such as moving inventory or staging an office move or a complex project such as building a product or a house.

Debrief: Did your attendees plan before they started moving?
What did you do when you got stuck? How would you describe the attendee process?
How do you think you could speed up the process? How could you make the process more harmonious?
What can we learn from this activity to perform better at work?

Case Study: Towers of Hanoi was used with a team before they had to conduct a large office move. They did the game twice with five disks. The first time it took them over 45 moves to complete it. With proper planning, clearly communicating to each team member, and assigning key roles, they were able to achieve the minimum of 31 moves. Each team member committed to a key role for the office move in the debrief such as looking for dependencies, preplanning the next four moves, and preventing violation of rules (safety). They created five categories of moving responsibilities. They chose the bottom layer to represent infrastructure that had to be moved first and the top layer consisting of items that could only be moved/installed after everything else. By creating categories, they were able to multitask better, move over critical items first, and complete the move in less than 50% of the previously estimated time! The side benefit is that they used a shared document to collaboratively create, update, and monitor status so that every teammate could see what was happening in real time. Team morale was extraordinarily high in how the move was conducted and was rewarded with an outing paid for by the CEO!

Grid Unlock—How to Work Together to Solve Problems

Goals: Get attendees to find their own way to work together and solve problems.

Grid Unlock is a classic "Magic Squares" challenge updated for a virtual meeting. In a shared spreadsheet, attendees enter nine numbers until you can get every row, column, and diagonal to sum to 15. This is a great initiative for analytical thinking, problem solving, communication, and cooperation that has the bonus of teaching a team how to collaborate on a single document.

Time: 15–30 minutes
Participants: 3–9 per team; use breakout rooms if there are more
Technology: Share Screen and Microsoft Excel on a Shared OneDrive, Google Sheets or other applications that allow simultaneous editing
Category: Improving performance, problem solving

(Continued)

Setup: Create a copy of bit.ly/evmgridexcel or bit.ly/evmgridsheets. Click "share" and get a link to the spreadsheet saved on your server. Chat the link to all attendees. If you use breakout rooms, have a different link for every breakout room.

Instructions to the Audience: Your team needs to get the correct code to unlock these contents. The correct code has every row, every column, and both diagonals that add up to 15.

Every attendee is assigned at least one number from 1 to 9. If you have fewer than nine people, you can assign two or more numbers to an attendee.

Once assigned, you are responsible for entering your number into the grid.

You have limited time to complete this challenge. (Suggested: 10 minutes)

Tips: Watch for how the attendees work together or don't work together during this process. Roles such as leader and data entry usually emerge.

Debrief: What happened? How did your meeting tackle this challenge?

So what? So what did you learn about solving problems as a group?

Now what? Now what will you do differently in your next meeting based on this activity?

Variations: You can repeat this initiative up to two more times and time each iteration. You can give two to five minutes of planning time before you start the stopwatch. Write down the times for each completion and calculate the % increase or decrease in time.

You can also involve more people and make this exercise more complex by creating a 4×4 grid that totals 34 or a 5×5 grid that totals to 65, but know that adding more people will slow down the problem solving and increase the difficulty.

Case Study: This is a great team-building game where a team really learned key lessons in planning, accepting failure, and using all their resources to create the best result in the end. This team approached Grid Unlock like most other teams—by trial and error—and took over 12 minutes to complete the entire task. During the debrief, the group agreed that they wanted to do better and one teammate asked what the fastest time anybody had finished the challenge was. The facilitator said about two seconds. While there were only five minutes of planning time for the second stage, the team realized they had three attempts and they all agreed to spend all the planning and execution time for the second attempt in figuring out the two-second solution, thus having a worse time in the second attempt. When they had figured out all the roles for each of the team members and they were all clear on the plan, when the clock started, every team member filled in their one or two boxes and called time. In just 1.87 seconds, the team had completed the Magic Square with a reduction of 99.7% of the execution time! What the team got in the debrief was how to ask game-changing questions, having the courage to fail during a trial to win the event goal, and approaching future projects with the mindset to radically succeed!

Meeting Mine Field—Collaborating to Complete a Goal

Goals: Work together and take turns navigating a hidden route through a 10×10 grid.

Meeting Mine Field is based on a classic team-building event, Gridlock, created by Rocky Kimball, in which a team takes turns trying to discover a hidden route through a 10×10 grid. This initiative is good for paying attention, group problem solving, allowing mistakes, and being efficient.

Time: 20–60 minutes
Participants: 5–10 per team; use breakouts for more than one team
Technology: Share Screen and Microsoft Excel or Google Sheets
Category: Problem solving, collaboration

Setup: Open Microsoft Excel or Google Sheets. Leaving one row on the left and one row on the right, highlight a 10×10 grid and click "Borders" on the toolbar to create a grid on the playing area. Send the spreadsheet or a link to one of the meeting participants.

Create a path on your own 10×10 spreadsheet. Make sure you can see it and that it's not shared to others.

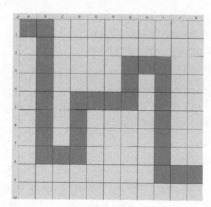

Instructions to the Audience:
Okay, one attendee, please open the document "Meeting Mine Field."
Your goal is to get from one side of the matrix to the other in the least amount of time and fewest acceptable incorrect steps.
You'll take turns and have one person calling the moves on the grid at a time.
If you move and are on the path, there will be no noise.
If you move and are off the path, you will get buzzed and you'll go to the back of the line.

(Continued)

The first time you make a mistake is a valuable learning opportunity and you will incur no penalties.

If you make a mistake more than once, you incur a one-minute penalty.

You can only move up, down, left, or right.

I'll give you two minutes to establish an order and plan and then the timer will begin.

Tips: As the facilitator, have the solution in front of you so you can buzz the team when they make a mistake.

On your own solution, mark when a team goes off the path, then add one minute to the penalty if they hit that square again. Mark the time when they exit.

You can reduce or increase the size of the grid to decrease or increase complexity and time to complete.

You can require the group to not talk (at all or only while they are on the grid) to increase difficulty.

You cannot allow the group to modify the grid to increase difficulty.

You can add Dead Ends (paths that do not lead to the end) to increase difficulty.

You can allow diagonal moves to increase difficulty. I often make time marks such as "3:45 team goes too slow to avoid mistakes" on my solution sheet to give me talking points for the debrief.

Debrief: What was your initial strategy?

Who took what roles to support the entire team?

What was fluid and what was frustrating?

Did some people move too slow or too fast?

How did your team feel about mistakes?

How many repeated mistakes did you make?

What were the team dynamics like?

What can we do in our meetings to get to our goal faster?

Case Study: I first used Meeting Mine Field with a team that was struggling and I wanted to use a collection of four initiatives to help them. Meeting Mine Field was sequenced to be first for the explicit purpose of diagnosing the team. I predicted that the team would have challenges in completing the task. This was useful, as the team thought they were a high-functioning team but the manager did not, so this initiative would let them know who was right. In this case, the team was hesitant to make any mistakes so they moved very slowly. Many of the teammates were not paying attention to what was going on so they racked up penalties by stepping on the wrong square more than once. At the end, the team was pretty depressed and one teammate remarked that this is exactly what happens at work. What was useful as a designer and facilitator is that I put three initiatives behind this one in a particular order. The first one worked on planning and was relatively easy. The second initiative focused on clear communication with medium difficulty. The third initiative focused on execution with higher difficulty. With this momentum, the team was able to learn key meeting skills, which they used to create success on the initiatives. They used that momentum to complete each subsequent challenge in record times. The meeting ended on a high note and all team members made strong commitments to each other to change how they work together. They found out that they would rather have the feelings of team success than working hard individually and having team failure.

Poll Survivor—Setting Meeting Priorities and Making Hard Decisions

Goals: Improve prioritization and group decision making.

Do you have meeting attendees who prioritize everything or nothing as important? Do you have a meeting whose attendees are having difficulties making hard decisions? Use this activity to help your attendees have a discussion and make new decisions about how to make hard decisions. Poll Survivor is a tested simulation used for survival training. This activity will put your attendees into a survival situation and have them prioritize what items they will take to maximize their chances of survival.

Time: 20–60 minutes
Participants: 2–16 per team; use breakouts for more teams
Technology: Polling
Category: Problem solving, decision making, collaboration
Setup: Set up a poll with the following 10 items:

1. Ball of steel wool
2. Small ax
3. Loaded .45-caliber pistol
4. Can of Crisco shortening
5. Newspapers (one per person)
6. Cigarette lighter (without fluid)
7. Extra shirt and pants for each survivor
8. 20×20-foot piece of heavy-duty canvas
9. Quart of 100-proof whiskey
10. Family-size chocolate bars (one per person)

(Continued)

Set the poll to Multiple selection so every attendee can vote for multiple items.

Instructions to the Audience: You and your teammates have just survived the crash of small airplane. Take time to read the scenario; then, by checking and unchecking the boxes in the poll, decide on the order of the items that your team will take. Items with the most votes will be picked first. We will rank your choices at the end. We will begin a timer (default 10 minutes).

Tips: It can be helpful to give reminders at the five-minute, three-minute, and one-minute mark to let attendees know how much time is left.

Recording the meeting and saving the chat log are extremely useful to highlight specific points of meeting inflection. Usually, you need to stop and start the meeting again to gain access to the video. You can use the video to debrief at a follow-up meeting.

The correct order is:

1. Cigarette lighter (without fluid)
2. Ball of steel wool
3. Extra shirt and pants for each survivor
4. Can of Crisco shortening
5. 20×20-foot piece of heavy-duty canvas
6. Small ax
7. Family-size chocolate bars (one per person)
8. Newspapers (one per person)
9. Loaded .45-caliber pistol
10. Quart of 100-proof whiskey

An easy way to score is to add up the numbers next to the top five items. The lowest score wins; the lowest possible score is 15.

Close the poll and share the results.

Debrief: What happened? How did you choose your items?

What did you learn from the process?

Was the decision unanimous or not?

Who was the leader? Who had a decision-changing idea?

How did you persuade each other to agree with your point of view?

What can you take forward in your team meetings to make better decisions?

Case Study: Chat Survivor was run at the American Society for Training and Development's 2011 International Conference. While they were face-to-face during the 10 minutes, participants could only communicate to each other over Twitter on specific hashtags, and then submitted their final answers to a shared hashtag. What was fascinating was the different feedback we got from the 20-plus teams. Some teams said it was very challenging to keep track and create consensus using only text. Other teams said it was very engaging and that they came to consensus very quickly as they were all in agreement over the major items. In the results, scores ranged from the 40s all the way to a team that had 16 (1 away from the best score possible). Most of all, these training professionals experienced the same team dynamics they have with face-to-face team building. They learned how their team makes decisions and how well they did with the best results possible. This activity gave insight on how they can make better decisions in the future.

10 | End Your Meeting on a High Note

Is the end of your meeting awkward? Do your meetings end on a low note? Do you have less energy at the end of your meetings? Do your attendees not know when to log off?

You've done all the work to create an engaging meeting; take the last step and end your meeting on a high note. It's very easy for work-minded people to forget this important step, but for recurring meetings, I think you'll see the benefits of investing in this step. You'll help your meeting establish rhythm and ritual by starting and ending every meeting in the same or similar way.

Erica Olsen, author of *Strategic Planning Kit for Dummies*, says:

You successfully made it all the way through your strategic planning meeting. You did it! You accomplished everything you intended. You have the key pieces of your strategic plan in place. You're feeling great. Everyone is slowly packing up and heading out the door, but you sense a feeling of exhaustion and maybe a little anxiety. You're wondering why.

What just happened is that you unintentionally ended your strategic planning meeting on a low note. In most cases, you have more to cover in your meeting than you have time for. You end up rushing the last part of the meeting to get it all done.

No matter where you are in your agenda, structuring the last half-hour of the meeting to end on a high note is critical to getting everyone excited about the new strategic direction.

The best way to get people jazzed about the plan is to have them visualize success and ensure that they're comfortable with the work product. What does success look like? Help your team feel successful by living the future today.

Ask your team to draw a picture of what the company may look like if you achieve your strategic plan. How many employees? What is the office like? Where are you located? Who are your customers? What's the media saying? And so on.

Then have your team explain its vision to the group. After the drawings and explanations are over, tell your staff members to hang their creations at their desks to remind them of the plan and their part in it. That way, everyone leaves the planning session feeling successful, brought into the decisions that were made, and not overworked.[1]

Here are more ways to end your meeting on a high note.

Applause—Celebrating Together

Goals: Celebrate.

Fast, easy, and inclusive. You can thank everyone and get everyone to applaud.

Time: 5 seconds
Participants 2–Max
Technology: Audio, video
Category: Closers

Instructions: Let's give a round of applause for our speaker.
Tip: If all of your attendees are on mute, ask them to hold their hands next to their head and then shake their hands. This is sign language for applause.

Kudos—Acknowledging Attendees

Goals: Have attendees notice something positive about other attendees.

As one of my good friends, Helice Bridges (http://blueribbons.com), says, people are not only hungry for food, they are hungry for acknowledgment. This simple closing gives each person time to acknowledge another teammate for their contribution. This raises team morale and has the side benefit of increasing relations between those two people as well as the receiving person perhaps noticing something about himself or herself that they didn't see before.

Time: 1–10 minutes
Participants 2–25
Technology: Audio, video
Category: Closers

Instructions: Every attendee gives kudos or acknowledgment to another attendee. Keep going until every attendee has received at least one acknowledgment.

Tips: Keep a timer handy if you need to limit time to end on time. If the kudos are authentic, this is worth asking your attendees to stay a few extra minutes to complete the activity.

Case Study: In one team-building event, we did this closing event and one woman posted that she was so grateful to the team and one person in particular who had helped her through her recent medical challenges. She mentioned how emotional she was from that support and the team responded with even more support for her. It showed that the critical piece of the meeting was supporting her in her personal life as well as her professional life. This support helped build one of the strongest team cultures as they were caring for each other. Every team member felt pride in being able to help her out and responded, knowing that she had given so much to the team and the company that they were glad to help her when she needed it. She has since given back much, much more to the attendees and the company now that she is healthy.

I Commit . . .—Public Commitment to Change

Goals: To choose one action that each teammate will commit to do after the team-building session.

This initiative was given to me by Dr. Simon Priest, PhD, as one of the easiest ways to do effective follow-up at the end of a program. Just revisiting these commitments within two to four weeks after the team-building session has the potential to retain 80% of the learning gains. In addition, by committing publicly to your team, you increase the odds that individuals will own their actions.

Time: 2–20 minutes
Participants: 2–25
Technology: Audio, video
Category: Closers

Instructions: One of the goals of this training is to take just *one* thing from this training and *do* something different. Knowledge is not power; new actions and results are power. And the one thing I know that is in your complete control is the choices you make each day. To gain the value of this training, what is the one thing you commit to do based on this meeting?

(Continued)

I'd like every attendee to finish the sentence "I commit.. . ." What do you commit to do different based on this meeting?

Tips: Record the commitments and send them back to the attendees to increase the chance of them following through with their commitment.

You can play back each commitment at the next meeting and ask for an update.

Case Study: In working with one team-building event, a teammate who was in charge of increasing cash flow committed to working with three different teams to decrease the time of a process that took four hours, because he had to walk around to each salesperson and get the status on where every project was at in terms of accounting. Because the company was already using a CRM (Customer Relationship Management system, such as salesforce.com), he met with leaders from sales, accounting, and operations and mapped out the process for a workflow into five different stages of accounting for each project. In addition, he created measurements of how long it stayed in each stage so that each team could be measured and held accountable. Finally, he rolled out this workflow with agreements from each of the teams. Amazingly, cash flow from closed projects improved, going from 64 days to 32 days on average, and the process of getting the information went from four hours to one second with just the push of a button!

Just Three Words—Powerful Closure Quickly

Goals: To provide closure quickly to your meeting.

Attendees reflect on the meeting and sum up their thoughts in just three words.

Time: 1–10 minutes
Participants: 2–50
Technology: Audio, video, chat
Category: Closers

Instructions: It's time to close this meeting; before we go, let's find out where everyone is at. Take a moment to think about this meeting and sum up your experience in just three words. Just signal me when you're ready. We'll end when everyone shares their three words.

Tip: If you need to speed this up even more or have a lot of attendees, ask every attendee to send their three words by chat.

Debrief: Take the time to highlight or ask about any unique or distinct words. Close by thanking all your participants and then end your meeting.

Case Study: One team took the three-word close to the extreme. They had just solved a very complex team-building challenge and their morale was very high. Three-word quotes came streaming in: "Never give up," "Success is yours," "Anything is possible," "I heart team," "Dreams come true," and other powerful messages came through. The trainer was moved that he was able to help the attendees so much. A week later, the trainer received a package in the mail. He opened the package and found that a team member had created a necklace on http://zazzle.com (there are other sites like Cafepress.com that can turn anything into a physical object) and added a note that was sent with the necklace: "THANK YOU for your gifts and skills as a trainer; our team was on a path to failure and with your help, I can tell you that the last week was one of my BEST weeks working with this team. We knew we had the potential. Thank you for seeing it, believing in it, and, most of all, making it come true."

Call and Response—High Energy, Engaging All

Goals: End with high energy from every attendee.

Call and response is a time-tested technique for getting attention and raising energy. Call and response is used in classrooms, military, churches, sporting events, and in many international cultures. The host gives the call and all the attendees give the response.

Time: 15 seconds
Participants 2–Max
Technology: Audio, video
Category: Closers

(Continued)

Instructions: I'm going to unmute everybody (click the button to unmute all). When I say (call), you all say (response).

Examples include:

Going. Going. (GONE!)
Scooby Dooby Doo. . .(Where Are You?)
Marco (Polo!)
Sea (Hawks), Sea (Hawks), Sea (Hawks)!
1, 2, 3 (We out!)
Good times never seemed so good. (So good! So good! So good!)
To infinity (and beyond!)
Stop. . .(Collaborate and listen!)
Peanut butter (jelly time!)
I want to rock and roll all night (and party every day)
Ben Kenyon with his Great Day Squad likes to close with: Great Day Squad! (We out here!)

Tips: You can draw from music, pop culture, movies, or company mottos. Just make sure it's a good fit for your attendees.

The Last Word—The Final Statement of Your Meeting

Goals: To allow every attendee a final remark.

Definitions of last word:

1: The final remark in a verbal exchange
2a: The power of final decision
2b: A definitive statement or treatment

The last word gives every attendee the opportunity to have their final remark for the virtual meeting. The last word allows everyone to have closure and give their impression or value of the meeting. A key feature is that everyone feels heard and, quite often, you will be surprised at what the quietest attendees say. Sometimes, they have the best and deepest insights.

Time: 2–10 minutes
Participants: 2–25
Technology: Audio, video
Category: Closers

Instructions: Ask every attendee to answer, "What did you get out of today's meeting?" Use air traffic control so attendees don't talk over each other. End the meeting after the last person answers.

Tips: Here is a sample of other Last Word–type questions. Feel free to use or develop your own questions.

How do you feel about today's meeting?
What's the one thing you remember about today's meeting?
Who would you like to thank for their contribution to this meeting?
What would you tell someone else about this meeting?
What are your final remarks?
What do you think we accomplished this meeting?
What makes you proud about this meeting?

Case Study: I have a friend who runs a training virtual meeting. At the end of her training, she uses The Last Word. At the beginning of her meeting, she started recording the meeting and everyone agreed to the video waiver. What she realized is that The Last Word was giving her the best testimonial in a very natural format without having to ask an attendee to stay after class to give a testimonial.

Draw—A Picture Is Worth a Thousand Words

Goals: To summarize your meeting with a picture.

"A picture is worth a thousand words" is an English adage meaning that complex and sometimes multiple ideas can be conveyed by a single still image, which conveys its meaning or essence more effectively than a mere verbal description.[2]

This fast closer can communicate a lot of information in a short amount of time even with a large number of attendees.

Time: 2 minutes
Participants: 2–Max
Technology: Audio, video, optional Share Whiteboard
Category: Closers

Instructions: Ask attendees to have a piece of paper and a pen at the beginning of the meeting. At the end of the meeting, ask them to draw a picture that represents the meeting for them. Ask them for a thumbs up when they are done drawing. Ask them to turn off their

(Continued)

virtual backgrounds if possible. When the majority is done drawing, ask them to hold up their pictures up in front of their face or shirt and keep them up until you ask them to put them down. If you have a lot of attendees, ask them to scroll through all the attendees to look at the other pictures while still holding up their own.

Tips: You can make comments or acknowledge pictures with people's names as you look at them. You can encourage an attendee to hold up their picture or adjust it so you can see it. If your attendees don't have paper, you can Share Whiteboard (Chapter 5), draw lines so there is at least one box per attendee, and ask them to draw in the box you assign them. If you want to take longer than two minutes, you can ask one attendee at a time to share their picture and describe what they drew.

Case Study: A Parks and Recreation group was having a virtual meeting on how to use virtual platforms. At the end of the meeting, the host used "Draw" to close the meeting. As all the attendees showed their pictures, the host saw the one shown here. He asked, "Why did you draw that?" The attendee said, "I live alone, so during this pandemic I've mostly been by myself. By learning how to use this virtual platform, I now know I can communicate with others. I have been so lonely and today is the first day I have hope during this pandemic. Thank you!" The host hadn't known that a simple closer could create so much meaning.

Q&A—Questions and Answers

Goals: To answer unanswered questions from the meeting.

The most important meeting is the meeting before the meeting and the meeting after the meeting.

—John Chen

I discovered at Microsoft that allocating extra time to showing up early and staying late at meetings meant I would get face time with important people from different teams.

One of the best ways to keep a meeting engaging is to allow people who need to leave to go and then open up to 30 minutes of Q&A. Anybody who has extra time can ask questions with a smaller audience. The host or a special speaker can answer questions that didn't get asked or answered during the main meeting. When Q&A is done or time is up, make sure to find a way to end on a high note.

Time: 2–30 minutes
Participants: 2–Max
Technology: Audio, video, (optional) chat
Category: Closers

Instructions: Remind the attendees that you're going to stay for up to 30 minutes after the meeting. Complete a Closer. Invite people who need to go that they can log off. Ask for any questions or comments that they'd like to make about today's meeting.

Tips: Use air traffic control to make sure that only one attendee at a time is asking questions. For large meetings, you may want to use a producer who will keep track of order if there is a large number of attendees who want to ask questions.

After Hours—The Party After the Party

Goals: Keep the meeting/party going.

If you have a meeting that was more like a performance or a conference, then consider closing with After Hours. Invite people who want to leave to depart; for those who stay, the host can help have an open conversation on any topic the attendees would like to talk about. Sometimes they talk about the meeting, sometimes they just socialize. For speakers, pretend that this is like staying after a meeting to talk to people who come up to talk to you after you

(Continued)

speak. This is a key time to engage, answer key questions, and network. Keep the After Hours open either as long as the host would like or for a fixed amount of time.

Time: 2 minutes to as long as you'd like
Participants: 2–Max
Technology: Audio, video, (optional) chat
Category: Closers

Instructions: Let your attendees know that there will be After Hours. End with a Closer. Invite attendees who have to leave that they can log off. Start After Hours and use any format that you'd like to keep attendees engaged. It could be comments. It could be Q&A. It could be open discussion.

Tip: You can play a video or use something similar to create a transition from the main meeting to After Hours.

Case Study: Daybreaker is a morning dance community of 500,000+ members in 28 cities around the world. They were one of the first to launch an all-virtual dance party. Over 2,000 people from all around the world showed up. For the Pacific Standard Time zone, the dance was scheduled from 8 to 10 a.m. For their first show, they were so excited to make it happen that they stayed on from 10 a.m. to noon PST, another full two hours. The numbers reduced to around 500 people online and they continued to engage more attendees that they did not spotlight in the first two hours. Many attendees said they became bigger fans of Daybreaker because they kept their After Hours going so long.

One Thing Better—Improving 1% at a Time

Goals: Create meetings that are better over time.

Don't think about doing one thing 100% better, think about doing 100 things 1% better every day.

– Pete Winemiller, vice president of customer experience, Oklahoma City Thunder, who lost his battle with brain cancer

Pete was in charge of customer experience at Oklahoma City Thunder and the Seattle Super Sonics, and the customer service he provided was legendary.

If you ever met one of Pete's paid staff or any of the 400 volunteers who helped run an NBA game, you would know that they had all attended one of Pete's legendary trainings. You would find a laminated tag on a lanyard around their neck. On the laminated tag was the one thing they were going to do 1% better during that game. Every staff member gets a new tag every game.

After Pete's 18 seasons with the NBA, David Stern, the commissioner of the NBA, said that Pete set the gold standard for the NBA experience, 1% at a time.

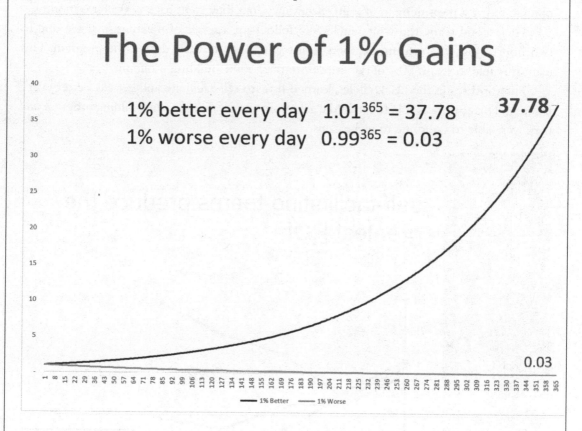

The Power of 1% Gains

1% better every day $1.01^{365} = 37.78$ **37.78**
1% worse every day $0.99^{365} = 0.03$

0.03

— 1% Better   — 1% Worse

Time: 2–10 minutes
Participants: 2–25
Technology: Audio, video
Category: Closers

Instructions: Ask every attendee to choose one thing that they will attempt to be 1% better at during the next virtual meeting. Use air traffic control to make sure people don't talk at the same time. End when every attendee has spoken.

Tip: If you are pressed for time or you have a large audience, you can speed this up by asking your attendees to chat their answer.

(Continued)

Why does this work? Meetings that self-facilitate or decide to get just 1% better every meeting outperform other meetings.

Here's the research why. Three teams attended a professional team-building session. The first team, the black squares, did nothing after the meeting. They achieved gains in a team development index, a measurement of team effectiveness, but they went back to 0 after 6 months.

The second team, the white circles, did follow-up, a series of meetings that are one to two hours long where team members revisit what they learned during the program. This team was able to retain 80% of the gains from their team-building program.

The third team, the black circles, learned how to self-facilitate and get 1% better every meeting. This team was able to retain the gain from a professional team-building program *and* they were able to continue to make gains.

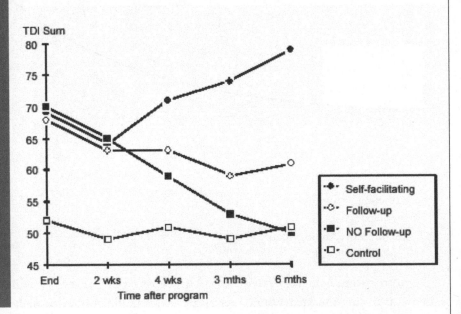

This closer can add significant value to your meeting. You can record the 1% commitments in the meeting notes or just hit record to get a video. Make sure to follow up at the next meeting, such as by playing the last meeting's video, and make sure that every attendee follows through.

Plus-Delta—What Did You Like? What Could Be Even Better?

Goals: Close your meeting and get immediate feedback.

Do you want a quick and effective way to end your meeting? Do you want to know what your meeting did well?

This activity is very quick and easy and can help you recognize what's working in your meeting as well as how to make it better.

Time: 2–10 minutes
Participants: 2–25
Technology: Audio, video, (optional) chat
Category: Closers

Instructions: Have every attendee come up with two pluses, or things that went well during the meeting, and one delta (delta, or Δ, is the symbol for change), or something that would make the meeting even better for them. Have every attendee share by taking turns or by chat if you need to finish in a shorter amount of time. The host can help the attendees decide what they are going to do differently in the next meeting.

Choose one of the deltas you'll try next meeting. Make sure to keep the meeting feature that the attendees identified with the most pluses.

Tip: You can speed this up and handle large groups by using chat.

Case Study: Tony Robbins is a top speaker with six internationally bestselling books; over 50 million people have attended his programs. After *every* program, Tony uses Plus-Delta to find out what went well with the program and what he can do better. He started this practice when he was charging less than $50 for his program and now his top tickets can sell for more than $10,000. His 50 privately held companies now have combined sales exceeding $6 billion a year and Plus-Delta had a place in creating his success.[3]

WWW—What, So What, Now What?

Goals: An easy way to remember how to debrief and move your attendees to action.

Do you want a way for your attendees to decide what they can do even better? Do you want three questions that inspire action? Do you want a closer that is very easy to remember?

WWW is a facilitation method taught by established facilitators. I've remembered it since I learned it and I continue to use it as a way to help attendees come to their own conclusion about taking action.

Time: 2–15 minutes
Participants: 2–25
Technology: Audio, video
Category: Closers
Instructions: Ask your attendees these three questions:

1. What? What happened during this meeting?
2. So What? So what did you learn during this meeting?
3. Now What? Now what do we do better next meeting?

One way to close is to have one third of the attendees answer What?, one third answer So What?, and the last third answer Now What? Keep track of who spoke and summarize what the attendees agreed on before you end the meeting.

Case Study: I learned WWW more than 19 years ago at the Association for Experiential Education (http://www.aee.org). This well-known reflection model was developed by Gary Rolfe, Dawn Freshwater, and Melanie Jasper, who did extensive research for their book *Critical Reflection in Nursing and the Helping Professions: A User's Guide* (2001). The University of Connecticut Center for Excellence in Teaching and Learning offers more questions that you can use in this model.[4]

11 | Fun and Games for High-Performing Teams

Create fun . . . and a little weirdness.
—Source: One of Zappos' Ten Corporate Values. © 2020, Zappos Insights Inc.

Virtual meetings are very efficient.
Virtual meetings take 66% less time than face-to-face ones.
Virtual meetings cost 85% less.[1]
Virtual meetings impact the environment up to 90% less.
Virtual meetings are virus free.
You can eat lunch with your family or walk your dog after your meeting.

The challenge with virtual meetings is that it's very easy to spend too much time getting work done and not spend any time having fun. If your attendees are experiencing work or virtual meeting burnout, consider using fun at your next meeting to increase morale.

Fun provides stress release. Fun can help you feel vital and alive. Fun can help you have a positive attitude. Fun can help you laugh, which has many health benefits. Fun can help you build strong relationships and social support.[2]

The best learning is fun. When you're having fun and something good is happening, you are put into a unique state—and when you are in this state, you are more likely to remember what is happening and what you are learning. Many of these activities are designed to be fun and educational, which is what makes them so effective.

Fun is a key indicator of winning teams. I have been doing team building for over 23 years and I have been doing video analysis of team building for the past 10 years. After reviewing over 50 terabytes of data, I discovered that a common trait of winning teams is fun. Winning teams have fun. Winning teams have attendees who are enjoying themselves and the other members of their team. In contrast, losing teams are not having fun. They are usually quiet, unhappy, or mad. Go to bit.ly/evmfun to see a short video contrasting winning and losing teams around how much fun they are having.

Dave Crenshaw, author of *The Power of Having Fun*, shared this research on fun:

A recent Gallup survey found that only about one-third of US employees consider themselves engaged at work. This means that about two-thirds could care less—or are even hostile—about the work they're doing and the company they're working for. It's even worse outside the United States, with over 80% of employees in the disengaged category.

Yet companies with highly engaged workforces outperform competitors by 147%. Each year, *Fortune* magazine enlists the aid of the Great Place to Work Institute to compile The Fortune 100 Best Companies to Work For® list. Companies covet and seek membership to this rare group. Talk about a recruiting boost!

For all employees who work for the companies on the list, the phrase "this is a fun place to work" most highly correlated among all survey statements with this phrase: "Taking everything into account, I consider this a great place to work." Translation: If you want a workplace that attracts and retains top talent, make it a fun place to work.

And if you want to love your work, find a way to infuse moments of fun into your day.[3]

I will add the caveat that your fun needs to be authentic and come from a place of psychological safety. You cannot put a fun event in a series of meetings that has serious unresolved conflict. I would suggest that you plan your next meeting to resolve that conflict first. You also cannot put a fun event into a culture that does not value fun. Make sure you meet your attendees where they are and have the goal to elevate them one or two steps higher in a way they will most likely appreciate.

If you want your virtual meeting to be engaging, look to put fun into one of your next meetings. These activities are ordered from easiest to more complicated. Start at the beginning of the chapter and look for activities later in the chapter if your attendees are looking for more variety or challenge.

Happy Hour—Share a Beverage Together

Goals: Enjoy a beverage together and get to know each other.

The words "happy" and "hour" have appeared together for centuries when describing pleasant times. In act I, scene 2 of William Shakespeare's *King Henry V*, he says, "Therefore, my lords, omit no happy hour/That may give furtherance to our expedition…" The use of the phrase "happy hour" to refer to a scheduled period of entertainment is, however, of much more recent vintage.

The *Random House Dictionary of American Slang* dates "Happy hour," as a term for afternoon drinks in a bar, to a 1959 *Saturday Evening Post* article on military life.

Happy hour culture has grown internationally. It's a marketing term for when a venue, such as a restaurant, offers discounts on alcoholic drinks and appetizers. As a business tool, many attendees would easily go to a happy hour, but would think twice about going to a free marketing seminar.

The key to a successful happy hour is great food and beverages and people who are great conversationalists.

Time: 30–90 minutes
Participants: 2–Max
Technology: Audio, video, breakout rooms
Category: Fun, networking

Instructions: Send out invites to a date and time with a meeting link. Tell everyone to show up with a beverage. As the host, run air traffic control to help make sure attendees don't talk over each other.

Tip: If you want a successful Happy Hour over time, hold it at the same day of the week, the same time, and the same meeting link. This lowers the requirements to get into the meeting and makes it easier for people to participate every week.

One of your goals may be to create more psychological safety; if so, here are some suggestions. Do not livestream; attendees feel more open if they are not being broadcast. Do not record; attendees feel more open if something they say will not be captured. What happens during happy hour stays in happy hour. If possible, get agreements from all attendees that what is being shared is confidential. This means that attendees agree to not post on social media or share with outside people.

Case Study: On March 13, 2020, Seattle closed all community centers, libraries, and schools and banned any meeting of 250 or more people. Joy Carpenter, a sales associate for a hotel, posted the following:

(Continued)

I realized something I've been processing this week.... 5 stages of grief while working in travel during the Coronavirus "outbreak."

1. Denial: "Is this really happening? Not everyone is going to go crazy, not everything is going to cancel."
2. Anger: "Stop canceling!! Why are you shutting down the offices and meetings?... it's the flu."
3. Bargaining: "Look, if you rebook this year, we will work with you. Do you have any idea what this is causing us to do to schedules, maintenance, and spending? You still owe us damages and cancellation fees. It's for the economy."
4. Depression: "This is it, no one cares. No one is truly listening to doctors or going to pay cancellation fees. No other city feels this as mine does."
5. Acceptance: "I don't care, do what you want, I'm going to drink."

Seriously...
You're welcome... save yourself the therapy bill and go have a glass of wine.

Joy started a virtual happy hour on every Friday at 5 p.m. PST. This was a safe place for people in the hospitality industry to talk about all the rapid changes that were happening with the coronavirus. It was soon opened up to everybody. As a group, they shared low points such as furloughs, layoffs, and quarantines. They celebrated high points like birthdays, new jobs, and health.

Most of all, it was deemed the virtual meeting that had the highest level of psychological safety. Attendees looked forward to Happy Hour, especially after a hard week. *Game of Thrones* was a TV show that was known for epic moments in every episode. Every Happy Hour affectionately had the *Game of Thrones* moment, which was hearing a story so big that it was like one of the jaw-dropping moments from the show. The safety to talk about your work, the people you work with, your family, and the family you live with became a key benefit, as being able to talk was helping the attendees' mental health. This Happy Hour was cited by many members as one of the primary ways they were coping with the challenges of the coronavirus.

You can register now to see if this happy hour is still going at http://geoteaminghappy-hour.eventbrite.com.

Charades—Improving Your Nonverbal Communication

Goals: Guess what the actor is doing without the actor saying a word.

This classic game plays well in virtual meetings. A charade was a form of literary riddle popularized in France in the eighteenth century. This acting game is a great way to extend nonverbal communication and raise energy by involving every attendee.

Time: 2 minutes per round
Participants: 2–50; can extend by using breakout rooms
Technology: Audio, video, chat, (optional) breakout rooms
Category: Fun, communication

Instructions: Choose one person to be the actor. Everyone else are guessers. The host private chats a word or phrase to the actor. Ask the actor to give a thumbs up when they see and understand what the host sent them. Count down 3, 2, 1 and start a 60-second timer, usually held up to the camera. Attendees can take guesses by saying a word or a phrase out loud.

Common charade rules are:
No talking or sounds by actor.
Silent mouthing, spelling, and pointing are banned.
Tips: A basic strategy is to start with easy words and work your way to harder ones. You can also teach basic charades strategy such as denoting how many words and then how many syllables are in each word.

Case Study: Go to bit.ly/evmcharades to see an example of charades, including easy words like *team* and hard words like *hydroxychloroquine*.

Reverse Charades—Improving Everybody's Nonverbal Communication

Goals: Play charades with more engagement and more energy.

Have you ever wished for a fun game where more people were engaged? Do you want a game that's high energy? Reverse Charades takes the game of charades and reverses it so only

(Continued)

one person is the guesser and all the other attendees act out the word or phrase. You can see the energy when you have 10–20 video windows all moving around in different directions and with different strategies.

> Time: 2 minutes per round
> Participants: 2–50; you can do more if you use breakout rooms
> Technology: Audio, video, chat, (optional) breakout rooms
> Category: Fun, communication
> Instruction: Choose one person to be the guesser; everybody else is now the actors.
> Have the guesser close their chat window and cover the area where chat alerts can show up.
> Test it by chatting "TEST WORD" and get a thumbs up that the guesser can't see it.
> Now chat to everyone the actual word or phrase.
> Ask actors for a thumbs up so you can see if all or the majority of people saw it.
> Count down 3, 2, 1 and start a 60-second timer, usually held up to the camera.

The guesser will now have multiple windows of information to guess from! You can remind the guesser to click the right or left arrows if there is more than one screen full of actors.

Tips: Start with easy words and move to harder ones. Another way to customize the game is to have all the participants private chat the host a collection of words and phrases.

Case Study: I was introduced to Reverse Charades at the North American Simulation and Gaming Association conference. Formed in 1962, it's one of the oldest gamification conferences. By turning charades upside down, it creates 100% engagement and a lot more energy as so many people are acting at the same time. I have used this for special events such as birthday parties where I ask people to private chat me one to seven words about the birthday person, who becomes the guesser. Each actor gets to tell a story about why they chose their clue about the birthday person and whether or not the birthday person got the answer. You get to know something new about the birthday person and it's just plain fun.

Go to bit.ly/evmreverse to see an example of Reverse Charades.

Hat Day—Fun on Your Head

> Goals: Bring fun and levity on your head.

While the first types of hats were developed for protection from inclement weather, shade from the sun, and a shield against falling rocks or weapons, hats gradually came to represent status, wealth, and authority. Eventually, hats were also used to make a fashion statement. Make a fashion statement and learn something about your attendees by hosting a Hat Day at your next virtual meeting.

Time: 1 minute
Participants: 2–Max
Technology: Video
Category: Fun, networking

Instructions: This easy and fun activity requires sending out an email before a virtual meeting and telling everyone to bring a hat to the meeting. Then wear a hat at your meeting.

Tips: You can pair this with an opener that asks why you chose your hat. Often, you'll hear great stories of where the hat came from and when they first wore it.

Case Study: To celebrate the first Virtual Engaging Meetings 3 class, I asked everyone to bring a hat to the class. Attendees from around the world, including San Diego, Vancouver, and Slovenia, showed up. Hats ranged from baseball caps to cowboy hats to Canadian flags. (Figure 11.1) Theresa Little, senior consultant at McKinstry, showed up in a unicorn hat. If you look closely at the cover of the book, you'll see Theresa's image with her unicorn hat—now that's fun!

Figure 11.1 Hat Day at the First Engaging Virtual Meetings 3 Training

Pajama Day—Work in Your Jammies

Goals: Be comfortable and have fun.

We've all made jokes about being in our pajamas when working from home. Onesies (a one-piece bodysuit made of knit cotton) became street fashion.[4]

Time: 1 minute
Participants: 2–Max
Technology: Video
Category: Fun

Instructions: Have fun with your group by sending an email to have everyone show up wearing their pajamas to the next meeting (Figure 11.2).

Variations: Tell everyone except one person. When everyone arrives at the meeting, attempt to have a regular meeting until the one person says something. You can make a betting pool to see how long it takes this person to make a comment. Make sure to convey this was done in fun as singling out one person could be construed as harassment in the wrong context—and that's *not* fun.

**Figure 11.2   Author John Chen declared Pajama Day after
60 days of stay-at-home orders.**

Virtual Backgrounds—Your Setting Can Create Pure Laughs to Serious Business

Goals: Change your background for fun or for business.

Do you want to be in a beautiful office overlooking the ocean? Do you want to be on the site of your favorite TV show? Do you want to clean up your office without doing the hard work or using a hard-to-set-up green screen?

One of the fastest ways to clean up or improve your background is with virtual backgrounds. A virtual background takes any picture or video and changes everything around your head and body to that new background. If you have a computer that is powerful enough, you can change your background right now.[5] If you have an older computer or want to get best results, you can use a green screen[6] or a large green mat behind you, like what's used in movies. The green screen allows the computer to easily replace the green with your virtual background.

Time: 1 minute
Participants: 1–Max
Technology: Virtual Backgrounds
Category: Fun, Communication

Instructions: Most systems allow a photo or a video for your virtual background and usually come with examples. In Zoom,

Step 1: Click the "^" next to "Stop Video."
Step 2: Click "Choose Virtual Background."

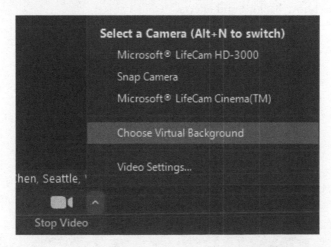

(Continued)

Step 3: Click a virtual background like "Beach." Usually there are five demonstration backgrounds.

Step 4: Click "I have a green screen" only if you have one. If this option is not available to you, your computer is not powerful enough to work without a green screen.

Step 5: Click the "x" on the top right.

On Microsoft Teams:

Step 1: Click ". . ." on the toolbar.

Step 2, Click "Show background effects."

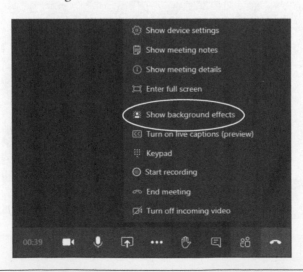

(Continued)

Step 3: Click on a background.
Step 4: Click "Apply."

Tip: Some companies have had contests for best virtual backgrounds. They have used replications of art pieces, the most isolated workplace, and backgrounds with matching costumes.

Variations: Another fun Virtual Background trick is to take the backgrounds of other attendees if they step out during the meeting. Dave Vaught, technical services manager at NW Event Technology (https://www.nweventtechnology.com), was one of the first to do this. I left a meeting and when I returned, he was sitting in my office!

Marni and Dave, Seattle

Go to bit.ly/evmbackgrounds for how to make a virtual background.

Case Study: While virtual backgrounds can be fun, they can help you get work done. Justin Reidt used a virtual background during his interview.

During preparation for the interview, Reidt discovered he'd be talking with Sean Gentry—a diehard fan of the Los Angeles Lakers. Since the interview would be taking place by Zoom, he made his background the Staples Center, where the Lakers play.

"I'm really glad I did it, because he instantly opened up," Reidt says. "He was like, 'Ah, man, you got me! You know what you're doing here, right?'" Gentry was so impressed that he shared a screenshot of the Zoom around the office and later posted about it on LinkedIn. Reidt got the job.[7]

Yoga—Stretch and Breathe

Goals: Provide a moment of stretching and breathing.

Figure 11.3 Yoga can be healthy and engaging, virtually

Want a little health in your meeting? Have a team member or a professional lead yoga to start your meeting (Figure 11.3). Yoga has been around for more than 5,000 years. It's a total mind-body workout that combines strengthening and stretching poses with deep breathing and relaxation. There is a type of yoga that suits your attendee needs and fitness level. You can also have the benefits of getting your attendees more connected together, as yoga is a form of Matching and Mirroring (Chapter 7).

(Continued)

Time: 2–90 minutes
Participants: 2–Max
Technology: Audio, video
Category: Fun, health

Instructions: The easiest workout is chair yoga that you can do in your computer seat. The next is standing yoga, although many will have to move or adjust their camera. If you want to do full-body yoga, I recommend emailing your attendees beforehand and advising them on a setup where they have a yoga mat and their camera positioned so you can see their entire body. You can have a live instructor or use one of the many free yoga videos online.

Need Productive Meeting Experiences? Try Mindfulness

There is no escaping it, our minds are full. Call it exhaustion, or stress being human today comes with it a lot of overwhelm. We must discern what meetings we will and will not attend. Then consciously or unconsciously choose how much energy we will bring to them. This is where mindfulness comes in. Mindfulness, at its simplest form is awareness. Mindfulness is the practice of being present in the moment. Neuroscience, and data demonstrate mindful people and companies have improved employee experiences, better workplace culture, create better customer experiences that result in better business outcomes. Mindful meetings need to be a part of every company strategy.

Before Your Virtual Meeting:

Have each participant set an intention. An intention is simply one word of how they will put their energy in motion on the meeting/convention or event. An example – my intention is to be focused. Depending on the size of the meeting, take aggregate of those intentions and find one word, or energy that all can agree on is the direction they want to set their energy in motion toward.

During the Virtual Meeting:

Set time in the scheduled agenda for "awareness" breaks. Here are three ways to do that. Every thirty minutes pause, breathe, have everyone mentally take awareness back into the room they are in and drink a glass of water.

At the End of a Virtual Meeting:

Make mindful moments to send people back into the "real" world in a positive way. Have people breathe, center and vision what they want to have happen. Invite them to close their eyes and vision what they want to see, feel and know for the project or topic that was the focus of the meeting or event.

Mindful meetings matter and so do you!

Holly Duckworth, CAE, CMP, LSP www.HollyDuckworth.com

Dance Party—Freedom of Creativity

Goals: Have a fun dance party.

Dancing is a way to bring energy to your next meeting. Dancing helps your attendees' heart, increases energy, makes you feel happy, and helps eliminate stress and depression.

Time: 2–60 minutes
Participants: 2–Max
Technology: Audio, video, share computer audio
Category: Fun
Instructions:

To share playing a music video (see Chapter 5, "Share Video"):

Step 1: Click "Share Screen."

Step 2: Check "Optimize Screen Sharing for Video Clip." This will also check "Share computer sound." Forgetting to check "Share computer sound" is a common mistake, so double-check it.
Step 3: Click "Share."

(Continued)

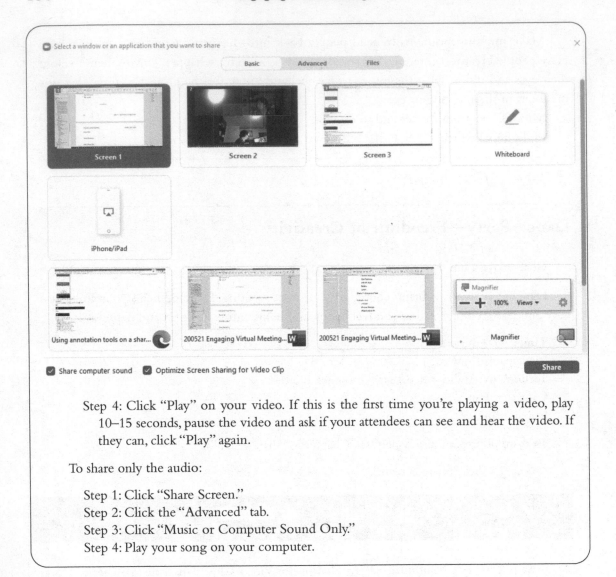

Step 4: Click "Play" on your video. If this is the first time you're playing a video, play 10–15 seconds, pause the video and ask if your attendees can see and hear the video. If they can, click "Play" again.

To share only the audio:

Step 1: Click "Share Screen."
Step 2: Click the "Advanced" tab.
Step 3: Click "Music or Computer Sound Only."
Step 4: Play your song on your computer.

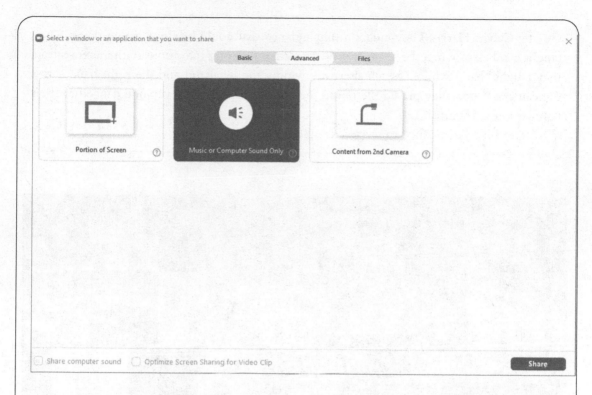

Tips: For a more engaging experience, use the Share Music or Computer Sound Only. Test setting your audio level on your video. If you set it at one quarter to one half the maximum value, it's about the same volume as your voice and it may allow you to talk with the music and still be understood. Because this option does not share your screen, you can use your screen to see your attendees in gallery mode dancing at the same time. See Matching and Mirroring (Chapter 7) for ideas to get people to dance at the same time or play songs with known dances like "YMCA." You can also ask for song requests by audio or by chat. Some virtual meetings have a professional DJ come in to mix their dance party and be interactive. Remember, some of your attendees may not like to dance, so give positive alternatives like clapping along with the music.

If you are live streaming at the same time, consider that many live streaming platforms have rules and regulations around copyrighted music. Playing copyrighted music may mean that your live streaming platform may mute all the audio during this portion and they also may end your live stream. Check the rules on your live streaming platform.[8]

Case Study: The US Power Team is a group of people who meet to support each other. They wanted an energetic way to start their meeting. When this group met together in the past, they would dance to start their live face-to-face meetings. They chose the song "Let's

(Continued)

Go" by Calvin Harris. They taught a simple dance that could be done sitting down. They taught hand claps when the snare drum is hit. When the song transitions to the next section, they taught "hand wipes," which alternates wiping the left hand and the right hand across the camera. When they played the music, the energy exploded as everyone danced to their familiar music (Figure 11.4).

Go to bit.ly/evmdance to see an example of this Dance Party.

Figure 11.4   US Power Team Dance Party

Karaoke—Sing a Song

Goals: Sing along with recorded music.

Karaoke or singing to recorded or live music was invented in the 1970s by Daisuke Inoue, who worked to popularize it in Japan.[9] Karaoke continues to gain fans around the world; I've hosted Quarantine Karaoke and had singers from all over the United States, Australia, the Philippines, and Saudi Arabia. Karaoke is fun because you either discover amazing talent from your attendees or you find out how bad some of them can sing (which can be entertaining).

Time: 3 minutes–4 hours
Participants: 2–Max
Technology: Audio, video, share video, share computer sound
Category: Fun, talent

Instructions: The easiest way to sing is to allow attendees to share their screen and make sure they click "Share computer audio." Have your singing attendee play a YouTube karaoke video with the volume on the video set to one quarter the maximum volume.

Tips: To be a good karaoke host, find out who wants to sing and establish an order. Remind singers to have their song ready (like play past ads) when their name comes up.

Resist the urge to be like a regular karaoke jockey and play all the music. There is a 0- to 3-second delay on most virtual platforms. If the singer sings when they hear the music, all the attendees will hear the lyrics 0 to 3 seconds behind the song, which is very non-engaging and frustrating.

More advanced setups include Enable Original Sound.

During a Zoom meeting, click audio settings->advanced and check "Show in-meeting option to "Enable Original Sound" from microphone."

Close the dialog box.

(Continued)

On the top left, click the "Enable Original Sound" box until it turns blue.

This prevents your microphone from adjusting automatically, which is good because when you sing louder than you talk, Zoom automatically reduces the volume and most attendees will have a hard time hearing you.

Make sure to test this setup. When it works, you can play music on loudspeakers and sing as loud as you'd like, which means you'll have the experience just like at a real karaoke bar. Your attendees will be able to hear you at full volume and get into the song with you. Most of the time, attendees should be on mute, but sometimes it's fun to have them sing the chorus with you off mute. Just know that you're going to hear them delayed, but it's engaging for them if they're into the song.

Case Study: The API (Asian Pacific Islanders) Heritage Month Celebration Committee in Seattle, Washington, was planning an APIs Can Sing karaoke contest. When the coronavirus canceled their 5,000-person live celebration, the committee worked together to create an APIs Can Sing Quarantine Karaoke Contest (Figure 11.5). There would be three semi-finals and the top three semi-finalists would advance to the finals featuring nine singers. The judges included Lady Scribe, founder of the Seattle Sound Music Awards, the Filharmonic, the all-Filipino a capella band featured on *Pitch Perfect 3* and the James Corbin show, Nasty Nes, the DJ who discovered Sir Mix-a-Lot, and The Wanz, Michael Wansley, the double-platinum Grammy award–winning singer who is the voice on "Thrift Shop" with Macklemore. Because the contest was virtual, space didn't matter. Contestants from Washington State, South Carolina, Baltimore, and Saudi Arabia entered. The youngest entry was a 12-year-old boy from the Philippines, who sang with a beautiful baritone. The winning singer was from Baltimore, who used to sing in live performances. Most of all, every attendee said they had fun and enjoyed bringing props and creativity to their performances.

Figure 11.5   The 2020 APIs Can Sing Quarantine Karaoke Finals

Book Club—You Get a Book

Goals: Read a book and boost your brain power.

Ever since the advent of book clubs in eighteenth-century England, when books were scarce and expensive, these organizations have been about more than reading. Book clubs were organized to help members gain access to reading material and to provide a forum for discussing the club's books.[10]

Time: 30–90 minutes
Participants: 2–Max
Technology: Audio, video
Category: Fun, focus

Instructions: Make your next meeting engaging by assigning a book or a section of a book before your next meeting and spend time discussing the book at the meeting (Figure 11.6).

(Continued)

Case Study: Jillian Cardinal created The Eventprofs Book Club.[11] She said, "Hi, I'm Jillian and I am an insatiably curious book-aholic. The idea of creating this community was planted while at an annual conference. We meet and network with so many interesting people. What about maintaining that connection in between those encounters? Could the conversation and thought stimulation continue? Why, yes it could. This is why I started The Eventprofs Book Club."

Jillian leads regular online events to discuss books, not just any book, but intelligent, interestingly written books that intrigue and inspire. Her book club is atypical, as reading is strongly suggested but not mandatory. People now look to her past and upcoming reads to help curate their "to read" lists. Her book club invites authors and thought leaders as co-hosts for each event to further deepen the discussion and create a truly engaging experience.

Figure 11.6   Silent Virtual Book Clubs Are Growing

Movie Night—Better Than the Drive-in

Goals: Watch a movie together.

Do you like movies? Your next meeting can be made fun by choosing a quality movie. This is a great way for attendees to spend time together. Through a movie, you can build new relationships, have a shared experience, educate your attendees on a particular subject, relax, and help motivate.

Time: 30–200+ minutes
Participants: 2–Max
Technology: Audio, video, share screen, chat
Category: Fun, networking, education
Instructions:

Step 1: Click "Share Screen."

Step 2: Check "Optimize Screen Sharing for Video Clip." This will also check "Share computer sound." Forgetting to check "Share computer sound" is a common mistake, so double-check it.

Step 3: Click "Share."

Step 4: Click "Play" on your video. If this is the first time you're playing a video, play 10–15 seconds, pause the video and ask if your attendees can see and hear the video. If they can, click "Play" again.

Step 5 (optional): Your audio can echo when you are sharing a video, so click "Mute" to turn off your microphone. If you want an experience like *Mystery Science Theater 3000*,[12] leave your microphone on and talk over the movie.

Step 6 (optional): If you want to see the reactions of your attendees, click "More" and then click "Show Video Panel." Note that your video panel will block the attendees' view of the playing video so drag it to another screen or make sure the video panel window is in a place that is not blocking an important part of the playing video.

See Chapter 5, "Share Video" for details.

Tips: Some streaming services block sharing through video platforms. Many tools exist to watch movies together that are allowed. One of the most popular currently is Netflix Party. Every attendee needs to have a Netflix account. It synchronizes video playback and adds group chat to any Netflix show for free.[13] It currently has 10 million users.

If you are using your virtual meeting platform, then click "Chat" and you can chat to everyone watching the movie. If you are the host, make sure to move any controls to another monitor so that it doesn't block the view for an attendee.

Just search "watch a movie together online" for all the latest solutions.

Talent Show—Your Meeting's Got Talent

Goals: Showcase your attendees' talent and entertain everybody else.

Like karaoke, talent shows continue to be a fun hit. *America's Got Talent* is in its fifteenth season and continues to draw high ratings. The show has expanded to almost every country. Your meeting talent show can discover unknown talent and learn a little more about the skills your attendees have.

Time: 30–120 minutes
Participants: 2–Max
Technology: Audio, video
Category: Fun, talent, networking

Instructions: Attendees take turns showing their talents such as magic, juggling, spoken words, or other talents. If the show is competitive, you can have one to five judges and each judge can give commentary after every performance.

Tips: Make sure to do a dry run with all of your performers and make sure all of the technology works.

Dinner Party—Celebrate and Learn More About Each Other

Goals: Eat a meal together and get to know each other.

Dinner parties are fun and casual. 78% of Brits believe that cooking food and sharing meals brings people together, no matter what's going on in the world. The Dinner Party Theory states that you should "invite the most diverse audience possible to a dinner party and then sit back and watch what happens." To create an engaging virtual dinner party, look for tips from Bustle.[14]

Time: 60–120 minutes
Participants: 2–50, more with breakouts
Technology: Audio, video
Category: Fun, networking, eating

Instructions: Set up so the camera sees all your guests in your location. Use a microphone that picks up the entire room or has a cord long enough to bring it closer to diners. Dress up like you're going out. Ensure that everyone arrives on time. Greet guests like they were coming into your home.

Tips: You can agree to have the same food and drinks to make it feel more like you're at the same restaurant. You can send one or more virtual backgrounds from a restaurant to give the image that you're all sitting in the same restaurant. You can also arrange activities, such as a tour of each home or any of the activities in this book that you can do before, during, or after your courses.

More advanced, you can log in multiple cameras to give the proper view for every guest in your house, such as one guest per camera. Make sure to only log one computer in for computer audio, otherwise you'll get a very non-engaging echo in your audio. You can then use computer speakers, so you can hear your guests, and a quality and/or movable mic, so the attendees can hear your different guests.

Case Study: Gousto, a UK recipe box company, launched a bid to bring one million people together over a virtual dinner party. This dinner party had four celebrities who cooked each course and invited guests into their kitchen. This dinner party brought people together and raised money for the Trussell Trust food bank charity.[15]

Trivia Night—What Do You Know?

Goals: Test your knowledge against other attendees.

Trivia nights are popular in bars and they can be fun for your meeting. This is an easy way to engage a large group. Trivia Night was known as a pub quiz and was established in the UK in the 1970s by Burns and Partner and became part of British culture.[16]

Time: 15–90 minutes
Participants: 2–Max
Technology: Audio, video, chat, forms or other type of data entry and scoring
Category: Fun, competition, trivia

Instructions: Get a collection of trivia questions. For a short game, get eight questions. For a longer game, get up to five categories of eight questions each. Answering can be as easy as using private chats to someone keeping score. For larger games and scoring, you can use Microsoft Forms or Google Forms to keep score. One key rule is no use of the internet to find answers unless you are teaching attendees to find answers using an internet tool or site. Ask one question at a time and use a timer to determine when to ask the next question.

(Continued)

When eight questions have been asked, attendees can click "Submit" and you can score the entries. Announce the results and move to the next category if you are doing multiple rounds.

Tips: It's easiest to use multiple choice for your quiz. You can allow open-ended questions but they take more time to score if you are not able to automate scoring. If you are looking to keep your trivia night fresh and innovative, try using teams, picture clues, audio clues, puzzle clues, bonus rounds, jackpots, and prizes.

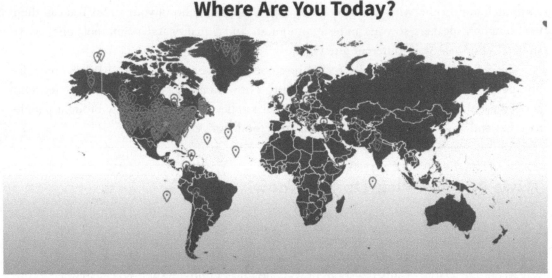

Figure 11.7   Where in the World Example

Where in the World—International Networking

Goals: Learn where attendees are calling in from visually.

This is a fast networking exercise akin to putting a pin in a world map when you arrive at a conference. By using the annotate stamp feature, you can visually show where all your attendees are calling in from to your virtual meeting (Figure 11.7).

Time: 5 minutes

Participants: 2–Max

Technology: Share screen, annotate stamp

Category: Fun, networking

Instructions: Share Screen and show a copy of a world map.

Step 1: Ask attendees to click "View Options" at the top.

Step 2: Ask attendees to click "Annotate."

Step 3: Click "Stamp."

Step 4: Choose a stamp, such as the arrow.

Step 5: Click to place your stamp on where you are calling from.

Case Study: Here is an example from Michelle Cummings, founder of Training Wheels (http://training-wheels.com), when she had over 500 participants at her virtual meeting. The majority of attendees came from the United States, but she also had attendees from Africa, Germany, Italy, and South America.

Go to bit.ly/evmwhere to see this example of Where in the World.

Memory Match Breakouts—Learn Where to Look

Goals: Network and play a game.

Remember the memory match game where you shuffle and put down cards and you and another person would try to match as many as possible? This is the video meeting version! Memory Match Breakouts combines one-on-one networking with a fun game.

Time: 10 minutes
Participants: 12–50
Technology: Audio, video, breakouts
Category: Fun, networking

Instructions: This program requires a minimum of 12 people. Decide on two people to be the guessers. Put everybody into breakout rooms of two people for two minutes and make sure to put the two guessers in the same breakout room. If you have an extra person, make them the referee. During the breakout, the two people decide on a body position to take. For example, you could do thumbs up, hands up, hands near your ears, and so on. The two people can use the remaining time to learn more about each other.

Make sure to return everyone at the same time. When everybody returns, they hold their unique body position for a total of five seconds and then go back to their normal positions.

The guessers take turns guessing two people they think are a match or had the same body position. If they don't match the people, it's the next guessers' turn. Keep score of correct guesses and the winner has the most correct answers at the end of the game.

Tips: Plan to play this game more than once and make sure every attendee meets with new people every round.

Jimbo Clark from InnoGreat (innogreat.com) was the first to create this game.

Go to bit.ly/evmmemory to see an example of Memory Match.

Poker Tournament—I'm All In!

Goals: Win all the money and have fun with your attendees.

Poker continues to be an engaging game of fun and socializing. In the 1837 edition of *Foster's Complete Hoyle*, R. F. Foster wrote: "The game of poker, as first played in the United

States, five cards to each player from a twenty-card pack, is undoubtedly the Persian game of As-Nas." In the early 2000s, poker popularity experienced an unprecedented spike due to online poker and hole-card cameras that showed how the top players were playing and turned the game into a spectator sport.

Poker is a game played with a deck of cards as you attempt to get a hand that is ranked higher than other players' hands. There is betting in every round and you have a choice to continue or fold every round. Poker can be competitive and engaging as you try to outwit your other attendees. It is a very social game where you can learn a lot about the other players as there is time to talk during and between hands.

Time: 30–300 minutes
Participants: 2–Max
Technology: Audio, video, poker applications
Category: Fun, game, competition

Instructions: The easiest way to play this game is to have a meeting on your virtual platform and play the game on a second platform such as PokerStars or Poker Bros. Have everyone log into the virtual meeting and then into the poker application. You are given a set of chips and the poker software takes care of enforcing all the rules. Bicycle, one of the top playing card manufacturers, lists all of the rules for poker.[17] There are many excellent videos to learn how to play poker (see bit.ly/evmpoker). You can play a "cash" game where you play for a certain amount of time for the same stakes. You can play a "tournament" game where every player starts with the same amount of chips and the stakes rise in every round until there is only one player left.

Tips: One of the best integrations I've seen is Live Game Night's Poker (https://livegamenight.com/). It combines poker and up to six players on video. It only costs $5 for eight hours of game play and will most likely continue to add features going forward. Make sure to check the legality of playing online poker in your location.

12 | Innovation

Why are innovation skills important?

The current dynamic marketplace has caused innovation to be recognized as the mandatory mantra for businesses to become increasingly competitive and provide the best and the latest solutions to the problems of industry. Following are some of the benefits of innovation skills for employees, one of the most valued assets of an organization:

They improve efficiency. As a result of the greater inquisitiveness being displayed, innovation skills enhance the ability of employees to recognize potential for improvement not only in their own field, but in that of others as well. They are also able to utilize the limited resources available to them in an optimal manner.

They overcome monotony. Innovation skills have the power to break monotony for employees, thereby adding to their sense of accomplishment as well as a sense of fulfillment. Such efforts to make work more interesting usually become the reason behind someone's having new and out-of-the-box ideas.[1]

If your meeting is stuck and needs innovation and new thinking, try these activities.

100 Uses—Use Something in Ways Not Intended

Goals: Brainstorm 100 uses for a common item.

This activity challenges your attendees to creatively use an item. This will warm up your attendees' creativity and lower their inhibitions for sharing their ideas with other attendees. 100 Uses encourages attendees to use every conceivable idea that is offered to reach the target number. It also teaches the value of building on other ideas like "Yes, and. . ."

Time: 10–15 minutes
Participants: 2–25; can handle larger groups with breakout rooms
Technology: Audio, video, chat, (optional) breakout rooms
Category: Innovation, brainstorming, creativity

Instructions to the Audience: I'm going to give you a common item (such as a pencil, newspapers, unused pizza boxes). You need to come up with 100 uses in chat in 10 minutes or less. Start a 10-minute timer and hold it up to the camera.

Tips: Delegate the role of counting to 100 to one of the attendees. Alternatively, you could share a spreadsheet to help count to 100.

Posts-its—Virtual Brainstorming

Goals: Brainstorm visually and at the same time.

Are you brainstorming a brand-new idea? Are you looking for creativity and patterns? Do you miss brainstorming with Post-its?

Time: 5–30 minutes
Participants: 2–Max
Technology: Share Whiteboard
Category: Innovation, brainstorming, problem solving

Instructions: See Chapter 5, "Share Whiteboard," for details.

To create the whiteboard and type the first Post-It:
    Step 1: Click "Share Screen."
    Step 2: Click "Whiteboard."
    Step 3: Click "Share."
    Step 4: Click "Text" on the annotate bar that appears.
    Step 5: Click on the whiteboard and start typing.

To have attendees add their first Post-It:

Step 1: Tell your attendees to click "View Options."
Step 2: Tell your attendees to click "Annotate."
Step 3: Tell your attendees to click "Text."
Step 4: Tell your attendees to click on the whiteboard and start typing.

Tips: After a period of brainstorming, you can organize the Post-its into groups or patterns.

Step 1: Click "Select" on the annotate toolbar.
Step 2: Click on any Post-it and drag to move it.

This is an easy way to see many ideas from all your attendees and find a way to organize them into major trends to see which ideas you should pursue as a group.

Here's an example of Post-its that I used to brainstorm the concept of this book.

	Engage and Interact with Every Attendee
	Never Lead a Meeting Alone
	Good Looks
Engaging Virtual Meetings	Air Traffic Control
	Get Productive With Virtual Tools
	End Your Meeting on a High Note

Add One Line—Adding Creativity

Goals: Get your attendees to add creativity to their solutions.

Are you stuck? Do you need your meeting to be more creative? Use this activity to help your attendees expand their thinking and create better solutions. This is a visual puzzle where you can create new solutions by adding a line.

(Continued)

Time: 10–30 minutes
Participants: 2–25; can handle more with breakout rooms
Technology: Share Whiteboard
Category: Innovation, problem solving, creativity

Instructions:

Step 1: Share Whiteboard.
Step 2: Choose the "Draw Straight Line" tool.

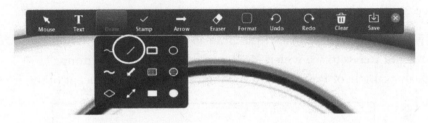

Step 3: Draw the following:

Step 4: Have a timer ready.

Instructions to the Audience:

We're going to work on creativity. (Share your whiteboard and drawing.)
Add one line to turn the whiteboard into a 6.
All attendees please:
Click "View Options."
Click "Annotate."
Choose the "Draw Freehand Line" tool.

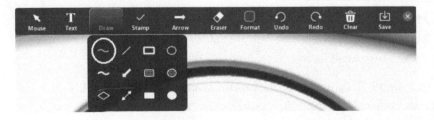

Click and drag to draw a line.

Click the "Undo" button to remove your line.

Remember you can only add one line at a time.

You now have 10 minutes to come up with as many valid solutions as possible. Please explain your solution to me and I will tell you if you scored a point.

Tips: Have a slide deck ready with each of these solutions and corresponding explanations.

If participants give a correct answer, award them a point and remind them to delete their line to start over.

Add One Line Solutions

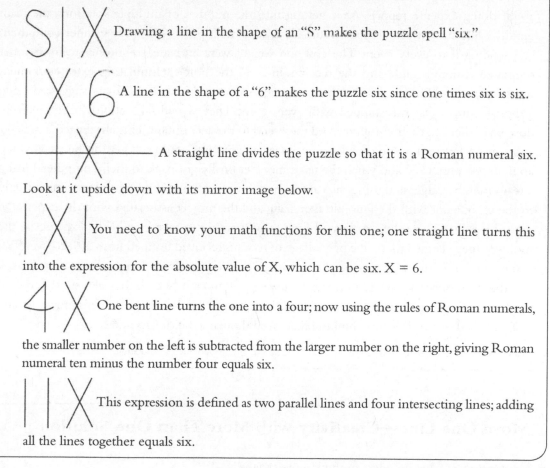

Drawing a line in the shape of an "S" makes the puzzle spell "six."

A line in the shape of a "6" makes the puzzle six since one times six is six.

A straight line divides the puzzle so that it is a Roman numeral six. Look at it upside down with its mirror image below.

You need to know your math functions for this one; one straight line turns this into the expression for the absolute value of X, which can be six. X = 6.

One bent line turns the one into a four; now using the rules of Roman numerals, the smaller number on the left is subtracted from the larger number on the right, giving Roman numeral ten minus the number four equals six.

This expression is defined as two parallel lines and four intersecting lines; adding all the lines together equals six.

(Continued)

Debrief:

How many solutions did you get before you stopped the first time?
How did great new ideas emerge?
What are barriers to new solutions?
What are supporters of new solutions?
How can we apply what we learned to our next real challenge?

Case Study: Move One Line (see below) and Add One Line were used with a team before tackling how to deal with travel receipts. The challenge was that the team was taking way too long to send its receipts after a project ended and, more importantly, many receipts were getting lost or not getting sent back to headquarters for proper filing. In addition, everyone grumbled about doing expense reports. After getting into the mindset of multiple solutions, the team rapidly came up with new ideas. Initial ideas came with purchasing new scanner equipment and sending it to every event. The cost and weight were an issue, so another team member suggested scanning or faxing the receipts in from the hotels, eliminating extra equipment but subject to additional cost if a hotel charged for a fax. Next, a teammate suggested using a digital camera that was shipped with every event. They would take photos of the receipts, download them to their computer, and then send to the accountant. This eliminated extra cost and weight, but took more time than necessary and receipts could still get lost between when an item was purchased and when the team member finally got back to their computer. Finally, a team member suggested using the camera on their phones and sending a photo immediately to the accountant with the amount, merchant, and the project associated with the expense in the subject line. This solution allowed each team member to take care of the expenses at the moment they charged them; the percentage of receipts received jumped from 30% to over 95% and expense reports could be completed from all the information sent in. It was easier to track and the team only had to add in things that were paid in cash (which they also started to send in photos of, like cash tips, to keep track of them, too!). Here's a case of where moving a line really created out-of-the-box thinking that saved thousands of dollars and hours.

Source: Sam Sikes, "Creative Mind Benders," in *Executive Marbles* (Learning Unlimited Corporation, 1998), p. 60.

Move One Line—Creativity with More Than One Solution

Goals: Get your attendees to think more creatively.

Do you need your team to do more with their existing resources? Use this activity to help them expand their thinking and create better solutions. This activity requires nonlinear and creative thinking to be successful. It will highlight how your attendees are stuck in one way of thinking and can help them reflect on how they need to think about their challenges differently.

> Time: 10–30 minutes
> Participants: 2–25; more with breakout rooms
> Technology: Share Whiteboard
> Category: Innovation, problem solving, creativity
> Instructions:

> Step 1: Share Whiteboard.
> Step 2: Choose the "Draw Straight Line" tool.

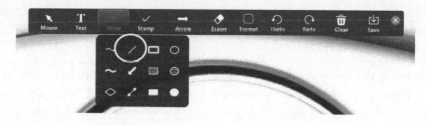

> Step 3: Draw the following:

> Step 4: Click "Remote Control" on your toolbar.
> Step 5: Click "Auto accept all requests."

> Step 6: Click the "Select" tool on the annotate bar.
> Step 7: Have a timer ready.

(Continued)

Instructions to the Audience:

We're going to work on creativity. (Share your whiteboard and drawing.)
Move any of the lines to make both sides of this equation equal.
The equal sign is *not* a line and cannot be moved.
You may consider the "V" to be one or two lines.
One attendee please:

   Click "View Options."
   Click "Request Remote Control."
   Click and move one of the lines, please.
   Now, please move it back to its original location.

You have 10 minutes to come up with as many valid solutions as possible. Please explain your solution to me and I will tell you if you scored a point.
Start a timer for 10 minutes.

Tips: Here is the current set of solutions. If an attendee is able to clearly explain an answer that is not provided and the answer does not violate a stated rule, then compliment their creativity, award them a point, and send me a jpg of their answer! I have a slide deck ready with each of these solutions and the corresponding explanation. Usually, as I show these, I can hear and feel the lightbulbs turning on.

The line is moved to form a square root symbol over a one; the square root of one is one.

A line is moved to form a multiplication symbol between two ones; one times one is one.

A line is moved to form a subtraction symbol; two minus one is one.

A line caps the "V" to form a triangular zero; zero one equals one.

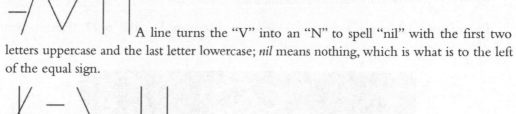

A line turns the "V" into an "N" to spell "nil" with the first two letters uppercase and the last letter lowercase; *nil* means nothing, which is what is to the left of the equal sign.

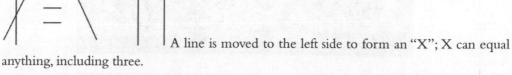

A line is moved to the left side to form an "X"; X can equal anything, including three.

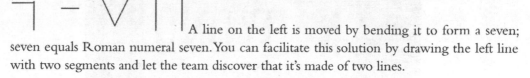

A line on the left is moved by bending it to form a seven; seven equals Roman numeral seven. You can facilitate this solution by drawing the left line with two segments and let the team discover that it's made of two lines.

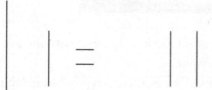

The "V" is straightened, counted as one line, and moved to the left side of the equation; two equals two.

License Plates—Innovative Communication with Few Characters

Goals: Create an innovative message with eight characters or less.

Does your meeting have challenges being innovative with limited resources? Do you want your attendees to learn how to do more with less?

Try this activity to test the creativity of your attendees in communicating with only 7 characters.

Time: 5–30 minutes
Participants: 2–300; use breakout rooms with 2–6 people

(Continued)

Technology: Audio, video, breakout rooms
Category: Innovation, creativity, communication, share screen

Instructions: Have you ever seen a clever license plate like this one? (Share Screen to show this photo)

By using the name of the car manufacturer, the car owner was able to communicate "To Infinity and Beyond!,"[2] a famous Buzz Lightyear catchphrase.

Using the limits for your license plates (in the United States, there is typically a maximum of seven characters on a license plate), work together as a group and communicate something important to other attendees.

This could be a key value, a phrase, or a project name; allow open creativity. When time is up, have one attendee ready to explain your license plate.

Tips: If there's more than one group, send them off to breakout rooms for six minutes to work on a license plate and make sure they have one representative ready to share their license plate and its meaning when they get back.

Office Move—Working Together to Switch Places

Goals: Have your attendees work better together by trading places.

Time: 20–30 minutes
Participants: 8–12; even numbers

Technology: Audio, video, share screen, Microsoft Excel or Google Sheets

Category: Innovation, collaboration, communication

Setup:

Step 1: Download the Office Move Template from bit.ly/evmofficeexcel or bit.ly/cvmofficesheets.

Step 2: Save the template to your server.

Step 3: If you have 10 attendees, remove all the Fs and 6s. If you have 8 attendees, remove all the Es, Fs, 5s, and 6s.

Step 3: Click "Share" and get a link to the Office Move document.

Step 4: Click "Share Screen."

Step 5: Chat the link to the Office Move document.

	A	B	C	D	E	F	G	H	I	J	K	L	M	N
1	**Office Move**													
2														
3	Start	A	B	C	D	E	F			1	2	3	4	5	6
4														
5	Current	A	B	C	D	E	F			1	2	3	4	5	6
6														
7	End	1	2	3	4	5	6		A	B	C	D	E	F
8														
9	Rules													
10	1	You can only move forward												
11	2	You must remain on a space												
12	3	You can only move into open spaces												
13	4	You can only move around a person the opposite side into the next open space												
14	5	You can only move around one person at time												
15	6	Only one person may move at a time												
16														
17		Use Ctrl-X and Ctrl-V to move												

Split your attendees into two groups.

Assign every attendee a letter or a number, 1 letter or number per attendee.

Instructions to the Audience: It's time for an office move and so the left-side team needs to exchange places with the right side. There are six rules that you cannot break. If you break a rule, you need to start over; you only have 10 attempts.

The six rules are:

1. You can only move forward.
2. You must remain on a space.
3. You can only move into open spaces.
4. You can only move around a person from the opposite side into the next open space.
5. You can only move around one person at a time.
6. Only one person may move at a time.

(Continued)

Assign each attendee one or more letters or numbers. They can only move their assigned letters or numbers. You can only move the numbers and letter in row 5.

An easy way to move is to put your cursor on the location you want to move from, hit Ctrl-X (to cut), move to your new location, and hit Ctrl-V (to paste). Are there any questions? Then, begin!

Tips: If the attendees get stuck, you can copy rows 3 to 5 to reset the letters and numbers. After every attempt, get your attendees to agree on what they are going to do differently in the next round.

Debrief: Look to see if the group plans, creates a joint strategy, or just moves without asking. A key discussion point is when a team is too overeager, moves, and ends up blocking the entire process. On the other side, the two teams can get into "analysis paralysis" by talking too long and *never* moving, thus never solving the challenge. At five minutes, call a time-out and discuss what is going on before continuing. Another interesting point is if you observe a team making an illegal move and you don't say anything. Do they police themselves or does no one on the team say anything? This can be an excellent ethics and integrity conversation that can be weighed on what the real-world consequences could be for an illegal move. Finally, look for team momentum as they recognize the pattern and people begin to move quickly.

Solution: The trick to finding and remembering a solution lies in this hint: once a side begins to move, everyone on that side moves unless a move puts one person behind another person from the other side (avoid doing this since it makes a two-person block against the other side). Here are the key steps to the 35-step solution for 10 people.

Move											
Begin	A	B	C	D	E		1	2	3	4	5
1	A	B	C	D	E	1		2	3	4	5
2-3	A	B	C		D	1	E	2	3	4	5
4-6	A	B	C	1	D	2	E	3		4	5
7-10	A		B	1	C	2	D	3	E	4	5
11-15	A	1	B	2	C	3	D	4	E	5	
16-20		1	A	2	B	3	C	4	D	5	E
21-25	1	2	A	3	B	4	C	5	D		E
26-29	1	2		3	A	4	B	5	C	D	E
30-32	1	2	3	4	A	5	B		C	D	E
33-34	1	2	3	4		5	A	B	C	D	E
35	1	2	3	4	5		A	B	C	D	E

Case Study: Two virtual teams that work together did Office Move. One team was here in the United States while the other was a development team in India connected by a telecon and the internet. The most obvious thing at the beginning was that everybody on every team was talking all at once and nobody was understanding anything because the teleconference line cut out when two or more people talked. Finally, an India teammate suggested a protocol of just one person talking at a time. They spent 15 minutes just talking over the ideas, but not moving at all. Eventually, they arrived at the strategy to the solution and both parties agreed to attempt it. Then, they started moving; it was the first time I had seen a team complete it on their first attempt. There was a *lot* of communication before someone made a move, but as each teammate bought into the plan and saw the pattern, the team moved faster and faster and faster. The final half of the moves took a mere three minutes to complete and the teams had switched places with no failed attempts!

In the debrief, they realized that the planning at the beginning paid off immensely and that they had not been doing that at work. They had been working on code and then "throwing it over the wall" to the other team at the end of the workday. There was a lot of work, rework, and frustration about doing it two different ways. This led to a meeting about defining goals and process and the team hit their first key milestone ahead of schedule for the very first time!

PART 3

Leading Large Virtual Meetings and Conferences

As meetings exceed 50 people, new and different challenges are created. Professional meeting planners know how to plan for meetings that engage 100, 1,000, 10,000, or more attendees. They have years of experience and thousands of systems to do everything from registration to feeding people to engaging people in keynotes, breakouts, and workshops.

Those systems don't exactly work in virtual meetings. Many conferences are being forced to move online. Many planners are suddenly declaring themselves virtual planners but don't have the skills to back up the claim. Many do not have the experience to take their face-to-face skills to the virtual conference world.

One conference attempted to do exactly what they would do in the real world, but all online. The virtual conference was two days long, eight hours per day. A variety of speakers presented sessions from 30 to 90 minutes all day. The conference trusted every speaker to be great virtual speakers, so they didn't give any training to them. They ran three sets of simultaneous breakouts after the morning keynotes and lunch. They turned chat off so they could save on staffing.

One attendee of this conference said it was painful to listen to speakers with bad audio, having trouble presenting their slides, and having no ability to connect with other people attending. One speaker moved and talked so fast that the attendee could not keep up. She said that after the last presentation on day 1, she went straight to bed and passed out until the next morning. If you are put in charge of a virtual conference, do not let this happen to you and your career.

There are professionals who have been practicing technology and engagement for years. I am in awe of many of those pioneers in the technology and meeting professional industries. They have been experimenting and learning the best practices of what works and what doesn't work.

The Green Meetings Industry Council's 2011 conference is one of the early conferences that I attended that explored what was possible. Elizabeth Valestuk Henerson and Mitchell Beer worked with an extensive team to create a fully gamified conference that was half face-to-face and half virtual.

During the planning process, then at the conference itself, organizers adopted a motto, first stated by Samuel J. Smith, co-chair of Event Camp Twin Cities 2010:

"Experimentation is our get-out-of-jail-free card. If we weren't having tech hiccups, we wouldn't be innovating."

The entire conference was gamified, dividing attendees into teams and competing to create a case study using knowledge gained at the conference. Every team was assigned an iPad, which at the time was in its first generation. Every session was live-streamed and used Twitter to allow attendees from around the world to attend and create new communication channels that the conference designers never anticipated.

One was that Samuel J. Smith (remember the quote above) was attending virtually from his home in Minnesota. Our team tweeted that we wanted more team members. Sam replied that he'd like to join and he immediately became a member of our team. I helped Sam engage in our team by setting up a computer on Skype and playing it through a set of speakers so everyone could hear Sam. We used Google Docs and Sam contributed significantly as we were simultaneously editing. Sam and I even recorded an interview on Skype and the organizers asked me to play it at the morning general session. Sam said it was one of his most engaging virtual conferences to date.

This is a conference that nine years after I attended it, I'm still talking about it. People remember exciting meetings.

Go to bit.ly/evmgmic to read the case study of the GMIC conference.

Go to bit.ly/evmgmicvideo to see an interview with a remote attendee who was recruited into a team by chat and became a valuable member of the team. Part of this interview was played in the opening morning keynote.

13 | Tips for Presenters, Trainers, and Sales

Do your meetings need to present concepts or plans for the attendees? Do you have learning or training goals for your meetings? Do you need to present to sell your company's product or services?

I wrote this section especially for you. Meetings that help or create revenue for your company are some of the most valuable meetings with the highest return on investment.

Since many people have honed their skills as face-to-face presenters, trainers, and salespeople, this is the chapter to read if you're new to the virtual world. This chapter will help you bring your specific face-to-face skills online and create a plan that will put you in the top 20% in the world and help you meet and exceed the goals in your company.

You have been introduced to the ENGAGE method. This chapter is how to use this method specifically for large presentations, interactive trainings, and valuable sales calls.

Engage and Interact with Every Attendee

Plan to Engage—Be Strategic

Decide on a strategy for how you are going to engage your attendee from the moment you log in to the moment you log off. Planning will help identify if you are talking too much or not enough. Planning can show you if you have a gap in engagement or if you're attempting to do too much.

Plan to engage every 10 minutes. Given a presentation of moderately interesting content, your audience's attention will "plummet to near zero" after 9 minutes and 59 seconds, according to biologist John Medina at the University of Washington School of Medicine.[1] "Before the first quarter-hour is over in a typical presentation, people usually have checked out," says Medina, who cites peer-reviewed studies to reinforce this observation.[2]

I suggest you present no more than 10 minutes of key material at the beginning of a presentation before you start to engage your audience and demonstrate what you're talking about.

In sales meetings, I suggest you open with introducing everyone and stating the purpose of the meeting in 10 minutes or less. Then I suggest you follow up, asking the client to add more to their challenge or problem. I plan anywhere from 30% to 80% of the talking to be done with the client, depending on the stage of the meeting. Often, I spend all of that time listening and not providing any solution yet without asking for time for reflection.

Engage Early—Log in Early

As I mentioned earlier, the most important meeting is the meeting before the meeting and the meeting after the meeting. There is no penalty for logging into a meeting and then doing other work if no one is there. There is usually a penalty if you show up to a virtual meeting late. What are you going to do, blame traffic?

In a training or presentation, logging in early is the same as a speaker who comes early to make sure all their equipment is working and now is walking through the audience, taking one-on-one time to meet them and ask for some of their real-time goals in coming to hear you speak.

In sales, if your client logs in early, you now have valuable relationship-building time. Be prepared by reviewing your client's public information, such as their website, LinkedIn profile, and any news written about them. This can impress your client, as you took the time to do research on them and know about their needs. There's nothing worse than asking a client "What do you do?" when most of that information is publicly available. In addition, if they are new to virtual tools, you can help them or show them a new feature, further gaining their trust prior to a sale.

Never Lead a Meeting Alone

Share Your Agenda—Get Everyone on the Same Page

Use the power of shared documents: take your plan and put it in an agenda that you share with every presenting attendee. Make sure you have planned every minute and transition. Ensure that there are clear roles and goals for every role. A shared agenda means that if anyone updates the agenda, everyone sees the change immediately, reducing the chance for a mistake.

Team Presenting—Decide If You Need Help

For presenting and training, having a producer will allow you to focus on your attendees. A producer can do everything from greeting guests when they log in to spotlighting the speaker to making sure your training video plays correctly to replying to all chats and more.

If you are selling, decide if you need a producer or if you can do it yourself. Team selling is more important an ever.

The *Harvard Business Review* reported that the number of people involved in B2B purchasing decisions climbed from 5.4 people in 2015 to 6.8 people in 2017. That's a 25% increase in the size of a buying committee in just two years.[3] This article also said that problem solving is a team sport, especially with the use of subject matter experts. Finally, they concluded that team assessment is more valuable than self-assessment. From a producer to take care of your technical challenges to subject matter experts timed to chime in to handle a client's specific challenge, these are things that planning can help you with in your meeting.

Dry Run—Rehearse for Best Odds

If you're meeting as a team, make sure you have a shared agenda and list the roles and actions for each role. To speed up dry runs, cut short presentations by presenting enough to know that it works and playing videos for a minute or less. Focus on goals, roles, and the transitions.

Seamless Transitions—Eliminating Awkward Pauses

Most problems happen in a virtual meeting's transitions. Forgetting to unmute, videos with no audio, and sharing a presentation that is not in presentation mode are some of the most common problems with virtual meetings. In the dry run, test to make sure you know all of the correct buttons to push. Ask for confirmation from your teammates on another computer. Arrange for nonverbal cues like thumbs up if everything is working well. Get rid of asking "Can you hear me?" or "Can you see my slide?" by the time the client is there. Establish a private line of communication such as private chat or texting to give each other real-time feedback. When all else fails, make sure the host is ready with material to fill the time in the event that something unexpected happens.

If it's important enough to record a video of your presentation, stop your meeting so the video of your meeting renders. Start a new meeting and share the video of your last meeting to review as a group. During this review, you'll be able to see and hear exactly what attendees will see and spot areas of improvement that you can implement immediately with your team.

Good Looks

Dress Rehearsal—Show Up Exactly Like You're Going to Show Up for Your Meeting

Ask all of your presenters to show up *exactly* how they're going to show up for the meeting. I have seen a lot of meeting problems where someone logs in from their kitchen or phone or car and says they'll be fine because they're going to log in from their office for the meeting. Then when the meeting happens, their backdrop has laundry in it, they're backlit because of lighting, and their video and audio stops intermittently because their Wi-Fi is having problems.

Showing up exactly how you're going to meet increases the odds that you can fix any existing problems and you'll have no problems during the actual meeting. If someone is having technical problems, check their hardware, software, and internet speed. Sometimes, they may have to use a different device for your meeting. Take the time to improve everyone's virtual presence, assuming that they will turn their video on during the meeting. Clean up their background, move the camera, improve their lighting. You can also make clothing suggestions. Your favorite hoodie is not the best fashion for your big sales meeting; your closet is less than two minutes from your computer, so make the best use of it.

Good Looking Backgrounds—What You Communicate to Your Attendees without Talking

According to a study cited in *Inc.*, an estimated 84% of all communications will be visual by 2018.[4] You, and your background, are your key visual communication during your meeting. The same study mentioned that people form a first impression in a mere 50 milliseconds. Malcolm Gladwell's book *Blink: The Power of Thinking Without Thinking* included extensive research on the ability of the human brain to make snap judgments based on one's life experience. In his book Gladwell writes, "You can easily judge a person's personality if you have the opportunity to see their living room for about 15 minutes as in the experiment of Samuel Gosling and his students." Every virtual meeting is like an invitation to your living room. Help attendees make the correct judgments about your personality.

Good Speech—The Importance of Sounding Great

Sound is the main form of communication for humans and animals. We humans communicate verbally with spoken languages besides body languages.[5]

National Speaker Association member Jay Baer says sound matters a lot:

> If the speakers at your online conference don't have fantastic lighting or great cameras, the event can still work if the content is outstanding.
> But if the presenter audio isn't solid, your audience will log off IMMEDIATELY.
> Just like with podcasts, sound quality for a virtual event is non-negotiable.

It is shocking how often presenters at online events just figure they can talk into their laptop, with no regard for room acoustics, background noise, dogs barking, people walking by, the neighbor's cockatoo, and more.

When you do presenter run-throughs, make certain they are conducted in the same room and with the same setup as will occur during the actual broadcast.

Also, consider purchasing USB headsets or microphones for all presenters, and sending them out two weeks before the event, with a link to a video illustrating how to use them.

Lastly, if the speaker cannot be in a circumstance that is acceptable for audio when their live presentation is scheduled, pre-record that session and then have the speaker log-in at the end of the recorded portion to answer questions.

(This robs the speaker of the opportunity to use audience polls or take questions via chat during the session, but is better than bad audio).[6]

Have you ever had a virtual meeting attendee interrupted by a dog barking, a child walking in the room, a lawnmower, or the neighbor's supercharged car? It is disturbing for your attendees or clients and it can also knock you off your planned presentation.

Take the time to create a good audio background. This means a quiet room. This means a locked door. This means no pets during meetings. This means sound insulation if needed. This means letting your housemates know when you're having an important meeting.

When you can't control all of your audio background, look for technology to help you. Just like a virtual background changes where you're meeting, noise cancellation can help you block unwanted sounds. Bit.ly/evmkrisp is one of the best I've found, giving a limited number of hours a week and reasonable payment plan if you want noise cancellation all the time. Note that I do not receive any compensation, but for using that link, I receive two months' free trial.

Buy the Best—Microphones That Matter

Have you heard a great speaker in a virtual meeting who sounded tiny or distant? Have you logged in, excited for a meeting, but struggled to hear the presenter even though you turned up your audio? Have you ever logged off of a webinar because you couldn't understand them?

If you are a regular presenter, trainer, or salesperson, buy the best microphone. Your voice is your business. This purchase will have one of the largest returns on investment. Here are two current microphones that I would bet my business on:

1. The IK iRig Mic HD2. At $79.99–$129.99, this is currently the only handheld digital condenser microphone for the iPhone, iPad, and Mac/PC (Figure 13.1). I have personally used this microphone for three years for iPhone interviews as well as for over 100 virtual meetings. I consistently get feedback from attendees that I sound the best in the meeting. (I do not get any compensation from IK.)

   You can find more information for the iRig Mic HD2 at https://www.ikmultimedia.com/products/irigmichd2/.

Figure 13.1   The IK iRig Mic HD 2 Microphone

2. The Blue Yeti is the world's number-one USB microphone. At $99.99–$129.99, this is the best multi-pattern USB microphone for recording and streaming (Figure 13.2). It has three built-in microphones and has four different patterns to capture the best sound for different situations. Many of my friends have this microphone and their audio is much better than the standard microphones on phones and laptops.

   For more information on the Blue Yeti, go to https://www.bluedesigns.com/products/yeti/.

Figure 13.2   Blue's Yeti USB Microphone

Technology changes fast, so click bit.ly/evmbestmic for the latest reviews.

Air Traffic Control

Planning air traffic control is important in training, presentations, and sales. Each meeting has a different pattern for presenters and attendees talking, so prioritize and plan air traffic control.

Prevent Collisions

The first thing to do is prevent collisions. For presentations, one of the easiest ways to prevent collisions is to have a plan on when to mute and unmute attendees. For training, make sure you take part of the first meeting to establish the speaking rules and enforce those rules. Most groups only need one or two reminders to follow the system.

Positive Handoffs

The next thing that will help a presentation, training, or sales meeting is to find a way to do positive handoffs. Audio cues about who is going to speak next are positive handoffs that will help you maintain air traffic control.

> "Up next, Mary is going share about our model."
> "And that's my last point, back to you, John."
> "Roxanne, now that you've heard about our services, what questions do you still have?"

Smooth Air

Smooth air means making sure the meeting feels smooth no matter what's happening. If someone's computer goes down, you can enact your backup plan quickly by talking about some other material you have until your backup plan can restore what you were looking at. Smooth air means your host is always ready to redirect the meeting based on the conversation. Smooth air means that you have a backchannel so your team can feed the host clues about what's going on and shift on the fly to an unexpected client direction. Smooth air is the feeling that your team always has your back no matter what happens.

Get Productive with Virtual Tools

Have you ever had a presentation where a slideshow was put up for 60 minutes and the presenter never stopped talking? Have you had a meeting where the culture was to never turn on video? Did someone take a poll and then never share the results? These are all examples of not using a tool correctly.

Virtual meeting platforms come with more and more tools. This is great news for you as someone holding virtual meetings. The key to an engaging presentation, training, or sales demo is that you use the best tool available to help your point.

Pick the Right Tool—If All You Have Is a Hammer, Everything Looks Like a Nail

Abraham Maslow said, "I suppose it is tempting, if the only tool you have is a hammer, to treat everything as if it were a nail."[7] This is one way of saying to pick the right virtual meeting tool for the job you have.

Let's take sharing PowerPoint, which is a very powerful tool especially because the majority of us are visual people.

Christopher Witt, author of *Real Leaders Don't Do PowerPoint*,[8] gave these three occasions not to use PowerPoint:

1. Don't use PowerPoint when you want to build a strong connection with your audience.
2. Don't use PowerPoint when you have a story to tell.
3. Don't use PowerPoint when you want to motivate and inspire people.

Picking the right tool here might be, for example, presenting your analytical data and working with your producer to stop sharing after the analytical data and then spotlight one of your presenters as they talk about how that data will make a difference in the client's business.

Tool Skills—Virtual Tool Mastery

One piece of research said that as many as 90% of first-time webinar presenters said that the actual presentation was the first time they used their virtual meeting tool—which contributes to why there are so many bad webinars.

Mastery is defined as comprehensive knowledge or skill in a subject or accomplishment. Make sure you have tool mastery before you use it in a high-value meeting.

For high-value meetings, pick tools that you have used and you're familiar with. A high-value sales meeting is not the best place to use a manual set four-room breakout room with breakout room facilitators for the first time. Only pick a tool when it fulfills one of your goals *and* one of your teammates has significant experience with your specific virtual meeting tool.

Minimize Tool Risk—Virtual Safety Glasses

When you choose a tool, take the time to see if you can minimize its risk. This can mean creating backup plans, using the least number of features or tools during a meeting, and rebooting your computer before a big meeting.

The Pagdiriwang Festival celebrates the anniversary of Philippine Independence. Normally, this is a two-day festival full of live performance, food, and drink. Due to coronavirus in 2020, the entire festival had to move online. With three days before their festival started, the organizers called me to help them with a technical issue. They chose sharing videos in PowerPoint as one of their primary tools. The videos were shaky and the audio was not clear. Not the setup for an engaging festival.

After reviewing their setup, we saw that many of their videos were linked to YouTube videos. This means that they had to be downloaded, played, and uploaded to everybody watching. The videos were big, which meant that if YouTube failed or the network slowed down, the videos could become choppy or unwatchable. We changed their presentation to use videos that were already downloaded and removed half of the risk for their meeting. The Pagdiriwang Festival completed two days of virtual programming successfully.

Take steps to minimize risk.

Creativity with Tools—Create Virtual Wow!

Do you remember the best presentation you've seen? Do you remember the moment your jaw dropped? Do you remember the key point at the time and still tell the story today?

Then you were an attendee at an engaging meeting. Often, wow presentations have an amazing element such as a visual, an illusion, or a groundbreaking concept. John Medina, author of *Brain Rules*, said, "We don't pay attention to boring things. We pay attention to things like emotions." Look at how you create emotion. Sometimes you can create emotion using a tool in a new or creative way.

Spotlight or Pin Video—Use a spotlight to change the window on the attendees' screen to show the speaker in a large size. Imagine this as putting a high-powered spotlight on a speaker for everyone logged in.

Virtual Background Slides—One of the downfalls of sharing your screen is that your video becomes one sixteenth the size of your full screen.

One of the fastest ways to remain at 100% of your size is to use virtual backgrounds as your slides.

Tracy Stuckrath, chief food officer at Thrive! Meetings & Events, and I were discussing her upcoming presentation and we were talking about the problem that when you share your slides, your video becomes one sixteenth the size of a full-screen video (Figure 13.3), which we agreed was non-engaging. We came up with the idea of using virtual backdrops for her slides. She shifted her content to one side and positioned herself on the other side (Figure 13.4). This allowed her to keep her video size at 100% *and* present her content with a beautiful image backdrop. This presentation was conducive to this strategy as she had five key points. I believe this is the first time I have seen virtual backgrounds used for presentations; look for video platforms to catch on and offer applications such as PowerPoint to be used for your virtual background. Until then, you can create a slide deck in programs like PowerPoint and use the File->Save a Copy feature. Select PNG format and save and every slide will be saved as a graphic image that can be used as a virtual background.

See Chapter 11 for more ideas and how to use virtual backgrounds.

Side-by-Side Slide Presentation—If you need the full power of your presentation platform, such as PowerPoint, Keynote, or Prezi, then use the side-by-side mode. When you go into your presentation, ask your clients to click on View Options->Side-by-side mode. Then drag the bar in the middle until you are the same size as the slide deck. Your presence is about half your normal size and allows your client to focus on the presenter and the material.

Figure 13.3   The small window on the top right is the size of the presenter when sharing your screen.

Figure 13.4   Professional speaker Tracy Stuckrath uses virtual backgrounds to maximize her speaking presence.

Disappear—Using the virtual background without a green screen gives you the ability to make things disappear. Just duck out of your video camera and take a picture. Make that picture your backdrop (Figure 13.6).

Figure 13.5   I have a sign with the word "PROBLEM" on it."

Then use any single-colored paper, such as white. As you move it out from where you are, you'll see your sign disappear. Here I have a sign with the word "PROBLEM" on it (Figure 13.5). If I was in a sales meeting, I could say our product helps your problem disappear and have the sign disappear before their eyes.

Figure 13.6   Demonstration of making a sign saying "Problem" disappear

Go to bit.ly/evmdisapper to see a video showing how to make a sign disappear.

There are hundreds of creative solutions that can be built with your virtual meeting platforms. Look for new solutions every day and consider sharing them at fb.com/groups/engagingvirtualmeetings.

End Your Meeting on a High Note

Shut Up!—Stop talking if your attendee is sold. End your meeting early despite your planning and agenda. Ideally, get your client to sign now if they are ready.

Respect Time—One of the best ways to end on a high note is to end early or on time to respect the attendees' time. No attendee has ever complained about getting 20 minutes of their life back.

Next Steps—An easy way to end a business meeting is to recap what happened and what the next steps are. The best way to succeed is to make sure you follow through with those steps. In team selling meetings, other teammates can prepare and send requested material during the meeting to show the potential client that you can respond quickly.

Last Word—Ev Williams, cofounder of Twitter, promotes a closing round. Give every meeting attendee 30 seconds to comment on the meeting.

According to Williams, the benefits of doing a closing round are: "It gives everyone, in a sense, a 'last word'—the chance to get something off their chest that they might otherwise carry around or whisper to their colleagues later. It creates more mindfulness about what just happened—and how things might go better next time. And it lets you know where the group is at emotionally, as well as potential issues to follow up on that weren't strictly part of the proceedings."

Video—Use the power of video to inspire. A video can have a higher ability to inspire because it has production value. Three hours, three days, or more can go into a three-minute video. The video can transport your attendees somewhere. It can show them a point of view they usually can't see. It can express a concept that words alone would not be able to do. By 2021, 80% of all content will consist of video.[9] Video is important because you can easily control most aspects of playing the video and once it's playing, there is little technical risk of it breaking. Use the power of video to end on a high note.

An Example: Engaging Virtual Meetings Training

I have a 60-minute training for *Engaging Virtual Meetings* that has 20 participants.

Goal: Learn the fundamentals of *Engaging Virtual Meetings* in 60 minutes.

11:30 a.m. My producer and I log in. I make my producer co-host. We test our audio, video, and screen sharing. We test whether we both have access to the participation map.

11:45 a.m. Attendees start arriving. My producer starts recording. I engage guests in talking. My producer greets new people by chat and renames them with Name, Location, Company.

11:55 a.m. My producer starts live-streaming to my Facebook page and confirms it started by private chat.

12:00 p.m. I share my screen and start my presentation. My PowerPoint has the real-time caption feature turned on, which immediately impresses my attendees. I present 10 minutes on the foundations of *Engaging Virtual Meetings*. My slides use silent rotating videos to further highlight the concepts I'm teaching. They also contain one research fact for every key point. Attendees find this information rich.

12:10 p.m. I demonstrate the attendee opener where every person introduces themselves. I stop sharing and use the gallery view so everyone can be seen. My producer and I use the participation map to ensure that everyone has the opportunity to introduce themselves, even the late-arriving attendees. My producer greets late attendees and makes sure they are caught up with what we are doing.

12:25 p.m. I share my screen and describe why chat is the second most important tool for engagement. I get everyone to chat. Most people chat their LinkedIn profile or their website, so if there is time, attendees can click to find out more about another attendee, creating engaging networking value. My producer helps those who haven't chatted yet to find their chat button. My producer lets me know that every attendee has chatted.

12:30 p.m. I go over the instructions for A to Z. I ask if there are any questions. If not, I unshare my screen and let the attendees figure out how to solve it. At 12:35 p.m., if the attendees keep doing the same thing over and over, I ask if they'd like to see the rules again. If they all say no,

I let them continue. If they say yes, I'll highlight the rule they are missing (which is that they are allowed to talk in between tries). My producer and I are looking for key learning points such as when someone takes leadership of the group. After they are done, I ask What, So What, and Now What? of three different people.

12:45 p.m. I share my screen. I go over why I gave attendees A to Z. The main reason is to show that meetings without rhythm fail. I give suggestions on how to create that rhythm in their meetings. I test for retention by asking attendees to recite my key points. I give instructions for The Last Word. I unshare my screen and give a reminder that I will stay here up to 30 minutes afterwards if anyone has questions. I give a reminder that if anyone needs to go right on time, to please give their Last Word first.

1:00 p.m. After the last person finishes their Last Word, I ask people to wave goodbye to our Facebook Live audience. I invite anyone who needs to leave to log out. I start Q&A and allow attendees to ask questions. Often, attendees will ask questions that were not covered in the class and I'll lead mini-teaching sessions to cover their topic.

1:30 p.m. I graciously thank the attendees who chose to stay late and invite them to my second-level class. I say goodbye and my producer makes sure all attendees log off or are removed. My producer and I hold a 10-minute debrief using Plus-Delta and decide what we are going to do better for the next meeting.

Observe how many times I engage every attendee. It's a minimum of five times in 60 minutes. I make sure to engage attendees even if they have their video or audio off. Planning for this helps your training be inclusive for people who are deaf or couldn't speak. All different styles of people say this training was engaging and they actually did something different after the training. While this training took more planning, it creates more results and now after hundreds of deliveries, this training has the ability to handle many different sizes and situations, all of them leading to a positive result.

14 | Tips for Emceeing and Hosting

Emceeing and hosting are critical skills for large virtual conferences. Make sure you select someone who has these skills. If you do not have someone available with the skills, consider using a professional emcee (MC). Here's how to apply the ENGAGE method to selecting your virtual MC or host.

Engage and Interact with Every Attendee

One of the most important skills is your MC's ability to engage with every attendee. Make sure your MC is warm, friendly, and inviting. Your MC should make sure they are encouraging the right virtual engagement tool at the right time.

Have your MC work with you and your committee as if you were the attendees.

Pretend you're an attendee who doesn't want to talk.

Make sure your MC knows the right level of engagement for your audience and isn't perceived as too much or not enough.

Never Lead a Meeting Alone

How well does your MC work with your team? Great MCs will ask for the agenda long in advance. MCs should research their speakers and be ready with great introductions. Your MC needs to work well with your producer and speakers to keep engagement up.

Good Looks

Your MC needs to care how they look. From their appearance and professional clothing to their background and microphone, a great MC should set the standard for good looks and be capable of coaching your speakers and attendees.

Air Traffic Control

Have your MC announce the next speaker and watch for smooth transitions.
    Have a speaker mute during their speech and see how your MC handles it.
    Play a video with no sound and see how your MC handles it.
    Your MC needs to be able to fill any amount of time with information that is relevant with your attendees and techniques that are appropriate for your audience.

Get Productive with Virtual Tools

Your MC needs to be familiar with your virtual tools. You do not want to hire an exclusively Zoom MC for a Microsoft Teams conference. Knowing the virtual tools you selected for your virtual conference will make sure the MC can use those tools to create engagement on your virtual platform.

End Your Meeting on a High Note

Look for MCs who bring energy. MCs will suggest engagement techniques that will help bring a boost after a long keynote. MCs will interact with the audience and get them to follow, such as applauding for a speaker. MCs have the ability to present or tell stories. By telling the right story at the right time, an MC can bring the education to an emotional level to help attendees retain more. MCs can facilitate learning. They can ask questions, get reactions from co-hosts and subject matter experts, and use gamification to test for retention. Most of all, MCs are fun. They can take any material and make it engaging and fun to learn. MCs plan and find a way to end your conference on a high note. Virtual MC Thom Singer is a unique MC who closes only with the material contained in the conference. He does not know what the keynote will be when the conference starts, but he curates the closing keynote from what happened and he creates engagement by customizing his closing keynote only with material that attendees have experienced.

Hoan Do is a virtual MC. He's a professional speaker. He is an award-winning inspirational speaker, author, and city finalist in NBC's hit show *American Ninja Warrior*. He shares his experience in being the virtual MC for a conference:

Background

Every spring the Washington Healthcare Authority hosts an annual in-person Spring Youth Forum to celebrate the accomplishments of over 150 youth and adults. The purpose of the event is to acknowledge the positive impact of local projects on the health and wellness of youth, families, and communities in Washington State.

Due to COVID-19, I was hired to help turn their in-person event into a virtual one. Serving as the emcee and keynote speaker, I was tasked with hosting a three-hour-long event to provide an inspiring message and acknowledge their work while keeping attendees engaged.

What Worked

1. Acknowledge and set the tone

   When our Virtual Spring Youth Forum began, I immediately acknowledged the uncertain situation we were all in. I then shifted the focus to highlight that this was the very first Virtual Spring Youth Forum ever and that we were going to have an incredible time, despite not being able to meet and connect in person.

2. Teach attendees how to engage

   After welcoming the attendees, I shared that this virtual event was not going to be me speaking at them but rather it would be more of a conversation. I shared with them instructions on how to use the chat function, which allowed them to answer and ask questions so that they could be involved during the three-hour event.

   One example of engagement was saying at the start of the event, "I would like to know where you are watching or listening in from. Enter in the chat box right now what city you are from." As the answers rolled in, I acknowledged each person who answered

(Continued)

by saying aloud their city. This encouraged everyone to participate and to see where other attendees were calling in from.

3. Let the audience be the star

Throughout different parts of our virtual event, we scheduled time for the focus to be all about the attendees. Half of my keynote was a live Q&A where the teens and young adults determined what they wanted to hear. During another part of the program, students spoke live when I asked them to share about their project and the lessons that they learned.

Results

The client was over-the-moon happy with the virtual event.

Some feedback from attendees:

"This was exactly what I needed."
"I had so much fun."
"Thank you for a great time!"
There was more than a 90% engagement rate for the three-hour virtual event.

Hoan Do, inspirational speaker | author | American Ninja Warrior
Empowering people to overcome their adversities by sharing practical strategies to develop resilience and mental toughness.
www.HoanDo.com

15 | How to Run a Virtual Workshop or Conference

Moving a 200-person face-to-face conference to all-virtual in less than eight weeks is a monumental task. The fact that it had never been done before only added to the challenge. Read about the ENGAGE model in action, applied to a conference format that had never before been attempted. Learn the lessons without the risk or pain of doing it yourself. If you were just placed in charge of a large virtual conference, let this be your guide.

Tips for High-Stakes Meetings and Board Retreats

Board retreats are high-value meetings. Although they may not be large (usually less than 25 people), they usually last one or two days and they require a large amount of planning, decisions, and work to do in a short amount of time.

Tara Liaschenko, CMM (Certificate in Meeting Management), is a Meetings Professional International board retreat facilitator. She is a past president of her local chapter and she facilitates over 20 board retreats a year for other chapters around the world. During 2020, she needed to modify her board retreats so that many of them ran 100% virtual; some of them ran part face-to-face, part virtual. During this time, Tara used a variety of techniques. Here, she shares her best practices.

Hybrid Board Retreat Tips

Face-to-Face Group
1. Everyone sits at their own 6-foot table spread throughout the room.
2. Everyone uses their own computer.
3. One computer is linked to the screen and projector.
4. Everyone has a microphone connected to the sound system.

Virtual
1. Every participant must have their cameras on (otherwise they are not focused).
2. Every participant needs to raise their hand when they want to speak, to prevent speaking over each other.

Fun
1. Incorporate fun icebreakers and activities; e.g., wear your craziest hat, wear your favorite shirt, pajama party (caveat of appropriate guidelines).
2. Bring a fidget-to-focus toy; e.g., slinky, play dough, spinner.

Tips
1. It's recommended to only do four hours a day over two or three days. Any longer and it's difficult to keep the participants focused.
2. Ask everyone to turn off their phones and close their email application.
3. Ask everyone to wear headphones if possible.
4. Remain on mute until you want to speak to reduce distractions.
5. If the group is quiet, call on people to share.
6. If they are talking over each other, tell them they have to wait to be called on to speak.

During my virtual and hybrid board retreats, I was able to build strategic plans, approve budgets, brainstorm new solutions, and assign follow-up for the year's goals.

Tara Liaschenko, CMM, creative executive officer, The Link Event Professionals, 2015 Meetings Professional International RISE Award winner

The Challenge

A Fortune 100 company planned a Worldwide Incentive Compensation conference in 2020. Two hundred employees from around the world were scheduled to meet in the United States for four days. This annual conference is critical to the company's strategy to update incentive compensation specialists around the world. This information is confidential and critical to the company's revenue.

The information is so secure that other employees cannot access it. The conference theme was Space Camp. The hotel contract was signed. The flights were scheduled. The planning was on the way. And then . . . coronavirus.

Stay-at-home orders were issued. Hotels and flights were canceled. The Americas, Asia, and EMEA (Europe, Middle East, and Africa) all shut down. Canceling the conference was not an option. The company had to innovate. This company would have its first all-virtual conference.

The Solution

The Fortune 100 company built a team with Geoteaming, including me. I was onboarded with just 12 days until conference launch. Together, we applied the ENGAGE model to enhance the planning that had already gone into the conference. Here is how we planned for conference attendee engagement.

Engage and Interact with Every Attendee

Timing—Preventing Virtual Meeting Burnout

The conference was still four days long, but it was reduced to six hours a day with a full hour off for lunch and 10- to 15-minute breaks between speakers. No speaker session was more than 45 minutes. Less time than a full conference and multiple breaks allow for maximum engagement as well as maximum knowledge transfer.

Co-Hosts—Live Engagement

The conference designer and I were designated as the conference co-hosts. Together, we opened and closed every day, helped manage every transition, and helped create engagement throughout the day. In addition, we could step in at any time during the conference to help with questions or if a speaker's audio was not working correctly.

See Chapter 14, about emceeing and hosting.

Watch Parties—International Engagement

The conference needed to engage attendees all around the world. The live content was recorded in the Americas. The strategy was to create a watch party to handle Asia and EMEA. The watch party would use videos recorded in the Americas with a live team to support the videos. An attendee in Asia would be greeted by a local co-host, watch a video played by the local producer, and engage in chat led by a local chat moderator. This combination of recorded and live interaction was designed to engage attendees and customized to how the information affected their regions.

The Americas would complete their programming and have two hours to update instructions for Asia. Asia would receive instructions such as when to start and stop a video and what to do next. Asia started their watch party at 8 a.m. Singapore time. Asia would complete their notes and send them to the EMEA team. EMEA would start their watch party at 8 a.m. London time. They would complete their notes and send it to the Americas team who would wake up, review their notes, and make any adjustments for the next day's programming. This conference ran 24/7 for four days straight.

Raise Hands—How to Ask a Question

Raising hands in Microsoft Teams is very easy. It's built into the toolbar that everyone can see. Raising your hand moves you to the top of the attendee list so it's easy to see who raised their hand. We all decided that we would use Raise Hand as the primary way to ask a question. A co-host in the opening session led an exercise where everyone raised their hand and then instructed everyone to use the tool throughout the conference. If you wanted to engage in this conference, everyone knew to raise their hand.

Chat Moderators—Presentation Engagement

Chat moderators were trained on how to engage attendees throughout the presentations. They entered in questions to create conversation. They researched and found answers to attendee questions. They monitored who raised their hand and let them know when in the program they could get to questions. They started GIF (short animated videos) chats to keep the meeting fun.

Surveys—Rating Every Session

Chat moderators sent out surveys after every session. This allowed attendees to give instant feedback, which was reviewed by the team to help make future sessions better.

Gamification—Engaging Education

Using Microsoft Forms, I was able to create a six-stage mission. The theme matched the conference theme of Space Camp. The content tested information that was presented as part of the conference. The overall mission could not be solved without Asia, EMEA, and the Americas communicating with each other.

BINGO—Rewards Listening to Speakers

Using a custom Microsoft Teams app, attendees could play BINGO by marking off conference key words as speakers said them and win prizes when they completed their BINGO card. This helped speaker engagement by having players listen for key words.

Never Lead a Meeting Alone

To handle a live conference and two international watch parties, we convened a team of 36 people to work together to help this conference. Here is how we organized that team to ensure attendee engagement.

Virtual Engagement Training—Getting the Team on the Same Page

We trained every team member on what virtual engagement is. From exercises ranging from Check In to Raise Hands to Chat Networking, every team member experienced what virtual meeting engagement looks like. Then, we flipped it around and had different members lead these exercises and we were able to coach them in the delivery of virtual engagement.

RunTheShow—Shared Agenda

We created and shared an Excel spreadsheet called RunTheShow. It was organized by four days and for the Americas, Asia, and EMEA. We used links to direct teammates to the resources they needed in the moment, such as videos and surveys. This shared spreadsheet meant that changes were sent immediately to every teammate.

Dry Runs—Practice, Practice, Practice

After virtual engagement training, we focused on dry runs. Dry runs are rehearsals for the conference. They helped the conference team understand what their new roles meant and the actual mechanics of the role. They helped develop practices such as raise hands and making sure that producers clicked "Include system audio." Many mistakes were made in the dry runs, but those mistakes prevented mistakes in the actual conference. The dry runs had the added value of team building where we bonded and became a closer team that paid off during the conference as we all supported each other.

Roles—Clearly Defining the Team and Expectations

In team building, goals and roles are part of the foundations of a high-performing team. Here are the roles that we defined for this conference.

Producer

The producer oversees the virtual conference. The producer is the definitive leader and makes the final decisions based on all information. The producer is in charge of the RunTheShow document. The producer makes sure that all other roles are delivering on time and starts a transition only when everything is in place. This conference used a co-producer, who assisted the producer and had the capability of becoming the producer in the event of a technical failure.

Co-Hosts

The co-hosts are the on-camera personalities. They engage the audience from the moment attendees log in. They give critical announcements and instructions to keep attendees on point. They can engage audiences until speakers are ready. They advocate for the speakers by making sure that their mics are unmuted and clear, their slides can be seen, and their video is on so their presentations can be understood.

Speaker Handlers

Speaker handlers work with keynote and breakout speakers. They ensure that they are online at least 15 minutes before they go on and that all of their technology is working. They communicate with speakers through IM, email, text, or phone as necessary to make sure they are online and ready before their time. If there are any challenges, speaker handlers communicate these to the producer so that the producer can make alternative plans.

Chat Engagement

Chat engagement engages the audience from the moment they log in on chat. Starting with hello, chat engagement engages all nonspeaking attendees, especially during presentations. Chat engagement asks for and curates questions from attendees. Chat engagement sends out all surveys.

Technician

The technician helps with any technical challenges with the production as well as advises on how to use the existing tools to solve new challenges that show up. For instance, our technician discovered a way to prevent attendees from getting lost during breakout sessions.

Breakout Captains

Breakout captains are like co-hosts for a smaller gathering. They engage the audience as they arrive at the breakout. They give instructions and make introductions. They can step in if a speaker has any challenges. They can call the producer for help if there are any challenges.

Video Production

Video production oversees recording the conference and packaging it for the watch parties. This includes start and stop times and instructions for the watch party. It can also let watch parties know if there is a change from the plan and how to insert other content if necessary.

Security

Security was there to ensure that only authorized people were attending presentations and that only authorized people had access to the content and streams. Security can also make recommendations for ensuring security, such as meeting links preventing access by uninvited attendees if forwarded from the intended recipient.

Command Chat—One Place to Communicate

One place was established for the entire conference team to communicate behind the scenes. It was called command chat and it was the one place for people to communicate when they were stepping away for a break, to confirm that a keynote speaker was ready to go so we could transition, and reminders for co-hosts to show up one minute before the end of a presentation to help transition from speaker to co-hosts.

This clear line of communication was like the radios at a face-to-face conference. It allowed for real-time updates and the ability to fix problems, so an attendee never sees it.

Good Looks

This was a conference for a Fortune 100 company; it needed to look professional. There are multiple ways to look good at a virtual conference.

Pre-Conference Emails

Short and information-packed emails were sent every week for eight weeks before the conference to prepare attendees and to create "bite-sized learning" in well-crafted and well-designed emails.

Speaker Training

Every speaker was given training on improving their background. A collection of beautiful space-themed backgrounds was provided. Every speaker tested their setup and did practice recordings to hear how they sounded. Some speakers needed to order new equipment before the conference to be heard clearly. Speakers were coached on timing and how to incorporate chat or Q&A into their sessions. Speakers were coached to stop sharing when doing Q&A to help create more connection with attendees. Special space backgrounds with the words "Command Center" were given to conference staff so they could be easily identified if an attendee needed help.

Presentation Consulting

PowerPoint was used by every speaker. Sharing your screen means that 80% of the screen is taken by PowerPoint. Templates were given to every speaker. Consulting was given to every presenter so they were able to create information-rich graphics that followed the best adult learning principles. The result was presentations that looked good and were effective in the goals of transfer of knowledge.

Multiple Screen Setup

Looking good includes being able to quickly see everything necessary for the virtual conference. The use of multiple screens allowed key conference team members to see and respond quickly to conference issues in real time. Here is how the screens were used (Figure 15.1):

   Screen 1: The RunTheShow spreadsheet was used so you would know what was happening next and if there were any resources you needed to get ready for an upcoming transition.
   Screen 2: Microsoft Teams showed the video or shared screen of the speaker and it showed the Attendees list, which would show if anyone needed to be muted or if anyone was raising their hand to ask a question. It also showed who was attending the meeting so you could look for speakers and other individuals.
   Screen 3: Using Microsoft Teams running the Microsoft Edge browser, the chat for the attendees is on the left. Command chat is on the right.

| RunTheShow | Microsoft Teams | Chat | Command Chat |

Figure 15.1   An example of how to use three screens to effectively run a virtual conference.

Phone: I used my phone as my fourth screen and that had a chat established with my co-host and producer so that we could coordinate internal decisions.

One aspect of looking good is the ability to respond to issues quickly. If an attendee said the audio is going bad, if a speaker is missing, or if a new change to RunTheShow happened, looking good with multiple screens allowed for decisions to be made quickly.

Psychological Safety

The invisible part of looking good is creating psychological safety. Every co-host created a welcoming environment. Every team worked together to ensure a safe environment in which to ask questions. Every team worked together to answer attendees' questions. Every team worked together to help achieve the attendee goals. Every team member watched out for other team members to ensure that people got sleep, food, breaks, and anything else they needed to make sure they could be there for the attendees. This psychological safety made sure the team looked good to the attendees.

Air Traffic Control

Air traffic control was one of the most important factors because the conference was being watched by 50 to 200 attendees at any moment. Air traffic control needs to think like a television station, where there is always engaging material and there are no awkward pauses. Here's how this conference did it.

Co-Hosts

Co-hosts are the primary way that attendees see air traffic control. They engaged attendees, getting feedback before and after speakers. Co-hosts do every introduction and take back control after every presentation. Co-hosts help moderate the Q&A by working with chat engagement to answer questions in the order that they are asked.

Speaker Handlers

Speaker handlers help with air traffic control by making sure that speakers are ready when it's time to start. Co-hosts may be busy engaging attendees while a speaker is getting ready. Speaker handlers can focus on the speaker and communicate with the producer to ensure they are ready. Speaker handlers give the producer confidence that when a co-host introduces a speaker, the speaker will take over immediately.

Get Productive with Virtual Tools

The selection of virtual tools is critical for conference success. With a first-time conference, we limited the virtual tools to prevent trying to do too much. Because this was a Fortune 100 conference with a company based on Microsoft software, we featured Microsoft tools that could get the job done.

Microsoft Teams

Microsoft Teams was the primary virtual meeting platform. This handled all the audio, video, screen sharing, chat, and document sharing.

Microsoft Teams Chat Running in a Browser

Microsoft Teams can also run in a browser by going to http://teams.microsoft.com. Click "Use the browser app." This was valuable because you could watch the chat in a separate window while the Microsoft Teams app was focusing on the presentation and the Participants window.

Microsoft Teams Apps

Microsoft Teams has the ability to have apps or other programs running inside of Teams. We used a customized Teams BINGO app and the Microsoft Forms app inside of Teams during this conference.

Microsoft Excel

Microsoft Excel powered the RunTheShow spreadsheet that held the schedule for the Americas, Asia, and EMEA. When the producer made a change, it was immediately visible to anyone on the conference team.

Microsoft PowerPoint

Microsoft PowerPoint ran all of the presentations.

Microsoft Forms

Microsoft Forms was used for the gamification and for the surveys.

End Your Meeting on a High Note

The original conference design ended with three breakouts. While the information was valuable, ending the conference in this way would mean that every breakout would have a different experience. It would be very easy to send out surveys and say goodbye but the conference would most likely end with low energy.

Brainstorming with the organizing team and pursuing many different ideas, the design team received good news. The Fortune 100 company's vice president had an opening in her schedule and she would now be able to give a closing keynote speech. Her team had been briefing her on the conference's updates in addition to the sessions she attended personally. We combined the closing keynote with a digital slideshow created by the conference's producer. The slideshow used screenshots and video that was captured from the four days and was set to music.

The Conference

If you're missing the adrenaline rush of planning a major conference, just plan a virtual one! Day 1 started and 150 people arrived for the live program. You could feel the excitement. Executive VPs kicked off the day with space-themed windows. I co-hosted with the company's conference designer. We made every attendee feel welcome, we made every transition look smooth. Breakouts increased engagement with the least amount of technical challenges. Everyone was on a conference high by the end of Day 1.

On Day 2, unexpected challenges showed up. An executive keynoter was ready at her home, computer logged in, lighting on, ready to present in 45 minutes. Then she disappeared. Space Camp, we have a problem. On command chat, we found out that the internet and power hard-line was cut to her entire neighborhood. I had established the role of virtual speaker handler. The handler was immediately on the phone to the keynoter. She had no internet. She had no power. Her phone was dying. She had no cell phone batteries. Her cell signal in her home was weak. The handler calmed the keynoter down and got the keynoter in her car with a charger. She helped her navigate to a place where there was strong cell signal. She arranged for another team member to present her slide deck, which was stored on Microsoft's cloud. With four minutes to go, she was ready. She delivered a powerful keynote with information that only she could present. If the handler hadn't found a solution in time, her entire section would have been canceled and recorded later. We built psychological safety by developing teams, communications, and trust that created plans B, C, and D and could solve any conference challenge in real time.

The Result

On Day 4, the conference finished with a surprise all-hands closing keynote with the division's vice president. Space Camp attendees felt educated, engaged, and uplifted. Space Camp generated 19 hours of education and engaged 2,500 chats. Space Camp earned a 4.7 out of 5 in the attendee overall survey. The Asia and EMEA watch parties said they felt as engaged or more engaged than the America Live program. Space Camp will be used as a model for all future conferences. The best feature of Space Camp was not planned at all. Space Camp was an emotional win in the physical distancing of coronavirus—every attendee felt uplifted in seeing each other again.

> You helped us create a sense of "contagious energy." I didn't expect this level of success for our first virtual worldwide event. THANK YOU!
> **—Conference designer and co-host**

> The overwhelming feedback was that people were surprised at how engaged everyone was as they were previously anxious it might be hard to engage whilst not watching live. They actually felt people were asking more questions due to the smaller audience and they appreciated that we were able to answer a lot of the questions between ourselves due to the different segment coverage we have as FCAs as well as the operations excellence team.
>   Thank you for making our roles easy by providing such concise training and instructions— we received a lot of praise from the group, but know that we were an extension of the preparation you put in. Thank you everyone for a great week! Hope you have a great weekend and catch up on the sleep you have missed!
> **—Host, EMEA watch party**

This virtual conference delivered on education, engagement, and energy!
  —Senior business manager

Kristin Clarke is a consultant to the National Association of Social Workers, Virginia Chapter. She was faced with a two-week turnaround from an in-person to all-virtual conference. Read how she used the ENGAGE method for her conference:

Kristin ensured engagement with every attendee, brought together a brilliant team including a seasoned technology partner, invested in speaker and staff training to make sure they looked good, assigned air traffic control to a moderator for every session, was productive with their meeting and expo tools, and ended on a high note with a successful experience and potential to grow their attendance and revenue for next year.

In early March 2020, the annual conference of the National Association of Social Workers Virginia Chapter was on track to reach its stretch goal of 400 registrants for March 26–28 in Williamsburg, Virginia.

With a COVID-19 pandemic quickly spreading across Virginia, however, Executive Director Debra Riggs, CAE (Certified Association Executive), had a tough decision—assume that increasing travel bans and growing fears of social workers would collapse attendance and require meeting cancellation, or take a risk and try a nontraditional shift to a virtual platform.

No one on staff had experience creating online education or events. Only one of its consultants had even attended a virtual conference. The meeting was in two weeks, and a lot of money was at stake.

Riggs turned to the NASW national office, which referred her to a former technology partner—CommPartners, Inc. After negotiations and deliberation, Riggs decided to take a risk and launched a whirlwind of staff and speaker training, revision of certain session formats, and rapid construction of a virtual exhibitor fair and learning platform.

Among the key questions: How could exhibitors still engage with attendees? How could registrants—nearly 25% of them veterans of 11-plus years of in-person conference training and networking—engage from home? Most members are Baby Boomers who don't consider themselves "tech-savvy"—would they still attend? Three hundred of them not only said yes, but later shared kudos and high evaluation scores.

Here are the top chapter tips from this experience:

1. Know your members and their likely comfort level with familiar and new technology, their expectations around engagement/networking, and their interest in and ability to learn in a virtual environment. That will inform how simple or advanced you can be when creating the engagement framework.

(Continued)

2. Find a superb technology platform partner that understands your goals, respects your budget and limitations, trains your staff and speakers, and offers ideas and troubleshooting that optimize the customer experience and help ensure a memorable meeting.

3. Focus on your organizational and engagement goals first rather than the technology capabilities. This applies to both your strategic plan goals (around education, innovation, competitiveness, leadership, etc.) and your operational plan goals (branding, budget, timeline, etc.).

4. Practice everything. Repeat. And again. Group training is great, but individual speaker coaching is essential to ensure each can interact with attendees, master tech options, and gain confidence in virtual instruction. Spend special time on engagement features such as pre-uploading polls and sharing results, handling live audio and/or video Q&A, and sorting breakout rooms.

5. Assign a moderator to every session to address technical or hacking issues, manage the chat and Q&A, and have the speaker's back. These can be volunteers, staff, or IT pros, but they should join the speaker at least 20 minutes prior to opening the session to test audio and lighting and answer any final questions.

6. Repeat attendee engagement instructions in each session: the break schedule, Q&A management, tech support availability, no live recording, chat room etiquette and transcript availability, etc. When people understand expectations and protocol, they relax and engage without fear or confusion.

7. Debrief quickly. It sounds obvious, but documenting what worked and didn't while fresh in staff memories is critical. For instance, the Exhibit Fair offered live chat only during certain conference hours, but attendees could visit 24/7. Would longer hours or video-chat have generated more leads through enhanced interaction? Would training exhibitors on possible engagement tools for booths be a future option, and at what cost? While a planned in-person networking reception was scrapped, would a virtual happy hour for informal dialog be doable? With such high scores, would a hybrid conference in 2021 be better than a strictly in-person event to engage more members and nonmembers short on time or money to travel?

While transforming a conference into an engaging virtual event made for a high-stress two weeks, the resulting insights and experience have revealed unrecognized opportunities to engage and include even more members in professional development and community-building, building positive momentum despite challenging times.

Source: By Kristin Clarke, consultant, Virginia Chapter, National Association of Social Workers. Retrieved from: https://www.naswva.org/

PART 4
Advanced Engaging Virtual Meetings

The more time you spend on a virtual platform, the more you will want to learn intermediate and advanced features. The advanced features give you more tools to make your virtual meetings look professional and be more engaging. Learn these tools and you can be seen as a virtual meeting master. People will seek you out to help design and lead big and complex virtual meetings. You could be part of a strategic role for your company.

16 | Advanced Tips

Virtual platforms have many features and they will continue to innovate. Here are advanced virtual engagement tools that can help you engage your audience. The best strategy is to try these tools for attendees who are at the intermediate to advanced level. You can find scenarios where these tools can help you get work done and are very engaging for your attendees.

Annotate—Collaborate by Marking Up Your Shared Screen

Goals: Give you and your attendee the ability to mark up shared information.

Annotating can help you remember more and be more productive. When you annotate, you are having a conversation with what you are reading. Annotating helps improve your reading comprehension, helps you jot down a reaction and connect ideas, enables you to filter the important details for research and recall, helps you better visualize the information, and enhances collaboration with others.

(Continued)

Time: 1–60 minutes
Participants: 2–Max
Technology: Share screen, annotate
Category: Communication, collaboration
Instructions:

Step 1: Click "Share Screen."

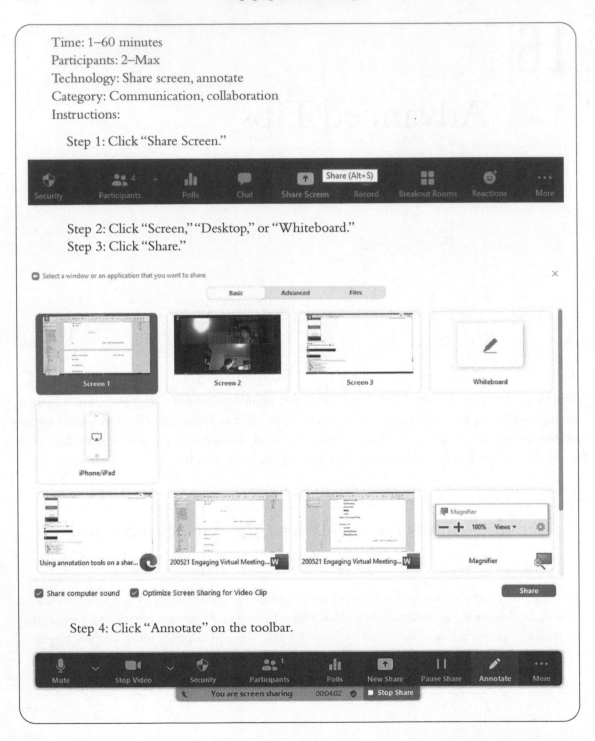

Step 2: Click "Screen," "Desktop," or "Whiteboard."
Step 3: Click "Share."

Step 4: Click "Annotate" on the toolbar.

Step 5: Click and hold down your mouse to draw.

For attendees to annotate:
Step 1: Wait for the host to share their screen.
Step 2: Click "View Options."
Step 3: Click "Annotate" (if this option is not available, the host has it turned off).

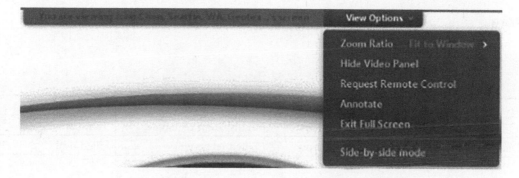

Step 4: Click and hold down on the mouse to annotate the shared screen.

On the annotate bar, there is a collection of tools. We will go through each tool and give examples of using the tool. To activate a tool, just click on the tool on the annotate bar.

Mouse

When you click "Mouse," the annotations tools are deactivated and your mouse can now click on your computer. This is useful to be able to move a document around before starting more annotations.

Select

The "Select" tool allows you to click on any annotation. You can move, resize, and delete any annotation. Let's say you drew some items while brainstorming and now you want to move them around into groupings; you can achieve this with the "Select" tool.

(Continued)

Text

Click the "Text" tool. Click on the shared screen. This creates a text box in which you can type a message. You can think of it like a Post-it note on the screen. Text is much easier to read than trying to draw characters for a word.

Draw

Click "Draw."
Here is a guide to the choices:

Freehand line	Straight line	Rectangle frame	Oval frame
Thick freehand line	One-way arrow	Transparent rectangle	Transparent oval
Diamond shape	Two-way arrow	Filled rectangle	Filled oval

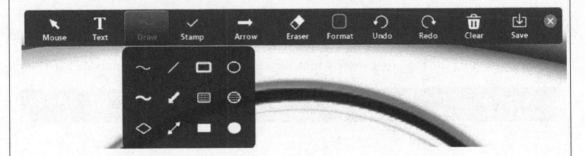

Do you know who John Madden is? He's an NFL coach and sportscaster who made annotation famous. He would play video of a football play and draw all over the screen to show where players were going and what they were doing.

This is what draw can do for your meeting if done correctly by either you as the host or an attendee you've given the control to draw on your screen. This can help highlight key items such as by circling or drawing arrows. You can also build models or workflows by using lines, arrows, boxes, circles, and ovals.

Stamp

Click "Stamp."
Click arrow, checkmark, x, star, heart, or question mark.
Click on the shared screen to place a stamp.

If you love the days of businesses using stamps for their process or love the stamps in your passport, you'll love stamps. You can use stamps to approve part of your document. You can use stamps to cast individual votes. You can use stamps to represent where you are on a map.

Spotlight

Click "Spotlight."
Click the laser pointer (only available to the host) or the arrow.

Move your mouse for the laser pointer to highlight something.
Click on the shared screen and an arrow will appear on the screen.

Have you ever had to help someone do something on their computer like change their settings? It's definitely challenging and frustrating, especially if your attendee is new to technology. There's help.

Ask your attendee to share their screen, then select your Spotlight tool. This can help you guide your attendee to the button or menu that you are trying to get them to click. Just move your mouse to the area you want them to click or be at. If you are using the arrow, click the arrow so it's pointing there. This will reduce the amount of time it will take to help your attendee.

Eraser

Click "Eraser."
Click an annotation and it will disappear.

If you have an annotation that another attendee drew and you don't want, click to erase it. If you are reviewing a document that attendees have marked up, you can erase one annotation at a time as you handle their feedback.

(Continued)

Format

Click "Format."
Click a color to change the color of your annotations.
Click "Line Width" to change the size of your line.
Click "Font" and you can change your text to bold, italics, and a different size.

If you have multiple people annotating at the same time, it can be a big help for everyone to be assigned their own color, the same color over multiple meetings. As your attendees annotate, they will know who is making the annotations by their color. This can also help if your text is too small for other attendees to read.

Undo

Click "Undo."

Did you make a mistake? Click "Undo." You can click "Undo" many times and it will keep removing what you created, one step at a time. In one of our activities that required adding a line, you can click "Undo" after you add a line and try to create a new solution.

Redo

Click "Redo."

Did you make a mistake by undoing too many mistakes? Click "Redo" and your annotations will come back, one step at a time.

Clear

Click "Clear."
Click "Clear All Drawings" to remove all annotations.
Click "Clear My Drawings" to remove only your annotations.
Click "Clear Viewers' Drawings" to remove all other attendees' annotations.

Save

Click "Save" to save all of the annotations.

Before you click "Clear," make sure to save or ask the attendees if you should save the annotations. Data storage is cheap, so if you're undecided on whether to save or not, just click "Save" and then you can find out later if you needed the annotations.

Click on "Show in folder" if you want to see where your annotations were saved.

(Continued)

Disable Participants Annotation

If you show your attendees Annotate, you should know that every attendee can annotate. If you have a large audience, quite often you see that annotations will take over your entire screen as attendees are just curious to try out this new feature.

Make sure you know where the "Disable participants annotation" or the "Stop Share" buttons are, which will stop attendees from making annotations.

Step 1: Click "More. . ."

Step 2: Click "Disable participants annotation."

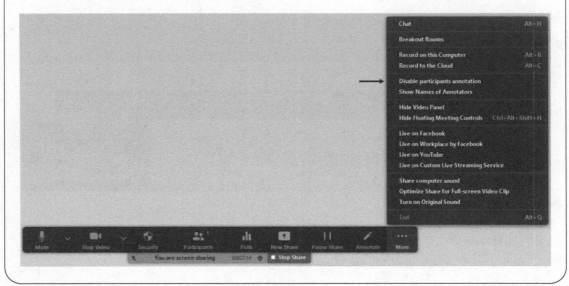

Remote Control—Give Control to a More Technical Attendee

Goals: Allow an attendee to control your computer.

Are you new to computers or virtual meetings? Do you wish someone would just show you instead of having to read a lengthy and technical manual?

Try remote control. You can give control of your computer temporarily and someone can show you how to do something new on your computer.

Time: 1–60 minutes
Participants: 2–25
Technology: Remote control
Category: Collaboration

Instructions:

Step 1: Click "Share Screen."

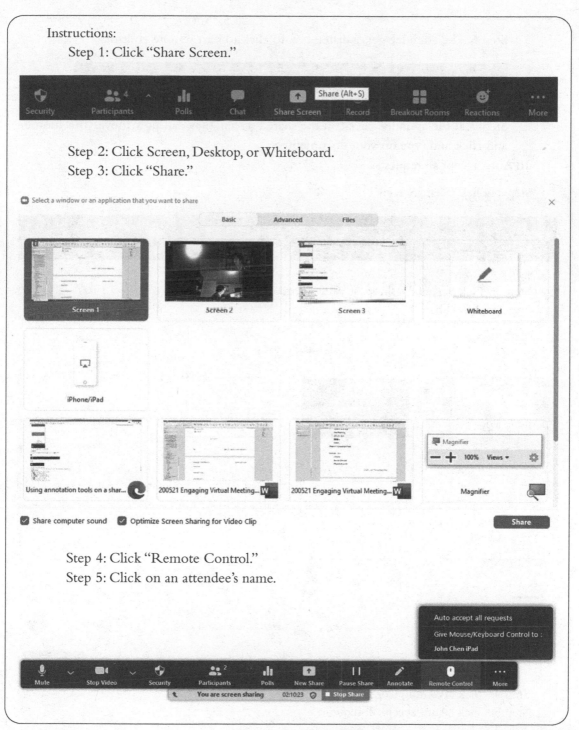

Step 2: Click Screen, Desktop, or Whiteboard.
Step 3: Click "Share."

Step 4: Click "Remote Control."
Step 5: Click on an attendee's name.

(Continued)

Step 6: The attendee gets a dialog box to click to start remote control.

Click to start the mouse/keyboard control of the shared screen.

Step 7: If the attendee clicks on the shared screen, they can now move your mouse and click and type on your document.

To Auto accept all requests:

Step 1: Click "Share Screen."

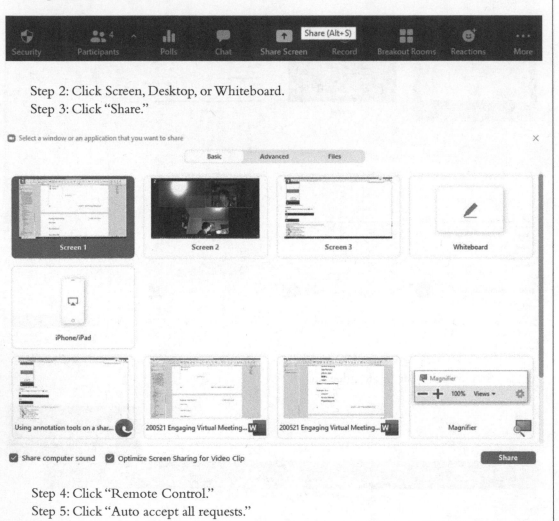

Step 2: Click Screen, Desktop, or Whiteboard.
Step 3: Click "Share."

Step 4: Click "Remote Control."
Step 5: Click "Auto accept all requests."

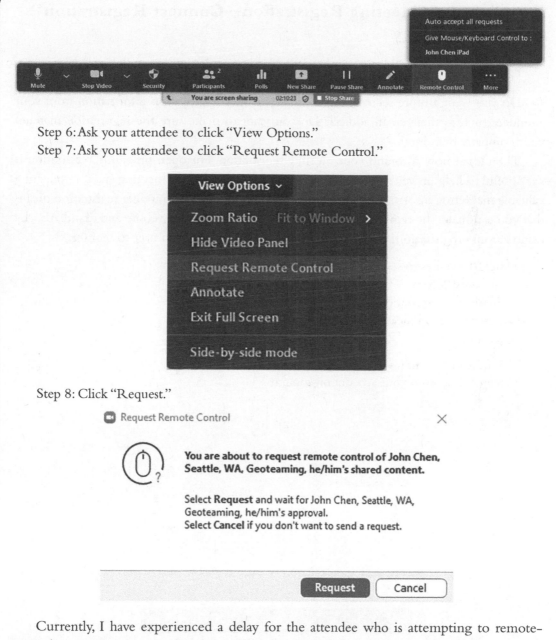

Step 6: Ask your attendee to click "View Options."
Step 7: Ask your attendee to click "Request Remote Control."

Step 8: Click "Request."

Currently, I have experienced a delay for the attendee who is attempting to remote-control your computer, so this does make this feature challenging for long-term work. A great application is if an attendee is having trouble and is not familiar with their technology, then you can take remote control of their computer and, hopefully, fix it faster. I have also found it useful for activities with limited motions such as Chapter 12's Move One Line.

Branding Your Meeting Registration—Connect Registration to Your Company

Goals: Add customized branding to your virtual meeting registration.

Do you want a more secure meeting? Do you want registration information from your attendees such as their email address? Do you want to make sure the registration matches your company branding?

Then learn how to brand your meeting registration. For open programs, registration is very useful to help prevent Zoombombers from getting into your meeting and for collecting valuable marketing information such as name and email address. Branding registration means that you can make the registration look like an extension of your website and brand. Also, by using Zoom's registration, it is extremely easy and fast for a Zoom user to register.

Time: 10 minutes to set up, 0 minutes for future meetings
Participants: 2–Max
Technology: Registration
Category: Communication, branding
Instructions:

This feature requires a paid Zoom account.
Step 1: Log in to your account on zoom.us.

Sign In

Email Address

john@geoteaming.com

Password

•••••••••   Forgot password?

Zoom is protected by reCAPTCHA and the Privacy Policy and Terms of Service apply.

Sign In

☑ Stay signed in   New to Zoom? Sign Up Free

Step 2: Go to "Personal."
Step 3: Go to "Meetings."
Step 4: Click "Schedule a New Meeting."

Step 5: Check the "Registration Required" box and save the meeting.

Registration   ☑ **Required**

Step 6: Click "Branding."

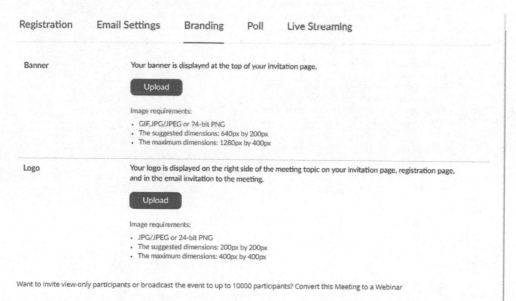

Registration   Email Settings   **Branding**   Poll   Live Streaming

Banner   Your banner is displayed at the top of your invitation page.

[Upload]

Image requirements:
- GIF, JPG/JPEG or 24-bit PNG
- The suggested dimensions: 640px by 200px
- The maximum dimensions: 1280px by 400px

Logo   Your logo is displayed on the right side of the meeting topic on your invitation page, registration page,
                and in the email invitation to the meeting.

[Upload]

Image requirements:
- JPG/JPEG or 24-bit PNG
- The suggested dimensions: 200px by 200px
- The maximum dimensions: 400px by 400px

Want to invite view-only participants or broadcast the event to up to 10000 participants? Convert this Meeting to a Webinar

Step 7: Click Banner "Upload" and select a picture that is 1280 pixels wide by 400 pixels high. You can use a program like "Paint" to edit a picture into this size.
Step 8 (optional): Click "Add Description" and describe your picture.
Step 9: Click Logo "Upload" and select a picture that is 400 pixels wide by 400 pixels high.
Step 10 (optional): Click "Add Description" and describe your picture.
Step 11: Go to the registration link for your meeting and review how it looks.

(Continued)

Engaging Virtual Meetings

Meeting Registration

Topic	6/23/2020 Engaging Virtual Meetings 1
Description	Are you working from home? Do your virtual meetings drain your energy? Is video exhaustion real for you?

Then you want Engaging Virtual Meetings. Engaging Virtual Meetings shows you the key secrets to having your attendees say, "I have more energy (rather than less) after 60 minutes meeting with you!". When you learn Engaging Virtual Meetings, you will learn how to:

- Create a powerful virtual presence
- Create a smooth flow so attendees don't talk over each other
- Network without saying a word
- Engage everyone even if only one person is talking
- Guarantee that everyone feels engaged and heard
- Powerfully close your meeting and take steps to make your next meeting even more effective

Time	Jun 23, 2020 03:00 PM in Pacific Time (US and Canada)

First Name*

John

Last Name*

Chen

Email Address*

john@geoteaming.com

Confirm Email Address*

john@geoteaming.com

* Required information

Register

The registration now has your banner at the top, your description and your company icon or logo. This can help to increase recognition and registration for your virtual meeting. Many users have reported that it has created more sales in the end by increasing registration to their programs.

Branding Your Waiting Room—Beautify Your Virtual Lobby

Goals: To customize your waiting room and give your attendees more value even before they arrive at your meeting.

When you come to a new office, you usually notice how the lobby is set up, what furniture has been chosen, and how you are treated as you arrive. In a virtual meeting that uses a waiting room, this waiting room is your new office lobby. Your attendees will start to make assessments about your virtual meeting from the moment they log in. This is how you can customize this experience for your attendees.

Time: 10 minutes to set up, 0 minutes for future meetings

Participants: 2–Max

Technology: Waiting room

Category: Communication, branding

Instructions:

This feature requires a paid Zoom account.

Step 1: Log in to your account on zoom.us.

Sign In

Email Address

john@geoteaming.com

Password

••••••••••   Forgot password?

Zoom is protected by reCAPTCHA and the Privacy Policy and Terms of Service apply.

Sign In

☑ Stay signed in   New to Zoom? Sign Up Free

(Continued)

Step 2: Go to "Admin."
Step 3: Click "Account Management-> Account Settings."

Step 4: Find the waiting room and turn it on.
Step 5: Choose which participants to place in the waiting room: Everyone (choose this one by default), Users not in your account, or Users who are not in your account and not part of your whitelisted domains.
Step 6: Click the pencil next to "Customize the title, logo and description."

Waiting room

When participants join a meeting, place them in a waiting room and require the host to admit them individually. Enabling the waiting room automatically disables the setting for allowing participants to join before host.

Choose which participants to place in the waiting room:

⦿ Everyone

◯ Users not in your account

◯ Users who are not in your account and not part of your whitelisted domains

Customize the title, logo, and description 🖉 ◀─────────

Step 7: Click the pencil next to the title and write your title.
Step 8: Click the pencil next to the logo and upload your square logo.

Step 9: Click the pencil next to the description and write your description.

Step 10: Click "Close."

Customize the waiting room UI

Meeting ID : 888-888-888

Let's have an engaging virtual meeting.

              { Your Meeting Topic }

Your meeting will start in a moment. Take this moment and think about your m ost engaging virtual meeting. What did it have? What did they do? What did y ou do? Could you share your most engaging virtual meeting practice during thi s meeting? I look forward to personally meeting you!

Logo should be in GIF/JPG/PNG format. The file size cannot exceed 1MB
Logo minimum width or height is 60px and cannot exceed 400px

Close

Step 11: Start your meeting and have a second computer, tablet, or phone log in to your meeting to review how your waiting room looks (Figure 16.1).

Let's have an engaging virtual meeting.

 | 6/23/2020 Engaging Virtual Meetings 1

Your meeting will start in a moment. Take this moment and think about your most engaging virtual meeting. What did it have? What did they do? What did you do? Could you share your most engaging virtual meeting practice during this meeting? I look forward to personally meeting you!

Figure 16.1   Geoteaming's Waiting Room

Customize Your Video Recording Waiver—Protect Your Company When You Record

Goals: Create a customized video recording waiver that protects you and your company even more.

Do you record your virtual meetings? Do you want to protect yourself and your company assets? Do you communicate clearly with your attendees?

Discover how to customize your video recording waiver. By putting a custom message here, you can clearly communicate to the attendee that you are recording, you can gain their acceptance by continuing in the meeting, and you can protect the company's use of the video.

Time: 10 minutes to set up, 0 minutes for future meetings
Participants: 2–Max
Technology: Recording
Category: Communication
Instructions:

   Step 1: Log in to your account on zoom.us.

Sign In

Email Address

john@geoteaming.com

Password

••••••••••   Forgot password?

Zoom is protected by reCAPTCHA and the Privacy Policy and Terms of Service apply.

Sign In

☑ Stay signed in   New to Zoom? Sign Up Free

Step 2: Go to "Admin."
Step 3: Click "Account Management-> Account Settings."

ADMIN

> **User Management**

> **Room Management**

∨ **Account Management**

Account Profile

Account Settings

Step 4: Click "Recording."

Meeting   **Recording**   **Telephone**

Step 5: Find "Recording disclaimer" and turn it on.
Step 6: Check "Ask participant for consent when a recording starts."
Step 7: Click "Customize."

Recording disclaimer

Show a customizable disclaimer to participants before a recording starts ⓥ

✔ Ask participants for consent when a recording starts   Customize

◯ Ask host to confirm before starting a recording

Step 8: Edit the title to "This meeting is being recorded."
Step 9: Edit the description to:

I give my consent for videos taken of me during this course to be used for publicity purposes. I understand that I will receive no compensation for such uses. I retain the right to have any videos discontinued from use in any or all of the above venues upon request and it is my responsibility to contact the program director to make this request.

Step 10: Click "Save."

(Continued)

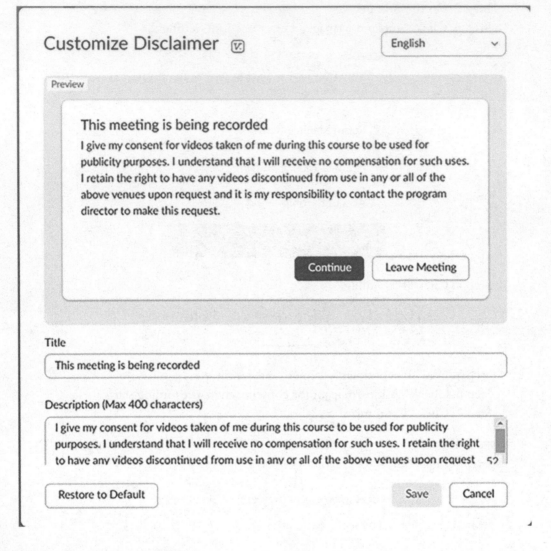

Step 11: Start a meeting.

Step 12: Log in to the meeting from a second computer.

Step 13: Click "Record."

Step 14: Review the video disclaimer (Figure 16.2).

I suggest you have your lawyer review your video disclaimer to ensure that it covers you and your company in your area.

This meeting is being recorded

I give my consent for videos taken of me during this course to be used for publicity purposes. I understand that I will receive no compensation for such uses. I retain the right to have any videos discontinued from use in any or all of the above venues upon request and it is my responsibility to contact the program director to make this request.

Continue   Leave meeting

Figure 16.2   How Your Attendees See Your Video Disclaimer

Record Multiple Video Views—Get the Right Shot from Your Virtual Meeting

Goals: Make sure you get the right shot or angle from your virtual meeting.

Do you need to create a video from your virtual meeting? Are you having the problem of your video platform not giving you the right footage at the right time? It's common for video platforms to only record what they see. For instance, in Active Speaker mode, it takes one to three seconds after someone starts talking to change to the speaker. Recording multiple videos will help you get rid of that problem. Learn how to get multiple views of your recordings. This will give you the ability to create great video edits of your virtual meeting.

Note that you get one gigabyte, which is about 30 minutes of recording time, of cloud recording space with a Pro Zoom account. If you want the ability to record most meetings, consider upgrading to 100 gigabytes of cloud recording space. This feature is only available on Cloud recording.

Time: 10 minutes to set up, 0 minutes for future meetings
Participants: 1–Max
Technology: Record
Category: Video

(Continued)

Instructions:

Step 1: Log in to your account on zoom.us.

Sign In

Email Address

john@geoteaming.com

Password

••••••••••   Forgot password?

Zoom is protected by reCAPTCHA and the Privacy Policy and Terms of Service apply.

[Sign In]

☑ Stay signed in   New to Zoom? Sign Up Free

Step 2: Go to "Admin."

Step 3: Click "Account Management–> Account Settings."

ADMIN

> **User Management**

> **Room Management**

∨ **Account Management**

Account Profile

Account Settings

Step 4: Click "Recording."

Meeting   **Recording**   Telephone

Step 5: Find "Cloud recording" and turn it on.
Step 6: Check all the boxes except for "Optimize the recording for 3rd party video editor."

Cloud recording

Allow hosts to record and save the meeting / webinar in the cloud

- ✅ Record active speaker with shared screen
- ✅ Record gallery view with shared screen ⑦
- ✅ Record active speaker, gallery view and shared screen separately
  - ✅ Active speaker
  - ✅ Gallery view
  - ✅ Shared screen
- ✅ Record an audio only file
- ✅ Save chat messages from the meeting / webinar

Advanced cloud recording settings

- ✅ Add a timestamp to the recording ⑦
- ✅ Display participants' names in the recording
- ✅ Record thumbnails when sharing ⑦
- ◯ Optimize the recording for 3rd party video editor ⑦
- ✅ Save panelist chat to the recording ⑦

Step 7: Start a meeting.
Step 8: Click "Record."

After your meeting ends, your meeting platform will notify you (usually by email) that your recording is done processing. Longer meetings take longer to process.

(Continued)

Name	Date	Type	Size	Length
GMT20200527-163845_John-Chen-	5/27/1954 9:38 AM	M4A File	57,100 KB	02:23:12
GMT20200527-163845_John-Chen-	5/27/2020 4:48 PM	Text Document	8 KB	
GMT20200527-163845_John-Chen-_2560x1440	5/27/1954 9:38 AM	MP4 File	1,778,930 KB	02:23:12
GMT20200527-163845_John-Chen-_as_2560x1440	5/27/1954 9:38 AM	MP4 File	163,138 KB	02:23:12
GMT20200527-163845_John-Chen-_avo_640x360	5/27/1954 9:38 AM	MP4 File	744,736 KB	02:23:12
GMT20200527-163845_John-Chen-_gallery_2560x1440	5/27/1954 9:38 AM	MP4 File	1,857,640 KB	02:23:12
GMT20200527-163845_John-Chen-_gvo_1280x720	5/27/1954 9:38 AM	MP4 File	979,834 KB	02:23:12

Figure 16.3   Cloud Recording Files

The following is an explanation of the filenames; sections of the filenames have been emphasized in boldface for descriptive purposes only (Figure 16.3).

GMT20200527-163845—This means that this video was created on May, 27th, 2020 at 16:38:45 GMT, which is 9:38 a.m. PST.

GMT20200527-163845_John-Chen-.m4a is an audio-only file. If you are creating a podcast or editing different video over the audio, then this file is already made for you.

GMT20200527-163845_John-Chen-.txt is the chat file. If your attendees chatted important information such as LinkedIn profiles for networking, you can see all the chats with who and when the chat was sent in this file.

GMT20200527-163845_John-Chen-_2560x1440.mp4 is the active speaker video. This is a full-size video of the attendee who is speaking as well as the full-size video of the screen that is shared, such as a presentation. This is the best file to use if you want the largest-size video of a speaker.

GMT20200527-163845_John-Chen-_**as**_2560x1440.mp4 is only the shared screen video; it does not have any attendees in the video. You can use this to highlight your presentation. It also can capture annotations from your attendees.

GMT20200527-163845_John-Chen-_**gallery**_2560x1440.mp4 is the gallery view. This has the video from all of your participants. This also has your shared screen and only shows the video of the attendee speaking in the top right.

GMT20200527-163845_John-Chen-_**avo**_640x360.mp4 is the active speaker video but in a much lower resolution. This may be easier to process but the quality of this video is not as good as the previous file.

GMT20200527-163845_John-Chen-_**gvo**_1280x720 is the gallery view only. This video has the gallery view of all your attendees and continues to give this view whether you are sharing the screen or not.

Here is an explanation of each of the settings:

Record active speaker with shared screen: Record both active speaker view and shared content on the same video.

Record gallery view with shared screen: Record both gallery view and shared content on the same video.

Record active speaker, gallery view, and shared screen separately: Select the recording layout types that you want to record as separate videos.

Note: By selecting this file type for cloud recordings, you will see the shared screen recording beside the active speaker/gallery view when viewing a cloud recording using the Zoom web portal.

Record an audio-only file: Only receive an M4A file with a recording of the audio.

Save chat messages from the meeting/webinar: Receive a TXT file with the transcript of in-meeting chat messages.

Note: For meetings, the chat transcript saved on the cloud will only include chat messages sent to everyone. For webinars, the saved chat will only include messages from the host and panelists to all participants. Messages sent between individuals are not saved on the cloud.

Add a timestamp to the recording: Add a timestamp of the meeting to your cloud recordings. The time will display in the host's time zone, set in their Zoom profile.

Display participants' names in the recording: Add participants' names to the bottom-right corner of their video.

Record thumbnails when sharing: Include a thumbnail of the presenter when screen sharing.

Optimize the recording for 3rd party video editor: Generate your cloud recording video files with a standard format that is compatible with 3rd party video editors. This may increase the file size.

Audio transcript: Automatically transcribe your cloud recordings.

Save panelist chat to the recording: The messages sent by panelists during a webinar to either all panelists or all panelists and attendees will be saved to the recording.

If creating an edited or recap video from your virtual meeting is important, these are important options to have to ensure you have the video content you need. Editing is becoming more and more important to create compelling videos from virtual meetings.

Case Study: The Actors Fund created the COVID-19 Emergency Financial Assistance program to help everyone involved with cinematic entertainment, such as musicians, editors, and sound mixers. They created a video from over 100 actors filmed in virtual meetings that became one of the most cinematic virtual meeting videos.

Go to bit.ly/evmactorsfund to see The Actors Fund video.

Microsoft Teams Share PowerPoint—Faster Attendee Review

Goals: To have attendees review a PowerPoint presentation faster.

Microsoft Teams has special features if you share your PowerPoint presentation instead of your screen. By giving every attendee control of the slide, every attendee can review the slide deck in any order they choose, which can greatly reduce review time, depending on the slide deck.

Time: 1 minute
Participants: 2–Max
Technology: Share PowerPoint
Category: Share, collaboration
Instructions:

Step 1: Click "Share."
Step 2: Click a PowerPoint presentation or click "Browse" if you don't see your presentation.

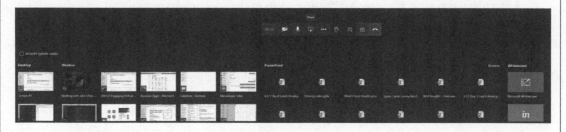

Step 3: Ask your attendee if they see your presentation.
Step 4: Your attendee can go forward or backward on their own in PowerPoint by clicking < and >.
Step 5: Your attendee can go back to the slide you (the presenter) are on by clicking "To presenter."

Tips: If you are using advanced features of PowerPoint, it's possible that your slides may not look the way you want them to. Make sure to practice before you do this in a meeting. If it doesn't work, just go back to sharing your desktop for your meeting.

More Advanced Tips

New features and tips are being developed every day. Go to http://engagingvirtualmeetings.com or join the Engaging Virtual Meetings Facebook group at http://fb.com/groups/EngagingVirtualMeetings where hundreds of professionals share advanced tips.

17 | The Future of Engaging Virtual Meetings

You now have the latest and best practices in virtual meetings. If you apply the ENGAGE method, you will be in the top 20% of all virtual meetings. You can be proud of mastering the current technology and best practices. Before now, face-to-face meetings always had the reputation for having the best engagement and most people preferred them to any form of virtual meeting. While they may still prefer them, most people must make new choices. When I say people, I mean that the entire planet is making the same choices now. For most, that choice is virtual.

This is one of the most exciting times in the history of virtual meetings. With everybody on virtual, the need for innovation is extremely high. By the time you read this, you will see more innovation in this industry than in the previous 20 years. As humans, one of our best traits is our adaptability. It's in our DNA. The saying "necessity is the mother of invention" could refer to virtual meetings; this is their time. I want to share with you my view on the future of engaging virtual meetings that can help prepare you for rapid change that is ahead. I want to help you get excited for the upcoming changes and help you find a way for you to lead the future. Here are my guiding principles for the future of virtual meetings.

Suddenly Everyone Is Interested

I predicted over 20 years ago that virtual meetings were going to be a big part of work. A partner and I built a company and attempted to sell training. It never sold. In March 2020, the coronavirus changed the entire world in just a few months and suddenly everyone is interested in virtual meetings.

Everyone around the world is having the same experience. Stay-at-home orders. Work from home. No travel. School from home. All of these factors mean that the entire population of Earth, currently at 7.8 billion, is interested in virtual meetings. This sheer demand means that the supply of virtual meeting tools is now very small, leading to new products and new innovations.

Be curious. Be interested in new platforms that come out. Join groups of like-minded people who will help keep you up to date. Watch the news for new companies with features that fix your current problems or enhance your company's capability. Do everything you can to be one of the most interested professionals/people; that's how you stay ahead.

Virtual Is Here Even If There Is a Cure

It's very possible that if a miracle cure for the coronavirus is found in the future, the world could return to its former state of traveling, eating out, and meeting in person. If this happened, it is possible that virtual will die or shrink again as face-to-face meetings regain in popularity.

There is significant research that even if a miracle cure is found, many people have seen the benefits of virtual and they are ready to make that a core part of their business.[1]

BENEFITS OF ONLINE CONFERENCES:

- ☑ Eliminate **travel costs**
- ☑ Reduce **environmental pollution**
- ☑ Reduce the **price of admission**
- ☑ **More targeted** event focus
- ☑ Allow conference organizers to **invest more into speakers**

Most of the conference resources used to go to the venue, food and beverage, and equipment. Now, virtual meeting planners can spend more on program design and speaker fees, meaning better education and networking.

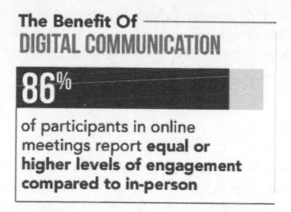

With the best virtual practices, attendees are finding equal or higher levels of engagement compared to in-person. We are humans; we are designed to connect. We want engagement. If we can find it in new ways, we will choose it. Imagine as a salesperson that you can do all of your sales meetings, sell as much or more than you did before, and save all the time and money on your trip.

With this research, I believe that virtual is here, even if there is a cure.

The Hard Stuff Is Easy, the Soft Stuff Is Hard

What does this quote mean? The hard stuff is technology such as networking, cameras, microphones, monitors, and more. The technology is now "easy," meaning companies know how to iterate and innovate to provide more and more and more. The 2020 iPhone has 7 million times the storage and 100,000 times the processer power of the *Apollo 11* computer that landed humans on the moon. Expect to see rapid innovations at lower and lower prices that will bring this technology to you.

The soft stuff is human challenges such as networking, collaborating, innovating, brainstorming, relationships, diversity, conflict resolution, teamwork, and leadership. These issues did not disappear with virtual meetings. In fact, many of these issues got magnified. Often, it created new issues that we didn't yet know about, such as virtual meeting etiquette. This soft stuff was hard in the face-to-face world. It's even harder in the virtual meeting world.

Look for significant innovations here. For instance, there are apps now that can track how much your attendees have participated and can detect automatically if an attendee is talking too much or too little. Video analysis of your virtual meetings will soon show patterns of when your attendees are efficient and when they are wasting time. Artificial intelligence (AI) will soon help with your meeting logistics, do away with chores like taking minutes, and can retrieve hidden business intelligence, which could be new opportunities to generate value and revenue. Look for technology to help with the soft stuff such as assisting and highlighting attendee behaviors that lead to the most business value.[2]

Think Cinematically

One advantage you have in virtual meetings is thinking cinematically. In face-to-face meetings, you think theatrically. That means that you are thinking about staging, lighting, where a person is located, how the meeting looks from all angles. In virtual meetings, you need to think cinematically because everything is created by cameras, angles, lighting, and how it presents on a two-dimensional screen. A good guideline is to think in "episodes." Audiences aren't captivated by an hour-long stream of a single camera pointed at a person on a stage. Instead, plan in segments and create a dynamic experience by changing cameras, angles, and views.

When you think cinematically, you pay more attention to what's in the video frame. You can hide items like lighting out of the frame. That lighting is improving what's in the frame, even though attendees can't see it. Think about entries and exits into different parts of your meetings. Think about what you can do with mobile cameras. You can transport your attendees with the right cinematic equipment such as gimbals and other stabilizers and give them a travel experience from their desk that is easy and amazing to watch.

By 2021, it is projected that video, including web conferencing,
WILL ACCOUNT FOR OVER 80% OF ALL INTERNET TRAFFIC

Thinking cinematically can help your virtual meetings be engaging by changing it up, using the best and unique angles, and bringing the power of a movie into your live meeting. Go to bit.ly/evmrethink to hear eight ways to rethink virtual events for the age of social distancing from Microsoft.

Virtual Is Going to Innovate Rapidly

In the simple economics of supply and demand, I see that there is a huge demand for virtual meetings and the supply is very limited in choices. Attendees can get work done, but now they are starting to ask for more. Companies are starting to respond and you should see rapid innovation for virtual meetings.

Here are current examples:

YoTribe.com attempts to solve networking by putting users in control. Attendees can move around and when they enter a circle of people, they join the conversation. This is a way to make networking more interactive and less structured than breakout rooms (Figure 17.1).

Figure 17.1   Adrian Segar and John Chen meet up on YoTribe.

Remo.co creates more real and authentic social interaction by using virtual tables so you can see a preview of who is sitting there. The preview allows you to see what's happening and decide if you want to join the table. Many formats, such as speed networking and conversation cafes, can be used on Remo.co. They also have sponsorship opportunities available to pay for the meeting or generate extra revenue (Figure 17.2).

VirBELA.com builds immersive virtual worlds for events, learning, and work. This platform can build a world like a corporate campus that includes boardrooms, conference rooms, halls, and closed meeting rooms. You can walk or run to any location, but you can also teleport to save time. Once you sit down in a room, you can use your mouse to look around the room. This is the first platform that uses stereo sound well. If you walk past someone, you can hear them get louder and then quieter as well as sounding as if they were passing next to you. There are a lot of features, from projection walls to locking doors, that bring the face-to-face metaphors back to the virtual world.

When I wrote my first book, *50 Digital Team-Building Games*, there was no dominant virtual platform. Zoom was just being created while Skype was starting to grow. Yotribe.com, Remo.co and VirBELA.com are three examples of new video platforms with potential viral growth. Any virtual platform could be the top platform in the future. Keep up and try new platforms to experience new features and decide which ones you like.

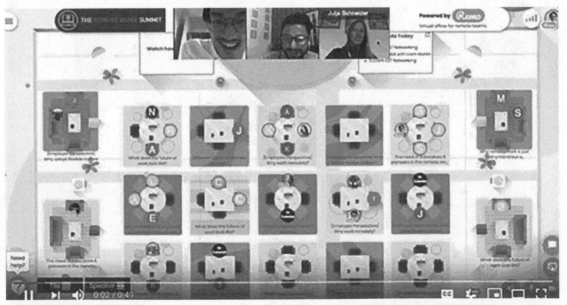

Figure 17.2 Remo.co allows attendees to choose who they want to talk to by using virtual tables.

Figure 17.3 Every person in this keynote is an attendee logged in on their computer.

The Theory of Bandwidth

The theory of bandwidth states that as you get more bandwidth, you can have a more realistic experience. Bandwidth is defined as the capacity of data transfer of an electronic communications system. If you have low bandwidth, you can only transfer a little bit of information. A text message of limited size like 140 characters can be sent with as little as 1,120 bits of bandwidth. Browsing a webpage takes on average one megabyte or 1,000,000 bits per page. Streaming audio like a phone call takes more bandwidth, such as 30 megabytes per hours or 240,000,000 bits per hour. Streaming video at higher resolutions (HD or 1080 p) uses 2,400,000,000 bits per hour.

As a virtual meeting uses more and more bandwidth, you can have an experience more like reality. Soon there will be a system so that multiple attendees can talk at the same time and be understood. Systems are using stereo and 3D sound to give the experience of space through hearing. Soon, you may be able to see a 3D image of every attendee. Haptics and tactile technologies may soon allow you to feel during virtual meetings. Maybe someone will innovate smell and/or taste to involve your other senses. You can communicate more information. You can get more work done if you take advantage of the extra information. Look for increases in bandwidth being provided. Many providers are offering gigabit or 1,000 MBps speed to residential houses. This is like having a high-speed superhighway that can carry a lot of cargo to your home. This will translate into more and more realistic virtual meetings that get closer and closer to real life.

Moving Closer to Reality

What you will see is virtual meetings becoming more engaging as they move closer to reality. Watch for augmented reality and virtual reality to redefine meetings for more and more attendees in the future.

Augmented reality is a technology that superimposes a computer-generated image on a user's view of the real world, thus providing a composite view. This means that the attendee has a device that sees their reality and then augments that reality with computer-generated images. Your desk could look like it has nothing on it, but when you turn on augmented reality, you could see screens, data, files, folders, videos, and any other kind of data. Your cell phone today can do augmented reality.

One of the top apps is Ikea Place. This retailer now allows you to see your home and put any piece of their furniture in your home so you can see what it looks like and if it fits. This app uses the camera on the back of the phone to show the room on the front screen of the phone, augmented by items that Ikea puts there.

I believe augmented reality can help us in day-to-day interactions. Imagine that as you are going to a meeting, you can look up an attendee on the internet and see their work history or recent articles by or about them. As you meet your attendee, perhaps she says she is an expert knitter. You don't know anything about knitting, but your augmented reality shows you the latest trends on Ravelry, a knitting community site. This can help you create rapport and connection with your attendee.

Virtual reality is the computer-generated simulation of a three-dimensional image or environment that can be interacted with in a seemingly real or physical way by a person using special electronic equipment, such as a helmet with a screen inside or gloves fitted with sensors. By wearing equipment that changes what you see and what you feel, you can create an environment around you, even though you're just standing or sitting in a chair. You can now quickly change or customize your virtual meeting. One minute, you could be meeting in an executive's boardroom. The next minute, you could be on a beach in Hawaii. Right now, your brain knows it's not as good as reality. You are missing the smells of salt and the ocean. You are missing the feeling of sand on your toes. As the technology continues to improve, this experience will get closer and closer to reality. Solutions such as multidirectional treadmills or other technologies may mean that you can have an experience that is very close to real.

While we can't predict the future, we can hope that technology, such as the holodeck from *Star Trek*, becomes reality. The holodeck could re-create any environment out of history and time. You could interact with everything in the environment as if it was real. You could have a virtual meeting in virtually any location and any time. When you were done, you could ask the computer to turn it off and exit through the door. If the technology becomes good enough to convince our bodies and our brains that we are there, our virtual meetings can become extraordinarily engaging, allowing us to do things we may not have the chance to do in the real world.

I want you to end *Engaging Virtual Meetings* on a high note. I hope that you are excited for the future of virtual meetings, as I am. I would love to hear that you got to the end of this book. I believe the future of engaging virtual meetings is connection. Great meetings connect people. I would love to connect with you. I want to hear what you think is the future of Engaging Virtual Meetings. Text (702) 879-8133 and let me know what you think the future of engaging virtual meetings is. I look forward to texting you back and meeting you in the virtual or the real world.

Do you want the latest advice on engaging virtual meetings?

You now have the basics that will help your virtual meetings based on over 35 years of experience.

Engaging virtual meetings change—rapidly. They are based on technology that will change constantly after the publication of this book. I personally invite you to join the community of other Engaging Virtual Meetings enthusiasts by joining the free Engaging Virtual Meeting Facebook group.

facebook.com/groups/EngagingVirtualMeetings

If you have any questions not covered in the book or you need a current answer to your virtual meeting challenge, ask it there and you will have access to a community of people who want to help you, including myself.

In addition, you can experience this book in action at one of our Engaging Virtual Meetings trainings. Register now at:

http://geoteaming.com/engagingvirtualmeetings

Endnotes

Acknowledgments

1 https://www.theverge.com/2020/4/23/21232401/zoom-300-million-users-growth-coronavirus-pandemic-security-privacy-concerns-response
2 https://www.geekwire.com/2020/microsoft-teams-hits-44m-users-huge-37-growth-spike-1-week-amid-remote-work-surge/
3 https://www.worldometers.info/world-population/us-population/

Chapter 1

1 https://www.theodysseyonline.com/11-reasons-why-wearing-bright-colors-is-beneficial
2 http://www.marketingprofs.com/short-articles/609/end-on-a-high-note
3 This is the most forgotten step. Always ask if attendees can hear the audio to check.
4 https://www.signingsavvy.com/sign/APPLAUSE/7950/1
5 https://www.inc.com/laura-garnett/acknowledgment-the-new-charisma-at-work.html

Chapter 2

1 https://www.usatoday.com/story/tech/columnist/2020/06/04/working-home-what-backdrop-video-call-says-you/3145490001/
2 https://www.speedtest.net/
3 https://www.business.com/articles/increasing-productivity-how-dual-monitors-can-save-you-time-and-money/

4 https://support.zoom.us/hc/en-us/articles/201362323-Changing-the-video-layout-Active-Speaker-View-and-Gallery-View

5 https://www.google.com/search?q=top+noise-canceling+headphones

6 https://www.ikmultimedia.com/products/irigmichd2/?pkey=irigmichd2

7 https://www.wsj.com/articles/how-to-sound-your-best-on-calls-from-home-11590917401

8 https://www.laptopmag.com/articles/best-usb-microphones

9 https://ref.krisp.ai/u/uafc542d3c?utm_source=refprogram&utm_campaign=114782&locale=en-US

10 https://www.studiobinder.com/blog/how-to-clean-camera-lens/

11 https://www.microsoft.com/store/productId/9P06SVLRLR66

12 https://apps.apple.com/us/app/webcam-settings/id533696630?mt=12

Chapter 4

1 https://support.zoom.us/hc/en-us/articles/201362603-Host-and-Co-Host-Controls-in-a-Meeting

2 https://en.wikipedia.org/wiki/Myers-Briggs_Type_Indicator

Chapter 5

1 https://www.okta.com/businesses-at-work/2020/

2 https://support.zoom.us/hc/en-us/articles/206476313-Managing-breakout-rooms

3 https://support.zoom.us/hc/en-us/articles/206476313-Managing-breakout-rooms

4 https://techcommunity.microsoft.com/t5/microsoft-teams-blog/bg-p/MicrosoftTeamsBlog

5 https://newsroom.cisco.com/press-release-content?type=webcontent&articleId=1853168

6 https://docs.microsoft.com/en-us/microsoftteams/teams-channels-overview

Chapter 6

1 https://en.wikipedia.org/wiki/Zoombombing

2 https://blog.zoom.us/wordpress/2020/03/20/keep-uninvited-guests-out-of-your-zoom-event/

3 https://docs.microsoft.com/en-us/microsoftteams/security-compliance-overview

4 https://mekshq.com/redirect-page-wordpress/

Chapter 7

1 https://www.signingsavvy.com/sign/APPLAUSE/7950/1
2 https://en.wikipedia.org/wiki/Dab_(dance)
3 https://www.aclunc.org/article/frequently-asked-questions-whats-pronoun
4 http://thecircular.org/why-are-quotes-important/
5 https://www.canr.msu.edu/news/what_is_the_best_way_to_begin_and_end_meetings

Chapter 8

1 https://www.td.org/insights/performance-consulting-tips-the-power-of-the-yes-and-approach
2 https://hbr.org/2009/05/real-leaders-ask.html

Chapter 9

1 https://en.wikipedia.org/wiki/Collaboration
2 https://en.wikipedia.org/wiki/Infinite_monkey_theorem
3 https://support.google.com/docs/thread/4715007?hl=en
4 https://answers.microsoft.com/en-us/msoffice/forum/all/how-many-users-can-simultaneously-edit-a-single/ef881dba-b69a-4552-b5fc-2f4f4a37a5cb

Chapter 10

1 https://www.dummies.com/business/business-strategy/always-end-strategic-planning-meetings-on-a-high-note/
2 https://en.wikipedia.org/wiki/A_picture_is_worth_a_thousand_words
3 https://www.tonyrobbins.com/biography/
4 https://cetl.uconn.edu/what-so-what-now-what-model/

Chapter 11

1 https://cmoe.com/blog/infographic-working-in-a-virtual-world/
2 https://www.verywellmind.com/the-best-stress-relief-3144573

3 https://www.tlnt.com/the-value-of-having-fun-at-work/
4 https://www.dailymail.co.uk/femail/article-2275285/Onesie-The-fashion-phenomenon.html
5 https://support.zoom.us/hc/en-us/articles/210707503-Virtual-Background
6 https://www.videomaker.com/article/c10/17026-how-does-green-screen-work
7 https://www.bloomberg.com/news/articles/2020-03-25/using-zoom-backgrounds-to-improve-morale-and-increase-business
8 https://www.facebook.com/help/1020633957973118
9 https://www.quora.com/When-did-karaoke-become-popular
10 https://www.atlasobscura.com/articles/1700s-book-clubs-drinking-socializing
11 https://www.theeventprofsbookclub.com
12 https://mst3k.com/
13 https://www.netflixparty.com/
14 https://www.bustle.com/p/how-to-have-a-zoom-dinner-if-you-miss-eating-out-with-friends-22665331
15 https://foodanddrink.scotsman.com/food/these-are-the-celebrities-hosting-the-uks-biggest-virtual-dinner-party-and-how-to-join-in/
16 https://en.wikipedia.org/wiki/Pub_quiz
17 https://bicyclecards.com/how-to-play/basics-of-poker/

Chapter 12

1 https://www.cleverism.com/skills-and-tools/innovation/
2 https://pixar.fandom.com/wiki/To_Infinity_and_Beyond

Chapter 13

1 http://www.brainrules.net/
2 https://www.forbes.com/sites/carminegallo/2014/04/30/why-powerpoint-presentations-always-die-after-10-minutes-and-how-to-rescue-them/#4037a74878ba
3 https://blog.hubspot.com/sales/team-selling
4 https://www.inc.com/larry-kim/visual-content-marketing-16-eye-popping-statistics-you-need-to-know.html
5 https://www.studyread.com/importance-of-sound/
6 https://www.jaybaer.com/7-virtual-event-success-factors/
7 Abraham Maslow, *The Psychology of Science: A Reconnaissance* (HarperCollins, 1966), p. 15.

8 Christopher Witt, *Real Leaders Don't Do PowerPoint: How to Sell Yourself and Your Ideas* (*Crown Business*, 2009).

9 https://www.acrylicdigital.co.uk/what-is-video-marketing/#:~:text=Video%20 content%20is%20extremely%20powerful,even%20from%20your%20own%20home!

Chapter 17

1 https://www.business2community.com/infographics/the-future-of-virtual-conferences-infographic-02308143

2 https://www.cisco.com/c/en_uk/solutions/small-business/tech-connection/workforce-productivity/how-ai-will-revolutionise-meetings.html

About Geoteaming

Meet John Chen, the extreme leader of Geoteaming. He climbs mountains, walks on fire, swims with dolphins, rides Harleys, and snowboards out of helicopters. John is a recognized thought leader on developing highly functioning corporate teams and an expert on digital team building.

As CEO, John leads his own team with an unparalleled passion for living and for people. More than 230,000 clients across the United States, Europe, and Asia have experienced breakthrough results and life-changing adventures with John and Geoteaming. John has harnessed the power of team through play with a purpose. As a connoisseur of technology and a strident adventurer, John has developed an innovative and adaptable approach to building team and leadership skills that strongly resonate with participants.

John is an accomplished author (*50 Digital Team-Building Games*, published by John Wiley & Sons) and winner of numerous professional awards and recognition, including two patents for software design. When you meet John, you will encounter a dynamic, energetic, and effective leader who builds strong bonds of friendship with those he meets.

You can reach John at john@geoteaming.com
Telephone 877.652.0875
Facebook http://facebook.com/ceojohnchen
Twitter http://twitter.com/geoteaming
YouTube http://youtube.com/geoteamingtv

Engaging Virtual Meetings

Engaging Virtual Meetings is a series of virtual trainings that put the ENGAGE method in practice.
Register at http://geoteaming.com/engagingvirtualmeetings

Virtual Meeting Planning

Do you have a virtual meeting that you need help with? From consulting to full-service execution of your virtual meeting, training or conference, ask Geoteaming's team from around the world to help your virtual meeting be very engaging and earn high ratings.

Find out more at http://geoteaming.com.

Virtual Team Building

Do you manage teams?
Did you just get asked to work from home?
Do you want to maximize your online teamwork?
Find out more at http://geoteaming.com/virtualteambuilding.

TeamOS

TeamOS, or Team Operating System, will help your team become one of the top 1% in the world. TeamOS is a five-step process to team success:

1. Team building: Your team executes our award-winning team-building program.
2. Analyze: Our recordings capture gigabytes of data. We analyze why the winning team won and what coaching your teams need.
3. Present: We present our findings to you and your executive team to create a custom message that will have the highest odds of creating team change in your culture.
4. Coaching: Your teams receive custom coaching, including video playback from their team-building program and a series of team-building coaching sessions to help your team succeed.
5. Results: When your team is ready, they replay our award-winning team-building program and if they have successfully implemented our coaching, they will become one of the top 1% teams in the world. Teams who have achieved top 1% status have achieved major goals such as a multimillion-dollar sales goal.

TeamOS is the culmination of 20-plus years of team building with over 2,100 companies around the world. TeamOS is a proprietary, research analytics–based, customized system that works.

Geoteaming TeamOS builds stronger, better-performing, longer-lasting, engaged, and purposeful teams.

http://geoteaming.com/project/teamos

Keynotes

Bring John Chen or one of our amazing facilitators to your next training session, breakout, or keynote and we'll turn this time into an interactive, engaging experience. Available on almost any platform online or for travel around the world, we'll work with you to customize your program and bring a unique experience to bring your program to life.

Contact http://geoteaming.com and click Request a Quote to speak to one of our account executives today!